BLUE RIDGE BOYS

War Time at the Blue Ridge School

BY PATRICK NAPIER

PREFACE BY DALE NAPIER

Mastersoft Media   Las Vegas * Houston

BLUE RIDGE BOYS

Printed in the United States of America

ISBN 10: 1497441242
ISBN 13: 9781497441248
10 9 8 7 6 5 4 3 2 1

Library of Congress Cataloguing in Publication Data
Napier, Patrick L.
    Blue Ridge Boys: A Story of Boarding School Boys During World War II
Patrick Napier
    p. cm.
    Does not include index
    ISBN 13: 9781497441248
1. Memoir – World War II

GV ?????

DEDICATION

This book is dedicated to my long-departed big brother,
John (Jack) Robert Napier Jr.

ACKNOWLEDGEMENTS

This book would never have seen the light of day without the help of my longtime neighbor, Dave Hitelman, who took the bits and pieces of my writing and collected them into a book. My nephew and Jack's only son, Dale Napier, edited and published the book on my behalf.

TABLE OF CONTENTS

PREFACE

As a young boy my father, Jack Napier, raised me on stories of his youth at a boarding school where he and his younger brother Pat spent the war years. He told me of some typical boys' hijinks, but he said a lot about the school's disciplinary system. Since Dad was a soldier I was raised to understand military systems, one aspect of which is reward and punishment. The code was all around us: when we lived on base, our yard was given a weekly inspection, and the result went on his permanent record. As yard mechanic #2, and the only non-supervisor, a lot of that was on my back once I entered my teen years.

As a result the merit/demerit system of the Blue Ridge (Industrial) School was of considerable interest. What Dad did not tell me was that as student council president, he was one of the primary designers of the system, and he may have been one of the few students happy with it. Uncle Pat and his friends had unfriendly things to say about it, with a result that is now amusing – partly because Pat and his friends were young boys at the time, and partly because it says so much about the hierarchy of human relationships, even within a group of young boys.

Blue Ridge Boys covers the summer of 1941 through the end of 1945, when their father (my grandfather) came home from the war in the Pacific, a lieutenant who had flown as navigator in a bomber and was known to golf with General MacArthur. The end of the war and their father's return was a logical time for changes, but there was an undercurrent that neither boy understood until much later. At the time neither boy realized it, but their dad was a very active man.

In 1943 their parents divorced. Bobby Napier, as he was known to his friends and family, remarried the same year and before the year was out, he had a fourth son (third son Jerry having been too young to attend Blue Ridge). Their mother Sarah remarried as well, and by the next year had moved to Miami, where the boys visited for the holidays in 1944 and 1945. After the war, Sarah and her husband moved to Los Angeles. Bobby settled down in South Carolina, where Jack, Pat, and Jerry were born. None of these undercurrents emerged until it was time for the boys to leave Blue Ridge.

Blue Ridge School exists today, albeit in a highly evolved form. In the 1940s it was little more than several large homes with teachers and caregivers on a farm, less than a hundred boys and girls. Today it is a college preparatory school, a well-developed institution with little evidence of its rural roots. Dad and Pat went to that school at the end of its first era – the last years of the founders' service, and the first year of the new regime. As such this story might be quite interesting to the schools caretakers today, if any were left to remember the old days. Instead, we'll have to remember for them.

One final note: Pat did not record these memories in entirely chronological order. The beginning came first and the ending came last, but the stuff in the middle has been jumbled in the mists of time. We enjoy it regardless.

Dale Napier
Las Vegas, Nevada
August 1, 2014

1941: "YOU'VE BEEN SHOT"

More than seven decades have passed since this story began. For more than four years during the war my older brother Jack and I lived in a boarding school in the state of Virginia, high in the Blue Ridge Mountains. The name of the school was The Blue Ridge Industrial School. The school exists to this day, as Blue Ridge School. When we first enrolled I was seven and Jack was nine.

Before Blue Ridge, Jack and I were living our lives with very little supervision. Our father was in the Army Air Corps and our mother worked in the local cotton mill. Getting into mischief and loitering around Main Street in the small city of Elizabeth City, North Carolina was the bigger part our daily activity. Smoking and sneaking into the back door of the local theater were` probably our most serious offenses until that fateful day in late summer of 1941.

Boredom really set in during the dog days of summer. I was with a friend we all called Stinky, but his real name was George. Why we called him Stinky I can't remember, but you know it couldn't have been good. On weekends, Stinky and I always shined shoes to make our own spending money. I had a dollar left. He came up with thirty-five cents.

"What in the hell are we going to do with a buck thirty-five?"

"We could hit the movie house."

"We've seen 'The Mummy's Hand' twice and that 'Frankenstein' movie scared the shit out of me."

Stinky had two older brothers, Harold and James. Harold had a rifle and had promised Stinky that he would take him hunting if he would supply the bullets.

"So, what do you think, a couple rabbits for dinner?"

"Sounds great to me!"

After we found Harold, he went home to get his gun. After we headed to the hardware store to get the ammo, we met Harold on the outskirts of town. Right on the edge of town was a blacksmith shop run by a black man named Luther. We stood watching him make horseshoes for awhile, until he got upset with us, and we went on our way. I didn't think about it at the time but as I thought about it later, three white boys with a gun could be quite intimidating, especially in those days.

Across from the blacksmith shop was a large cornfield. All the corn stalks had been cut and hauled away, leaving only short stubbles. In the center of the field was a large elm tree with a mule tied to it. I turned to Harold.

"Why would someone tie up a mule out here all alone?" I asked him.

"That's a real mystery, but what do we care?" At about that time James, Stinky's other brother, showed up. Claiming the gun was his, grabbed it away from Harold and shot at something in the field out by the tree. Since I was still interested in the mule, I walked out to where it was tied. On the way I bent over and picked up what James had shot, which looked like a quail. I heard the pop of the gun, and that was the last thing I remember.

My grandmother later provided the details of what happened next. She told me that the boys left me out in the field. The blacksmith had called the police when he first saw us with the gun. The boys ran when they saw the police, who arrived shortly after I was shot. That old Negro saved my life. When they arrived the police took me to the hospital in the squad car.

———

I lay in the hospital in a coma for seventeen days. When I awoke I couldn't talk or use anything on my left side. My left leg was in a cast, to keep it straight while I was in the coma, since they didn't know how long I would be out. I don't know how long I was like this. After a long time my speech slowly returned.

———

My grandmother said she got a phone call from my mom, saying that I had been shot and they didn't know if I would live. My grandmother came from her home in Augusta, Georgia on a Greyhound bus. When she got to the hospital she went straight to my room, where she saw my doctor.

"Now I don't mean to alarm you ma'am," he said, "but I think you need to know the truth. When I first saw Patrick I thought the bullet had just grazed his head. After I saw the X-rays, it was evident it had penetrated his skull. I didn't give him much of a chance to survive."

This information hit her like a ton of bricks but she had to keep a stiff upper lip. She went out to the lobby to break the bad news to my mother and try to calm her down. Later she told me there were two Catholic sisters praying for me through that first night.

After I made it through that first night my mother was informed that I was still in the coma. I was still not expected to survive, and if I did I would probably have brain damage.

———

My grandmother stayed with me for the whole length of time I was in the coma. I remember the day that I came to. Lying facing the window, I could see movement outside. It was a beautiful sunny day, but I had a very bad headache. My grandmother was sitting behind me so she didn't realize I had awakened. After a while I noticed there was another bed in the room with a person in it. In a very short while a woman came in to see the patient in the next bed.

A pile of comic books was lying at the foot of that bed, and I guess the woman saw me staring at them.

"Young boy, would you like to have some of the comics?" she asked.

I wanted some and tried to answer, but I couldn't talk. I was scared. I didn't know what had happened to me. I started to cry and just lay there. When my grandmother heard the woman talking to me she let out a scream. Several doctors and nurses came running in, which scared me even more because I had no idea what was going on.

The doctors were checking everything about me. It took a while before I was able to understand why my leg was in a cast. I thought I must have broken it. After a while my mother came in, crying. It was a day or so before they told me what had happened. I could hear alright but still couldn't talk. I could see but everything was fuzzy.

After six or seven days I could say a few words but couldn't put together a complete sentence. "Grammy, how?"

"How what, Patrick?"

"Long."

Eventually she caught on to what I was asking.

"Patrick, you've been here for over three weeks," she said.

"Wha hap?" I tried to ask.

"Well, Patrick, I don't know all the particulars, but someone shot you. The police found you in that large cornfield across the road from Luther's Blacksmith. Luther saved your life. He heard the shot and went out and stopped your bleeding. He directed the police to where you were lying. The boys who shot you ran and Luther wasn't sure who it was. The police will probably talk to you later. The police are the ones that drove you to the hospital."

She didn't tell me about the bullet entering my brain because it might scare me too much.

———

4

I stayed in the hospital about two months. They gave me five shots—one in each leg, one in each arm, and one in my stomach, three times a day. All that while they had me on a liquid diet because I couldn't swallow too well.

For the most part I enjoyed the liquid diet because I got to have Coke, soft foods and ice cream. Before long they put me in a wheel chair and had this man take me around the hospital to see all the other patients. After a while I got to where I could walk, talk, and eat a normal diet.

On Labor Day morning my doctor, Dr Josh Hammels, walked into my room.

"Pat, I have some wonderful news! You're going home!"

"Really? When?"

"Sometime this week your mother will be here. She has decided to send you and your brother Jack to a boarding school in Virginia."

"Why, Doctor Hammels?"

"It will be for your own benefit, Pat. She has asked me to help her make the arrangements."

———

I remember the trip from Elizabeth City to the school near Charlottesville, Virginia. My brother and I were excited about going somewhere in a car—that didn't happen too often in our lives. At the school my mom and the friend who drove us went inside to talk to the people while we waited in the car.

I don't know what my brother was thinking but I was wondering what was going to happen to us. We had never been away from our mother before. We didn't know anybody at this place.

I asked Jack, "Are they going to lock us in? I think I'm afraid of this place."

"Now, why would they lock us in? It's just a school, not a jail."

"I know, but it looks scary to me."

After a while my mother and her friend came out with a lady who identified herself as Mrs. Mayo. She asked, "Who are these two handsome young men?"

"This is Jack who is nine," my mother said, "and his younger brother, Patrick, who's seven."

Mrs. Mayo smiled real big.

"Welcome to Blue Ridge." She said we would be going up to Crawford House.

"Where's Crawford House?" asked Jack.

"It's about a quarter of a mile from the rest of the school," Mrs. Mayo said. We need to get started. It is late in the day, and we have to walk up this hill in front of us to get there."

She went back into the office. She came back with a boy about Jack's age, who she introduced as Daniel.

Daniel Anderson was a real clean-cut kid with well groomed blonde hair and sparkling blue eyes. No wonder Mrs. Mayo used him to greet new families.

"Daniel, this is Jack and Patrick. I need you to take them up the hill to Crawford House and see that they get settled in for the night," then added, "Mrs. Napier, you're welcome to go with the boys if you like, if you don't mind the climb."

My mom said "Thanks, but I think we'll pass this time. That climb looks a little intimidating and we do need to get on the road. It's a quite long drive back home."

With that mom kissed us both goodbye. She warned us to keep on our good behavior and to make her proud. Then she was gone.

———

Once mom was gone the loneliness really set in. I didn't understand why we were being deserted or how long it would be before we would see Mom again.

Daniel was a nice boy. He was friendly and asked us all sorts of questions during the trek up the fairly steep hill to Crawford House. Jack did most of the talking with Daniel during the climb because I was always quite shy, especially with strangers.

Crawford House was a large two-story building that housed twenty-four boys. At seven years old I was the youngest in the house. I probably would have been in the main house but my mother wanted us both to stay together.

———

After a month or two I got used to the things we were supposed to do and not do. I learned to keep the school rules, such as washing our hands and combing our hair before each meal. After cleaning up we had to stand inspection before the housemother. If your hands were dirty or hair not combed she would make you go back and do it right. If you were late for dinner she would make you stand while everyone else was eating, with your hands held out in front until she thought you had learned a lesson, sometimes as long as twenty minutes.

There was a bulletin with all the boys' names on it. Mrs. Mayo would write down all the things we did that was wrong. All week long we would check to see how many marks we had. If by the end of the week we had eleven or less we were okay. If you had more than eleven you couldn't leave the vicinity of the house, which meant we couldn't go to the country store or go on hikes. These rules would change as time went on.

———

After a while I understood what I could do and when I could do it. When I got to know some of the other boys, they taught me a lot. They would ask me to join them on hikes down to the pasture.

For the most part my closest friends were a year or two older than me. They wanted to get to know me and how it was that Jack and I were sent there.

One of the boys, Earl Martin, had a patch of blonde hair that grew in every direction. He was the epitome of the country boy, tall and gangly with a sprinkle of freckles. He asked me to hike with him down to the pasture, about a one-mile trek. Once there, he took out a crumpled up pack of Camels from the top of his sock and asked, "Do you smoke, Patrick?"

"Not usually," I said. I told him how I would always pick up cigarette butts, but that was only a puff or two, at a time, and added, "call me Pat if you want to."

"Okay, Pat. Enjoy a whole new cigarette. You just have to straighten it out a bit."

It had been a while since I had smoked, so when Earl offered me one I took it and lit up. The Camel tasted strong and made me a little dizzy at first, but I was okay after a while.

Before we finished our smoke four other boys walked up— Daniel Anderson, Buddy Watson, Eddie Lail, and Benny Lambert. They were all interested in my past and how I wound up here. I told them all about Stinky and the trouble we would get into and how we shined shoes to make extra money. I also told them what I knew about being shot and being sent to the school.

After hearing my story they treated me more like I was a member of their little group. After a week or so we were going everywhere together. The five of us stayed close friends for the first year.

A Typical Day at the Crawford House

That first evening when Daniel took me and Jack up the hill, we got our first glimpse of Crawford House. I felt the size of our new home was quite intimidating. I remember saying to Jack, "This is the biggest place that I have ever seen!"

Jack replied, "Me too." he asked Daniel, "Does everyone live in this house?"

"No, only boys your age. There are two other buildings just like this. Girls live in one. The other one is what we call the big boy house."

We walked into the north end of the house. We passed Mr. Mayo's room. Mr. Mayo was the housefather for the boys and Mrs. Mayo was housemother for the girls.

Mr. Mayo's room was on the right. On the left was a large playroom. The front room, as we called it, was where we went for fun activities, especially on inclement days when we couldn't go outside.

Next, on the left, we passed the wash room; on the right was a large laundry room. Beyond those was a large open room where there were six picnic tables that seated six boys each.

At the south end of the building on the left was a large kitchen on the left side. At the far right side of the dining room was the staircase that led to the upper story, where our living quarters were. A large open bay held twelve army style beds on each side of the aisle. There were storage rooms at each end of the building.

The housefather would see we were all awakened at seven a.m. We were expected to be washed and ready for inspection before breakfast at eight, but it wasn't that easy for some. Four boys had to clean the sleeping areas while four other boys had to help serve breakfast. These jobs lasted one week; we had to take turns doing them. The worst job of all was emptying the night pails.

We didn't have indoor plumbing in our building in those days. Since the outhouse was a couple hundred feet from our house, this was quite a scary walk in the dark, especially for a boy of seven. At nighttime we used two enameled white pails (one for each side of the hallway) with a lid and a bail, as a toilet during the night. These pails had to be carried out, dumped into the outhouse, then washed out, before breakfast.

Since nobody wanted this job, it was used as a punishment. If one of us was heard cussing we would be put on "night pails". Once you were put on night pails you stayed on it until someone else was caught cussing. One could stay on this detail for quite a while. No one liked it but it sure cut down on the cussing.

There was a bulletin board outside of the house-dad's room. Every Sunday night he would put up a new list of who was to be assigned to each chore for the upcoming week.

Jack and I were both lucky that they didn't put us on the chore list for the first month. I guess that Mr. Mayo wanted us to learn our way around. I remember the first chore we had. Jack was given the job of slopping the hogs. We kept two large hogs in a pen, out in the woods, that had to be fed in the late evening. We took the meal leftovers from that day and mixed it with grain. Sometimes this could be dangerous because at times the pigs would root their way under the fence and get out. It wasn't that they wanted you, but they were hungry and wanted the slop, and you were in the way. Mr. Mayo asked me to go with Jack that week, just to learn the ropes.

Another one of the chores was to keep the coal buckets filled. The coal burning stoves in the house had buckets that had to be filled and carried in, sometimes more than twice a day.

The yard had to be mowed and watered in the warm months, and raked in the fall. All of us had to pitch in and do this. We all had to help plant and maintain the large garden as well. We grew just about all of the vegetables we consumed at the school. With so many chores to be done we didn't have us too much time to get into trouble.

———

School always started at nine a.m. sharp. At lunch time we walked back up the hill to eat, usually peanut butter and marmalade sandwiches and a glass of cold milk. After two or three more hours of school we had to carry laundry back up the hill to the house. We did get a couple of hours of play time after getting the laundry up, until supper. Most boys would either play marbles, roll to the bat, or just sat around and talk. In my case, our little group would sneak out in the woods and smoke.

It wasn't long before all of these jobs became a daily routine. Even at the tender age of seven I was able to do my share...at least I thought I was. In the summer we had to work in the cannery as well as pick all the different kinds of fruits and berries we canned.

———

Saturday we all looked forward to because we were free to do whatever we wanted, within the rules of the school. The housemother let us have a small amount of money to buy candy or ice cream from a small store about a mile away.

Parents would send money to the school for the housemother to keep on account to provide for incidental needs throughout the year. She would keep track of our account, so on Saturday she let us spend what she thought we could afford,

Some of the kids didn't have parents or maybe others couldn't afford to send money. If that was the case then the housemother would ask us to donate some of our money to their account.

She would always see to it that every boy had a small amount to spend on Saturday.

I remember that my dad used to send Jack and me money that had Hawaii written on it in big black letters.

After we got our money we could hardly wait to get to the store. I would always get a Bit-O-Honey and a Clark Bar, then decide what cigarettes to buy. The four of us would chip in and get what we could afford. Lucky Strikes and Camels were twenty cents, Chesterfields eighteen cents, but Marvels were only ten cents per pack, so that's what we usually wound up getting.

After we got our candy and cigarettes we would go up into the mountain or just follow the creek bed and see what we could get into.

———

When the days were getting cool, Jack and I had been at the school for about three months. During that time I had to rely on Jack a lot, because I would sometimes forget to do things, and he would help me. I didn't realize it at the time but I was slowly becoming introverted. Often times, while the other kids were playing, I would like to go off and be by myself. I would try to forget that I was in a school with rules that I had to go by. I would sit and watch the things around me—the wind blowing the broom sage; a rabbit scampering across the field. When I saw it disappear into the woods I would wonder where it was going. If I saw a hawk circle in the sky, I would wonder how it would be to fly.

Sometimes I would just look at a tree and watch the leaves move in the breeze. It felt so good just to be by myself and enjoy the scenery.

Jack would always find me. He would remind me that I either had a chore to be done or maybe it was time to eat, so I had to leave my reverie behind. Jack was always finding me, no matter where I had wandered off to.

Understand things could be hard for me. Sometimes I would think that I was just plain dumb when I couldn't do things like the other kids. Jack would sit and talk to me and say, "Pat, you were injured in the head and it's going to take a while for you to completely recover, so just be patient. But you're doing fine. I promised Mom that I'd always help you."

———

As time went by, I would go with the other boys. Jack would always ask me where I was going and who I was going with. After he learned that I would be with someone he knew, he would say, "Have a good time."

After I got to know the other boys I mimiced them, acting the way they did. Before long I didn't need so much help from Jack. Eddie Lail and Earl Martin were a year older. They helped me a lot. Earl looked skinny but was stronger than he looked. Benny, at eleven, had been in the school almost two years. He knew all the ropes. Benny knew the people that lived in the cabins scattered around the mountains. He knew who was friendly to young boys like us, and who didn't like anyone on their property. He knew the best places to go to find the nuts and berries that grew around the school and where to find the best apples and cherries. One thing that I remember about Benny: no matter where we were, he could find a food source. If we went on a hike I wanted to be with him!

Large round chunks of solid salt were attached to stakes and placed at different places around the cow pastures. I never knew exactly why but it had something to do with the cows' health. It was referred to as a cow-lick. Benny taught us how to use a pocket-knife and chip off a small hunk of the salt then put in our pocket to be used on wild apples or cherries to make them more edible. He taught us a lot of things about what to eat and what not to eat.

One of the most important lessons we learned was what to look out for when we went in the woods—like poison ivy, poison oak, and sumac. Kids that came in contact with one of the poison vines had blisters and itchy skin for days. Benny was proud of his knowledge of the mountains and the people that lived there, and he spent a lot of time talking about it. I remember the day in late October, just before Halloween, we were walking on a ridge and could see the school in the distance. Below us to the left we could see several small cabins.

"That cabin down there with the tin roof is where old man Thomas lives," Benny said. "Stay away from there! He hates kids! The large cabin in that clump of pine trees is where an older couple lives…very friendly. Sometimes we can even get cookies."

On and on he went. He knew everybody, or so it seemed.

Benny was more like Tom Sawyer than anybody that I have ever known. He even had a homemade corncob pipe. That day on the ridge as we sat on a large rock overlooking the cabins below, Benny pulled out that pipe and lit up. I thought it looked so neat.

"Where did you get that pipe, Benny?"

"I made it."

"How I do get one?" I asked.

"You have to make it. I'll have to show you how. You'll have to find a corncob and cut in half, and dig out the pith, all but about an inch from the bottom, next get piece of hollow grapevine about five inches long. With the small blade of your knife put a round hole, just a tiny bit smaller than the grapevine and push it in the pipe just above the pith that was left in. And there, you have it. Your very own corncob pipe! All you need is some tobackie and you're in business"

"Where do you get that?" I asked.

"Well, you have to buy it with your Saturday money," he said, "but no tobackie….no problem."

"What do you mean, Benny?"

"Well, first off: when you smoke you throw your butts away, right?"

"Yeah."

"Well, don't. Save them in your pocket, and when you have enough, empty that tobackie into the pipe. Works great! But sometimes when I have no tobackie, at all, I put in dried corn silk or rabbit tobackie."

Rabbit tobacco was a weed that grew all over the place. Benny showed us where to find it, but it had to be cut and dried. After that, when it was crumpled up it looked a lot like tobacco. The taste was awful, but after a while, I sort of got used to it. At least it was free and it tided me over until Saturday.

———

The weather started to turn cold now, and it wouldn't be too long until we would have to stay close to the house because it would get cold in the mountains. Benny said there was a spring house, about seventy-five yards or so from the house, where we could go and have a smoke and it should be safe as the housemother never went out there.

The little shed was built over a natural spring just inside of the wooded area. The shed was about five feet wide and twelve feet long. Year round there was a steady stream of very cold water bubbling up from the ground. The remarkable thing about the shed was it acted like a refrigerator, where they put canned fruits and vegetables on shelves.

I had been smoking with Stinky, my buddy, before I was shot. I still missed him and wondered what he was doing. I didn't blame him for running and leaving me in the field after I was shot. I probably would have run too if I thought the police would be there.

I hadn't given it much thought but I guess my brother Jack still held a grudge, because he had a run-in with Stinky and his two brothers while I was in the hospital; but he never talked about it.

As the weather worsened we had got our first snowfall and had to stay in the house. We could only go outside if we had to use the outhouse, and we had to bundle up for that.

In the front room of the house we had books and games to play with during bad weather, but I had not learned to read so I mostly just looked at the pictures. I could make out some of the words, but not enough to read. Sometimes the housemother would read to us, which I liked. On those occasions we would almost always eat our lunch in the front room, which usually consisted of peanut butter and jelly sandwiches and milk. The jelly was extra good because it was canned here at the school. We had a herd of cows and a dairy, so the milk came from the school too. One day the cows got into a garlic field, so the milk didn't taste so good, but we had to drink it anyway.

After several days in the front room, at last the sun came out, the weather warmed up, and they let us out to play. A few inches of snow remained on the ground. Some of the boys had snowball fights but I didn't care too much for that because I was always the smallest one there, and it was too cold for me anyway. I went inside to stay warm and to be with other boys my age. My mother had sent me a coloring book, so on these bad weather days I would take it out.

Almost all of the crayons were used to a small nub, especially the popular colors, so I began using a black pencil to fill in the pictures, shading them in a way to give them a more of a third dimension. Soon it was more fun than coloring with crayons. Shading became my favorite playroom activity.

In the wintertime it was always dark after supper, but that was the time that I wanted a smoke. Going out to the springhouse was a real scary situation, so I would usually ask Buddy and Eddie to sneak out with me. Finding and staying on the path was difficult in the dark, but we were always able to feel our way. Weird noises came out of the darkness that gave me the willies. As long as we could see the lights of our house, somehow it gave us the nerve to finish our smoke. Once we snuck back into the house, it was usually was bedtime.

One of the most difficult chores we had to do was carry the laundry back up the hill to the house. We did this after school. The housemother would say, "You'd better not get it dirty!" I had heard other boys talk about carrying the laundry before, but it was a first for me. I remember the first day I was told to help carry the laundry. Like most boys, we played around and took our time getting it up the hill, so we were late getting back. Mrs. Mayo was very mad.

"Okay, young fellows, you can go to the dairy and bring up a couple containers of milk before you eat supper!" The next day we had more chores to do because there was some dirt on the laundry. Mrs. Mayo caught every little mistake we made.

As we lugged the large milk containers up the hill, Buddy turned to me.

"I'll be glad when tomorrow rolls around."

"Why's that, Buddy?"

"It's Saturday! Where's your mind?"

"I'm working too hard to think," I said.

"Well, we get some money in the morning to go to the store. How about this: candy, a few marbles, and some real cigarettes.

You know I'm sick of smoking rabbit tobackie, so if we pool our money we can get a sack of Bull Durham pipe tobackie."

"I'm glad you reminded me. I had forgotten about Saturday. It makes this damn chore not so bad," I said. "And you know, it would make me happy if I never have to light up rabbit tobacco again."

"I'm with you."

———

Come Saturday morning after we standing in line to get our spending money (usually about thirty-five cents), Buddy, Eddie, and I headed to the country store. During the night Mother Nature had deposited a couple inches of beautiful new snow. The temperature was just above freezing so the white stuff was just perfect for making snowballs. The mile walk was usually tiring but today, with the snow to play in, it was a pretty fast trip. When we arrived there we got our candy, cigarettes, and pipe tobacco and played around outside of the store. I was so glad to know there was a whole different world out there away from the school.

Now there was a good-sized creek called Cripple Creek that ran past Crawford House, on down the hill, and past the country store. We loved to play there, catching crawdads and wading when the weather allowed. But on this wintry day, we foot-skated on the frozen areas, and followed it all the way back.

I had never followed the creek back to the house before, so I got to see some parts of the school that I didn't know about. A dirt road went past the girls' house, which was where the creek ran across the road.

We had three ways to go to the country store…follow the road, go along the creek, or take the path. The path was the shortest as the road had a lot of turns, and it was almost a straight shot.

On the way back up the hill we met my brother Jack and some other boys were in his age group. He said that he was glad to see me and that they were on their way to the store. After that he and a couple of his friends were going on a hike the next day and wanted me and my friends to go too. We were to all meet at the spring house after church. After we had a smoke, sat, and rested a while, we continued up the hill to Crawford House. With time to kill before supper time but it turning colder, all I wanted to do was to get warm, so I headed to the front room to find a book with pictures.

———

Sunday we all had to go to church. I had never had much use for church, maybe because it always felt like some sort of a chore. At the time I was shot I had been going to a Catholic school. A priest in the hospital gave me a piggy bank to put money in, but as far as the church was concerned it was always the same old thing. After a while it was though I had heard it all and I felt it was a waste of time, so mostly, I just sat and daydreamed.

After we had got back to the house, Mrs. Mayo dropped the bad news on us, saying, "No one is to leave the hill. It's already getting colder. A big storm is due later on this afternoon and I don't want to go out rounding you guys up at the last minute!"

Well, we were disappointed because it blew our hiking plans right out of the water. Buddy walked over to me.

"Pat, that's a bunch of shit, it's not that cold! We won't even be able to go to the spring house for a smoke."

"Well, I think I know how we can smoke," I said.

Buddy and Eddie looked surprised that I might have come up with something ahead of them. Both asked, "What do you have in mind?"

"We can always go to the outhouse can't we?"

"Yeah, but do you know what would happen to us if we get caught? We would never get off the penalty list!"

"I know Buddy, but hear me out. You know that large boulder behind the outhouse?"

"Sure."

"Well, here's what we do, we take turns being lookout, as you can see the entire path from there."

Eddie looked at me.

"Well, I'll be damned, you ain't so dumb after all."

"That's a great idea," Buddy said, "but we'll have to wait until after it's dark because Mrs. Mayo ain't no dummy and I know she will see the smoke coming out."

"I might be dumb, but I sure ain't stupid," I said.

That brought a big laugh, and I think from that day they began to respect me and treat me like I was one of them.

The storm did come in, and the housemother was so right. It deposited about eight inches of new snow and brought high winds and icy-cold temperatures during the night. I don't believe we stuck our noses out for the two days. We used the night buckets instead of going to the outhouse, and mostly ate sandwiches in the front room.

After supper on our second day of the storm it had quit snowing and the wind had died down. Mrs. Mayo said we could go as far as the outhouse, but not to dilly-dally because the temperature was still awfully cold. That was music to my ears because I was anxious to try my new plan of smoking in the outhouse. My friends and I had come back to the front room, sitting around; just waiting for darkness.

Soon it was seven.

"Let's do it!" Benny said. Away we went, Benny, Eddie, Buddy, and me. Now I have to say, the plan was a thing of beauty. We all had our smoke, peed and were back in less than thirty minutes. I felt like a star, but I found out the next night that stardom is not a permanent thing. The evening started out almost identical to the night before. The temperature was a few degrees colder and we were pretty well bundled up as the four of us made our way to the outhouse. Benny and I had our smoke. We were standing up on the rock watching the path when we saw the light from a flashlight making its way toward us. He knocked on the board in the back.

"Get your asses out of there, someone is coming!"

Eddie and Buddy came to the back with us and waited. At this time we were whispering as someone went in and sat down.

"Who is it?" asked Buddy.

"Don't know. It's too dark," I said.

Right then Eddie slipped and his knee hit the back of the little house. The next thing we heard was a scream and the door slapping shut due to the closer spring. We saw the light bouncing up and down rapidly as someone ran down the path, and then, "Oh shit!" "Son-of-a-bitch!" We could see the light from the flashlight fall on the path.

Benny didn't hesitate; he got there in seconds. He picked up the flashlight, held out his hand to help her up, and just about died on the spot. There she stood with her robe and fur coat wide open and her panties around her knees. *It was Mrs. Mayo!*

He had never even seen a picture of a naked woman before, let alone a real one.

"Turn off that damn light!!"

"I can't, my fingers are too cold."

"Well, turn it away while I fix myself!"

But Benny couldn't make a move. He was petrified. There he stood with the light on her navel and staring. She finally turned away and got herself in order. Then she tried to act like what had just happened *hadn't happened.*

"Thank you very much for coming to my aid, Benny, you are a real gentleman," she said.

But he still couldn't talk.

After thinking about the situation a couple seconds she asked, "Where were you coming from, Benny?"

"Fr-fr-from Crawford House ma'am, I had to pee."

"Are you sure you weren't coming from the outhouse, young man?"

"N-n-no ma'am, *I had to pee.*" he wished he hadn't said that again.

"It's cold out here. I'm going in and I suggest that you do the same. Thanks again for helping me."

"It was my pleasure, ma'am."

Of course, that was the story that Benny told. I don't think that any of us believed it one hundred percent, but we were very reluctant to smoke in the outhouse anymore.

———

Winter was in full swing. The weather was still getting colder and it snowed more, but we still had to go to school. With the ice and snow on the ground it was a longer walk down to the school. Sometimes when the wind blew it would make it hard to see. I remember sitting in the class and looking at the snow, and thinking about the long walk up the slippery hill. No matter how much I disliked being in class, it was better than being out there.

Mrs. Pierce would almost always catch me daydreaming and say, "Wake up, Patrick!" My teacher, Mrs. Pierce, was an older heavy set woman. She had her gray hair in a bundle on her head, and had steel-blue eyes that could see right through you. Mrs. Pierce was probably the most intimidating person I had ever known. I even had the feeling that she could read my mind. The first week or so, I wouldn't look her in the eye and was afraid to answer questions. I would hang my head down and sneak a peek in her direction, but she would always catch me looking. Her cold-blue eyes gave me shivers.

I didn't realize it then, but Mrs. Pierce was probably the best thing that happened to me at the school!

———

When the weather let up about a week before Halloween, we all met at the main hall for a Halloween carnival. The whole school joined in for the festivities. We had apple-bobbing and a lot of other games, including some that I had never heard of. Later on that day we made our own costumes and they awarded a prize for the best one. We felt proud as someone in Crawford House got first place. When everything settled down they had a dance, which for the most part involved the older children. While they were dancing I hung around the food table of sandwiches and pumpkin pies and ate my fill.

During the dance Mrs. Mayo walked up to the stage and said she had an announcement. Everyone was quiet and waited.

"We have a student that was born on Halloween," she said. She pointed to me and asked me to stand up.

I didn't expect that, because I had not told anyone. I was a little proud and a little embarrassed when the whole school sang "Happy Birthday" to me. Later on, walking up the hill with my friends, Buddy and Eddie, one of them asked me why I didn't tell them that I was born on Halloween.

"I don't know when you guys were born," I said.

They just laughed…and that's the last I heard of that.

Home for the Holidays

Thanksgiving was the next big thing at the school, but I wasn't going to be there for the big dinner being planned. Jack and I were going back home for vacation. The housemother had made the arrangements for us and purchased the train tickets. I had mixed emotions about being away from the school for a month. At least half of the kids would have to stay, as there were some kids that had no parents to go home to. Others couldn't afford the trip, but one of the big things was the weather, because so many people didn't want to drive on the slippery roads. Jack and I were lucky we were able to take the train, and then the bus the rest of the way.

I would miss those kids that I had lived with for the last five months, as they had become like brothers to me. I wondered what kind of big dinners they would have for Thanksgiving and Christmas, but on the other hand, I missed my mother and wanted to see her and the rest of the family. I kept telling myself, "This is going to be fun." We said our goodbyes and hopped in the car with Mrs. Mayo and headed to the train station in Charlottesville.

———

The ride on the train was new and exciting to me and after spending a couple of hours exploring the other cars, I found myself sitting and staring out the window at all the farms, fields, animals, and beautiful scenery—mostly the mountains and trees. That's where I fell asleep until my brother woke me.

"We're here, sleepyhead!"

My mother was there waiting when we got off the train. She gave me a big hug and a kiss and said we had to get bus tickets to Augusta, Georgia to visit our grandmother and Aunt Emma. We had just enough time to get tickets and something to eat before catching the bus.

The bus wasn't nearly as comfortable as the train, but there was a lot of talking going on that made the time fly by. Aunt Emma was there to meet us when we got off the bus and couldn't stop talking about how I had grown and how I had recovered from my shooting accident, and kept hugging me. I didn't realize it before, but she had spent a lot of time with me when I was in the coma.

I spent a lot of time catching up on the family news. I had little memory of them because of the shooting. My little brother Jerry, who was only five, was like a stranger because my Aunt Emma had taken care of him most of the time. I did remember my cousin Patricia who was pretty close to my own age. She and I spent a lot of time together.

My Uncle Ralph was in the Coast Guard and he took Patricia and me up in a PBY rescue plane. I don't think that I will ever forget that. Patricia was the first girl that I enjoyed being around. She was game for whatever I wanted to do. After we got back home from the plane ride we sneaked off and had a smoke together. How cool was that? She said that she enjoyed it but her face was pretty white, so I wasn't so sure.

———

The second Sunday we were home, all of the adults were excited and listening to the radio. If anyone said something they'd be shushed up. Jack and I didn't know what was going on. My mom finally pulled us aside and said that the *Japanese had bombed Pearl Harbor.* Of course I didn't know what or where Pearl Harbor was, but it sounded bad because a lot of Americans had been killed and a lot of our ships had been sunk. Later on that day we listened to President Roosevelt and heard that he had declared war against Japan.

Without any doubt, that turned out not to be a very good Christmas. Everybody we saw on the street was talking about the war, and there were servicemen everywhere. My mother told us we were lucky to live in a country where we were safe.

Jack and I didn't ask for too much for Christmas because what we got we would have to carry back to school. I think I got about a half a dozen coloring books (I asked for colored pencils instead of crayons), a bunch of comic books, a sack of fifty marbles, and a dart board.

Everything turned out okay, since we did get to visit all of the family. Jack and I felt like the family were thinking of us as more than a couple of discards. Anyway, that's the way Jack put it.

———

After Christmas it was time to head back to the school. I was feeling anxious, because I wanted to see my friends and find out how their vacation went. I was surprised at how much I had missed them.

Jack and I caught the bus at Augusta. I was surprised and a little embarrassed when Patricia kissed me goodbye.

"Write me," she said.

Mom kissed us and told us to watch our manners and for Jack to take care of me, and to keep a close watch on the train schedule to Charlottesville.

The train ride back was a lot different than the one coming from school. It was more crowded and half of the seats were filled with servicemen in uniform. There was a car on the train that sold beer and a lot of the soldiers and sailors spent most of their time drinking. They played banjoes, guitars, and Jews' harps, and sang at the top of their voices. Jack and I were seated close to them and we enjoyed it too. All that entertainment made the miles tick away very fast. In no time at all we were pulling into the Charlottesville station. Out of the window I tried to see the car that was to take us back to school, but it was nowhere in sight. I turned to Jack.

"I don't see the school car anywhere out there. I hope we're not deserted."

"Relax, the car's out there, somewhere," he said. "They would never desert us!"

The train came to a stop and as we got off, sure enough, there stood Mr. Mayo.

"Welcome back to school, boys!"

"Have a nice holiday?"

"Sure did, Mr. Mayo," Jack answered. "We didn't see the school car and Patrick was afraid we were deserted."

Well, parked right there in front of us was a brand-new Ford station wagon, the kind with wood panels that people referred to as a "Woody". On the side of both front doors was printed... BLUE RIDGE SCHOOL.

THE WAR BEGINS

After the holidays I couldn't wait to see my friends. Unfortunately, that would have to wait because I got back on Sunday. I was the first of my group to return; my friends didn't return until Monday. I didn't mind being alone because I wanted to count out my marbles and add my new ones to my stash, which now had ballooned to two hundred and ten, the most I had ever had at one time. I also wanted to do some shading in one of my new coloring books, which I had looked forward to for a while.

That night I lay in bed and wondered about the war, and wondered how it would affect my life. Would it still be going on when Jack and I grew up? Would we have to go and fight?

The next morning at breakfast the housemother said that when we say our blessings to include a prayer for the brave men who were going to fight the war.

—

By afternoon everyone had gotten back from vacation. Benny, Eddie, Buddy, and I sat around the front room for hours talking about our vacations and what gifts we had received.

"I'm having a nicotine fit," Benny finally said. "Anyone up for heading to the spring house?"

The four of us headed to the spring house for a smoke. It was just like old times with everyone joking around. As we back up the hill we met Earl. After everyone greeted him back he walked over and talked to Eddie.

"How would you like to make a bet and win a few marbles?" he asked me.

I was kind of afraid that they were trying pull one over on me.
"What are you talking about?" I asked.

"Well, we're sure the odds would be in your favor, but I'm willing to bet you that Daniel can piss twenty-five feet."

"Impossible!" I said. "There must be some kind of a trick. Is he going to be standing on a hill and pissing over the edge?"

"No, it's not a trick. *He pisses on level ground.*"

"Okay, Earl, I'll make the bet." In my mind I almost knew something was wrong. Earl went to get Daniel, and I went to get my marbles. We agreed to meet in the back of Crawford House.

They had brought a lot of other boys with them, close to twenty boys watching as we counted out our marbles. We let Benny hold the stakes while someone paced off the distance and drew a line. Everyone stood back and waited.

Unbeknownst to me, Daniel had never been circumcised. When he peed he held his foreskin closed until it formed a balloon. When the balloon got as big as he could stand it, he took his other hand and squeezed it, all of a sudden.

The boys watching all agreed there were drops that fell across the line. I couldn't believe what I saw. No matter what they said, I had been fooled and felt embarrassed that I could fall for such a trick.

As Benny counted out my marbles and gave them to Earl, I looked at Earl and Eddie and said.

"I'll get even with you two!"

Later on we went back down to the spring house for a smoke. The others could tell that I was still peeved about the peeing incident, so Buddy put an arm on my shoulder.

"Pat don't feel so bad, most of us fell for Daniel's incredible trick, and lost the bet...even I fell for it."

As I lay in bed that night I thought of how I had been taken. I laughed and realized it was kinda funny - a good show and it only cost me a few marbles. But I wondered if the other kids would make fun of me at school the next day. I wondered if the girls knew about and if they would think it was funny.

———

A few days after vacation, everything was back in full swing again. We had given up on my idea of smoking in the outhouse, and were braving the weather, going down to the spring house when we got the urge to smoke. After school on our third day back, a couple of the boys had gotten a sled for Christmas and wanted to go up the mountain for a sled ride. I had never been on a sled before, but the others all told me how much fun it was; as it turned out, sledding was more work than fun. Each time a boy went down it took him twenty minutes to pull the sled back to the top. To add to the misery, it was snowing and blowing right in our faces. On my second ride down, I picked up some pretty good speed and was actually enjoying myself when the sled hit a rock that was sticking up about six inches. The sled stopped but I kept going, sliding on my stomach and face over a hundred feet to the bottom of the hill. I wasn't hurt, except my face was red and chapped for a week. I just about lost all interest in sledding, especially because I had given the other kids fuel to tease me again.

When we got back to Crawford House that evening we were all pretty well frozen and covered with snow; I was the worst. The housemother put some greasy stuff on my face and fixed us all hot chocolate and made us stay in the front room, where it was the warmest, for the rest of the evening. The next day the snow was still coming down and the wind had picked up so that you could hardly see to walk. I was happy because they closed school for the day.

The rest of that winter, after New Years, it was either snowing, sleeting, or just too bitterly cold to stay outside for any length of time. After school, Mrs. Mayo would say, "Now I want you boys to go straight to the house and stay there where it's warm until supper, and I don't want anyone coming down with their death of cold."

I didn't know that anyone could die from a cold, but I don't think anyone wanted to argue with her. One thing the bad weather did was cut down on our smoking. Only about once a day the group of boys that I ran with would bundle up and walk down to the spring house. I didn't mind staying inside too much because I kept pretty busy. I had my new coloring books in which I could do a lot of shading, and after I had read all my comic books I traded them with other boys for new ones. But Benny came up with the best idea of all: He went and talked to Mrs. Mayo, and she agreed to paint a permanent circle on the front room floor to play marbles on. One day I asked him how he was able to get her to do that.

"I saw something in her that others didn't," he said.

At the time I didn't get it, but later on Eddie told me, "He's talking about the time he saw her naked. Don't you get anything?"

I thought to myself, "I don't think that I could ever look her in the eye again, let alone ask her for a favor." But that was Benny... more nerve than anyone I ever knew.

As the weeks went by, the weather warmed up as winter gave way to spring. We were able to walk to school without our coats.

"I've got to get out of here," Earl remarked one day, one of the warmest so far. "Let's all go for a hike!"

"Where to, Earl?" I asked.

"I dunno, anywhere. Let's ask Benny."

"Maybe he has an idea," I said.

You see, Benny knew the mountain. He knew the trails and where they led to, where friendly people lived, and of equal importance; the distance to where things were.

One of the guys found Benny and brought him into the front room.

"So, Benny," Buddy said, "some of the guys want to go on a hike. Could you help us out?"

"Sure, I'm game. It's getting warm and I can't wait to get out of here, but we have to wait until Saturday. It's going to take time to get to anywhere we want to go. And I'll say this: it will be a lot more fun if we can spend the night. I know of a farm we can hike to, that I went to once before, and they let me sleep in the barn and help with the chores the next morning. I helped feed the animals and they fed me breakfast."

"Count me in on all of that," Eddie said, "but I don't think that the housemother will let us stay out over night. You know how she is about us being out in the dark."

"She let Benny go before," I said.

Benny, at twelve, was older than we were; I was only eight.

———

Friday night, after supper, when we went down to the spring house to smoke, Eddie said that Benny told him that Mrs. Mayo said we could go on a day-hike. We could leave early Saturday morning but needed to be back by supper Saturday night. The cook would make us sandwiches for lunch we could take with us.

Saturday morning we were all up at around six o'clock and on the trail by seven. Benny led us down by the pasture and along the creek. It was a nice warm day. Buddy wanted to get in the creek and cool off. Benny didn't say anything, he just stood by and let us find out for ourselves. When he stepped in the creek he let out a yell and jumped out of the water.

Benny laughed.

"What's the matter, Buddy?"

"That water is so cold that I think my feet turned blue!" Buddy said.

"I'm not surprised. That water runs down from the snow on top of the mountain and will stay cold until late summer. Even then it won't get much warmer," Benny said.

"I thought we were going to visit one of the farms you were telling us about," Eddie said.

"Don't worry, we've got time for farm visiting but I wanted you guys to see how cold the water is, and how tough it's going to be when we go frog hunting."

We headed to the farm that Benny said was the closest—Mike and Betty's farm was close enough we would be back to school before suppertime.

When we got to the farm Mike was out in the barn. Benny told him we were some of the new boys that would be coming to visit.

"Well hello, boys. I'm always glad to meet friends of Benny. Will you be spending the night?"

"Not this time, Mike. The housemother said that some of the boys were too young to stay away overnight." Benny said.

After Benny had introduced all of us to Mike, he said we were welcome to stay as long as we liked.

Betty, a very nice woman who looked to be in her thirties, came to the barn and said that she was going to start milking the cows and we could watch. I had never seen anyone milk a cow before and wondered how it was done. As we watched she sat on a stool and started. I saw her slap the cow's bag a couple of times, then she pulled on one of the cow's tits and the milk came out in spurts. After a while she changed to another tit and did the same thing. Before long before the bucket was almost full. Watching Betty milk, it wasn't difficult at all. She asked us, "Would you like a taste of fresh milk."

"Sure," I said. She gave me a small cup.

I was surprised by the warmth, but it was good.

Buddy took a sip but didn't like it.

Benny said that sometimes the milk would taste different, depending on what the cow had eaten. Then he said that he wanted to take us to an old cabin that wasn't too far from there, and that no one had lived in it for a long time.

We said goodbye to Mike and Betty and headed to the cabin.

The cabin was made out of logs and only had one room with walls covered with old newspapers. Benny said it had been built back in the Civil War days and that the dates on the newspapers went back to the 1880's. I looked at the dirt floor and the fireplace made of stone. The one window had no glass in it.

I wondered who had lived here and what had happened to them. I turned to Buddy.

"If walls could talk what a story these walls would tell," I said.

When we left I couldn't help but think about that old cabin all the way back to Crawford House. We made it back before suppertime and stayed out of trouble this time.

The next day was Sunday. After breakfast we had to get ready for church. I don't know why, but I hated to go to church and I think that most of the boys felt the same way. I knew in my heart there was a God and I also felt that he watched over me, but church was just a place where people went to show their appreciation. I could do this in my own way, and dressing up didn't make Him love me more. However, every Sunday we had to get dressed up, attend church, listen to the sermon, sing hymns, then stay and listen to the teachers tell us what all had happened the last week. This took away from our playing time, since by the time we got back to Crawford House at one o'clock, we didn't have much time to do anything.

Summertime is Frogging Time

As the weeks went by and summertime finally arrived, it was hot and we could go barefooted. Benny had told us back in the fall that he would teach us how to catch frogs. At first I didn't think too much of the idea, but it was better than sitting around the house doing nothing.

Benny, Eddie, Buddy, and I had gone to the spring house for a smoke when Eddie turned to Benny.

"Well, Benny, how do you feel about taking the three of us out to catch a few frogs?"

"You know, Eddie, you took the words right out of my mouth," said Benny. "When are you talking about?"

"How about tomorrow?" I asked.

The next day, the four of us got together after breakfast to talk about the frog hunt.

"Since we need to do this at night, we will all need a good flash-light," Benny said.

"I have one, and so do most of the others," I said. "We need them when we go to the outhouse at night."

"Yeah, I know about that," Benny said, "but the batteries need to be strong. I think they need to be Ray-O-Vac. They're the best."

Buddy got all excited about catching frogs and couldn't wait, but I didn't care too much about the thought of picking up a frog with my bare hands, so it wasn't all that exciting to me.

Well, we couldn't find the Ray-O-Vac batteries that Benny wanted but we spent all that day and the next getting strong ones in our flashlights.

The next night we got permission to be out at night, but we had to be back before ten o'clock.

"That should give us plenty of time to get some good ones," Benny said. He took us down by the creek. He told us he would spot for frogs by shining his light and when he saw one, he would make it jump.

Buddy got in the creek first, not too far from Benny, while Eddie and I waited on the bank. Buddy kept complaining about the water being so cold, but then Benny spotted a frog and made it jump. Buddy got up close and grabbed it in the air but it slipped out of his hands.

"I was afraid to squeeze it, it's so soft!" Buddy said.

Benny laughed.

"That's the art of this thing...you have to squeeze it enough to keep it in your hands."

Before long Benny spotted another one. This time it was Eddie's turn to try his luck, but just as he grabbed the frog he slipped on a rock and fell in the water.

"How's the water?" Benny asked, and we all laughed.

Eddie was pissed.

"Let someone else try it for a while, until I warm up a bit."

We hadn't caught any frogs and probably had scared some of them away, so Benny thought we should get away from the water awhile and have a smoke. Eddie got out of the water and we sat on the bank and lit up. As we sat there and waited, we heard all kinds of strange animal sounds we hadn't noticed before. One of the sounds was like a woman screaming and Benny said it was a bobcat or a mountain lion. I looked at Buddy and Eddie and they both looked scared to death.

"The animals we hear are actually too far away to be worried about," Benny said. "You will always hear them at night. Besides, they would be just as afraid of us as we are of them."

I wasn't so sure of that.

After that, Benny said "Let's get back at it if we're going to get any frogs!"

Now it was my turn to get in the water and try my luck.

Benny spotted one.

"Here it comes!"

I couldn't believe it: I grabbed it and held on to the frog on my first try.

"That's the way to do it!" Benny said. I felt proud that I was the youngest one there and had caught the first frog.

We kept taking turns grabbing frogs. Before long we wound up with ten frogs and I had completely forgotten about cold the water and the scary animal sounds. I was surprised that the frogs weren't slimy like I thought they would be.

When we got out of the water we had a smoke.

"The next time we do this I'm bringing a coat," Buddy said. "I've been cold since I fell in."

We put the frogs in a potato sack with the end tied and put it in the creek until the next morning. Benny said that he would show us how to clean them, then we headed back to Crawford House.

The next day after school, we had to carry the laundry up the hill. After we had Benny show us how to clean the frogs.

"Stand back!" Benny said. He whacked each frog on the head with a stick and cut off the legs, one by one. With his knife, he cut under the skin to get it started, and pulled the skin off of each leg.

"They're ready to fry," he said. "We'll get the cook to do that in the morning."

"I don't know if I can eat them but I'll try," I said.

"These are considered a delicacy," Benny said. "People pay a lot of money for frogs' legs."

The next morning we took them to the cook, who fried them, and I had my first taste of frog legs. I was surprised at how good they were. Buddy and Eddie liked them too and we decided we would like to go frogging again, but that would have to wait until another day.

Drawing Abe

I didn't like going to school. My teacher, Mrs. Pierce, was a full-blooded Cherokee Indian. I didn't care at all for her; she seemed mean, so I just sat there and made believe that she couldn't see me. I've always liked to draw, so that's what I did to make sitting in the class more bearable.

One day she came over to me.

"What are you doing?" she asked. She took the picture I was drawing and went back to her desk. I was afraid she would come back and give me a slap and keep me after school. Instead, to my surprise, she asked me how I drew the picture. I told her that I had a book with the picture of a cowboy in it, and I drew it from that. She asked me where the book was, and I told her it was at Crawford House.

"You mean to tell me that you drew this picture with nothing to look at?" she asked.

"I remember what it looked like and I just started to draw," I said.

"I want you to draw me a picture," she said. "I will give you something to go by." She handed me a book with a picture of President Lincoln and left me alone. I had never done anything like this before and I started to draw. After I finished she took my drawing and went back to her desk.

I started thinking I could do a better job, I started to draw it again. Since she had taken the book back I had to do it from memory. I felt my second picture was a lot better because I had added shading to make it more lifelike.

After class was over I took the picture to Mrs. Pierce, telling her that this one was a little better.

"This is remarkable!" she said. "I know that you've been injured and that you have had a difficult time learning, but I think that I can help you. Do you think that you can stay after school so I can work with you?"

"That could be a problem," I said. "The housemother has us take up the laundry after school."

"Patrick, if I talk to Mrs. Mayo and get her permission, would you be willing to stay with me?"

I jumped at the chance.

"Oh, boy would I!" Who wouldn't rather learn art than carry laundry up the hill? The next day Mrs. Pierce told me that she had talked to Mrs. Mayo and they agreed that I could stay after school three days a week.

When Mrs. Pierce showed so much interest in me it actually caused me to have a lot more interest in her and I started listening to everything she said. She told us about the Cherokee Indians and how they lived and that they would have to hunt for their food, so consequently they had to save and conserve all their food. The men did the hunting and the women did all the cooking, gathering of firewood, and building of the teepees. She also told us how they would grow their vegetables in tremendously large gardens in the summertime, and what they didn't eat, they would store underground to be eaten in the winter. She said that they would dig a hole and line it with broom sage, put in the vegetables, cover them with more broom sage, to keep it from freezing and fill the hole with dirt. Then when winter came it would be dug up and the tribe would have fresh vegetables.

She taught us a lot of other things, but the one thing that stuck in our minds was the burying of the vegetables, which was hard to believe. After school, the day she told us that story, we decided to try and bury some vegetables, to see if it really worked. We had a large victory garden, so we asked Mr. Mayo if we could pick some to bury. He surprised us by agreeing, saying it was a good project for us. He suggested we also get some apples from the orchard, so we did.

Soon we had quite a pile. Mr. Mayo watched us dig for a while.

"This is your project, and it looks like you're on the right track so I'll leave it to you," he said, and left.

We worked a lot more than we had anticipated, but finally got the hole big enough and deep enough. We gathered armloads of broom sage to line the bottom and sides, lay in our food, put a lot of sage on top, and add a large rock on top of that. After we finished filling the hole with dirt, we drove a stake in the ground to mark the spot, so we could find it when the ground got covered with snow.

———

The hardest thing for us boys to do was to wait for good things to happen.

"Is winter ever going to get here? I'm going nuts!" Eddie said.

"Me too!" I said.

"It's probably not going to work anyway, so just enjoy the warm weather while we can," Benny said.

Before we forgot all about our project and went looking for mischief, which was always just around the corner. I remember one day, not long after summer break, we were all sitting around under an apple tree. I was eating an apple after rubbing salt on it. Eddie was playing with a piece of cornstalk and put a small rock at the end of it. When he pulled back on the stalk and let go, it flipped the rock, which would go quite a ways. Buddy, seeing what Eddie was doing, began doing the same thing. I followed suit and had more fun than I had had in a while. Before long we all had a willow branch and played our own little war game, hiding behind trees and flipping apples at each other.

"This is fun but I have an idea. Let's see who can flip the farthest," Benny said.

We all thought that was a great idea, but Benny was the oldest and strongest and easily out distanced us.

One of the problems with this fun game was: sometimes the apple didn't come off the end of the stick and it would wrap around and smack you in the back and hurt like the devil. Another problem was, you could never accurately control the direction that the apple was going.

"I wonder how far a really big and strong boy could flip an apple this way?" Buddy asked.

"That's simple," Benny said. "Let's get Shorty."

Shorty was seventeen and lived in the big boys house. Benny had gotten to know him when he went to a ballgame and Shorty was playing. He noticed Benny smoking and bummed a cigarette. They had said hi ever since.

Well, I went with Benny as we headed to the big boys house in search of Shorty but he wasn't there. Someone said that he was down to the ball diamond. That's where we found him, taking batting practice.

Benny stood behind the backstop

"Hi Shorty," he said between pitches.

"Do I know you, kid?"

Benny was quite upset.

"Of course you do. We shared a cigarette during a game, not long ago," he said.

"Oh, that's right! It's Benny, isn't it?"

Benny felt better.

"Me and Pat here understand that you're the strongest kid in school," he said.

"Could be," he said and added "What of it?"

"Did you ever flip apples?"

"No," he said. "What are you talking about?"

Then Benny went through the whole routine of how we flipped apples

"That sounds like fun."

"Come over to the orchard with us and you can give it a try." Benny said.

"Okay, will do. Got any cigarettes?"

"A few, Shorty."

About fifteen or twenty minutes later Shorty met us at the orchard. He cut a long willow branch and trimmed off the small side twigs. Benny gave him a medium sized apple and Shorty slipped it on the end of the stick.

"Maybe you should try a few throws until you get the hang of it," Benny said.

"This looks simple enough to me. Stand back and learn how to do it!" Shorty replied.

The four foot piece of willow was drawn back to where I thought it was going to break and I stood there in awe, thinking, "We'll never see this apple again."

As Shorty released the end of the limb all eyes were on the expected trajectory of the apple.

Kersplat!!

I didn't see the apple. That's when we saw Buddy lying flat on his back with the apple's remains, now little more than apple sauce, laying next to his head. He was out cold, his face was white as a sheet, and I remembered the accident that landed me in that school. All of a sudden a cold chill went down my back and I thought, "he might be dead!", but that's when he moved. I looked around and Shorty was already about twenty-five yards away, running down the path towards the ball field.

"Hey, Shorty, I think Buddy's alright!" I yelled, but Shorty acted like he didn't hear me and kept on running. Buddy opened his eyes.

"Where am I?" he said in a mumble. He tried to get up but was too dizzy to stand. "What happened? Why can't I walk?" Benny tried to explain about Shorty's failed attempt to flip the apple, but you could see it wasn't getting through to Buddy.

"What happened?" he kept repeating.

Since it was getting late, we had to get back to the Crawford House and wash up for supper or we would all be in trouble.

A few minutes later Eddie asked him if he could walk, but I don't think he could hear. That's when we noticed that his face was swelling up. Eddie and I pulled him up and tried to help him walk. At first it looked like we would have to carry him up the hill but his dizziness would not go. He finally walked on his own, albeit a little wobbly.

After we got back to Crawford House the housemother took one look at Buddy and assumed that he had been in a fight.

"Okay, boys, what did you do to Buddy?" she asked.

She walked him into the front room and had him lie on the couch, and sent Eddie after the housefather.

When Mr. Mayo came in we explained about flipping apples using a willow limb, and how Buddy accidently got in the way and was hit. I think he finally believed us. Mrs. Mayo gave Buddy an ice bag to hold on his face.

"You boys are never to do anything that stupid again or you will be restricted for a month!" she said. "And you have about five minutes to get washed for supper. I want to see some clean hands and combed hair!"

"Not you, Buddy. Benny will bring your supper to you."

Buddy took a few days to get back to normal. After a week it was practically forgotten, except for the teasing, which we always did to each other, such as, Buddy, Buddy ain't got sense enough to get out of the way, or hey, Buddy I hear that you were in the wrong place at the wrong time.

———

Teasing was a big thing at the school but mostly we liked to tease the girls, mainly for how they dressed. In the summertime we got to wear overalls, and go barefooted but the girls had to wear shoes and dresses so we would call them "goodie two shoes!" For the most part they tried to ignore us but you could tell that they didn't like it. We teased the most about the perfume that the girls wore. When a girl passed we would say, "What do I smell? It must be a skunk!"

And they would say something like, "It must be you!" but when we laughed it made them even madder. It was easy to see why they didn't like us.

I think the most fun we had teasing the girls was in the cannery. On one occasion we had to can tomatoes. We sat in chairs at this long table and we were separated from the girls, as every other chair was a boy. I guess it was a way to keep the girls from gossiping and the boys to stay out of fights. It seemed to work, but it gave the boys a good opportunity to tease the girls.

Our job was to peel the tomatoes for canning, but before we could do that they had to be steamed for a short while so the skin would easily slip off. After they were skinned they could become quite slippery and have a tendency to slip out of your hand, and then other times it would squirt out juice if you squeezed a little too tightly.

We were going along just fine when, I guess one of the girls got squirted in the eye and she threw a tomato at one of the boys, and he took offense to that and threw a tomato at another boy. That boy thought it was a good opportunity to smear a tomato in the face of the girl next to him and before long everybody was throwing tomatoes with reckless abandon.

One of the girls, Rosy, was nine or ten but rather small for her age. One eye was crossed and she had to wear thick-lens glasses. She was a pitiful sight to begin with, but when I looked at her during the melee, I didn't know whether to laugh or feel sorry for her. She had a tomato hanging on her glasses and juice running down her face. While I looked at her, somebody hit her right in the face with a tomato and she started crying. Some of the other girls tried to help her but they got bombarded too. Then the door flew open and there stood Mr. Mayo. Everybody froze in their tracks and it got as quiet as a graveyard and nobody dared to make a move.

He just walked in and looked around.

"It looks like you've been having a good time! But just look at this mess! You've wasted a lot of tomatoes and this place looks like a garbage dump!"

Someone laughed but shut up just as quick. I didn't know about the girls but as for the boys, I knew there was going to be hell to pay. For a while he walked around a bit and mumbled to himself.

"It looks like every one of you is going to share the blame for this mess and here's what we're going to do: I want this place look-ing like it was brand-new!" he said. "You'd better get started. It will be done before you leave, if it takes all night! Is that understood?"

"Yes sir!" we all answered.

We had no idea how to get started on what was such a big proj-ect, but then one of the older girls stepped up.

"First, we have to pick up all of the tomatoes from the walls, stove, table, and floor and put them in buckets, after we start wash-ing up all the tomato juice and stains. Lastly we mop the floor," she said.

I was so glad that someone knew how to get started. I think she saved all our butts. The girls wound up doing most of the work as none of the boys had any idea of what to do.

By the time it looked like we were about to get done it was past midnight and we hadn't had any dinner. Mr. Mayo left us alone to do the work. When he returned he said we had done a good job and we had to come back the next day to finish canning the toma-toes, but for tonight we had to make it back up the hill and could have sandwiches before we went to bed.

Getting the girls home in the dark was difficult, but almost impossible to get up the hill to Crawford House, stumbling over rocks and into each other, with no flashlight. We finally made it.

After a couple sandwiches, I think we all passed out when our heads hit the pillow that night.

The next day, at breakfast, Mr. Mayo said that each of us would get five demerits by our names on the bulletin board, which meant we wouldn't be going on any hikes for a while. Most of our free time was spent in the front room playing marbles, reading comic books, or in my case using my colored pencils in my books.

A couple of days after our big tomato fight, Mrs. Mayo walked into the front room and noticed several of us boys playing marbles and other games. She stood there for a couple of minutes until we all stopped to see what she wanted. She looked at me and my friends.

"Did you boys learn anything from the punishment that Mr. Mayo gave you?" she said.

We were all quiet, for the most part, until Benny spoke up.

"Yes, Mrs. Mayo, when we have a tomato fight we should have it outside instead of in the kitchen."

She just stood there and shook her head in disgust.

"Benny, you are not to ever throw tomatoes!" she said.

Buddy, Eddie, and I shot each other glances: Benny had just gotten away with one. If either of us had smarted-off in that fashion, there's no telling how long we'd been on detention. I believed it had something to do with what Benny saw on the outhouse path that night. She certainly didn't want Benny to talk about it. She must have figured the best way to stop it was to be nicer to him.

We had to stay around the house for the next two weeks, but we could still go down to the spring house for a smoke if we didn't stay too long. The worst part was not getting our Saturday money and going to the store. For two more weeks we had to conserve our cigarettes and even smoke rabbit tobacco, which made me sick.

In the second week of detention I noticed that some of the other guys were doing push-ups.

"What's going on?" I asked Benny.

"Everyone's getting ready for May Day," he said.

"What's May Day?" Buddy asked.

"It all takes place on the first day of May. It is a big celebration that the school has every year. There are a lot of fun games and they give prizes for the winners of each event! And all of us want to beat the girls."

Benny also said that if we wanted to enter the contests we would have to let the housemother know.

"I've never been in a sports contest before. I don't believe that I could do anything well enough to win," I said.

"There are some events that didn't need any experience to enter," Benny said. "The wheelbarrow race is probably the best one."

"What's that?" I asked.

"Well, let's walk over to the garden and I'll demonstrate."

Benny sat in the front end of the wheelbarrow with his feet dangling beside the wheel.

"Now, pick up the handles and push me across the yard. Faster!…Faster!. You have to go fast, keep your balance, and above all… don't hit anything!"

At first I didn't want any part of this thing as just those few minutes hurt my hands.

"The more we work at this the tougher your hands will get. By the time May Day gets here, you will be in good shape," Benny assured me.

I still had my doubts about that but I reluctantly agreed to go through with it. Benny saw Mrs. Mayo and signed us both up for the wheelbarrow races. For the next couple weeks we practiced everyday but my hands didn't get any tougher. I even think they got worse.

The day finally arrived and it was time for the race to begin. Benny wheeled me for the first half which was down to the end of main house, where we changed places and I had to wheel Benny back to the starting point. Benny was bigger and stronger than me and gave us the lead.

"We've got a good lead, just give it all you've got!" he said. I hit a rock and fell down when the wheelbarrow flipped to one side.

"Get up! We can still make it to the finish line before the other guys if you hurry," Benny said. I started again; I couldn't believe it, but we just barely beat out Eddie and Buddy and came in first.

Benny laughed and jumped up and down. I was just glad it was all over as my hands were killing me, but then again, I was glad we did it, and we won. Buddy and Eddie were good sports and said we did a real good job and would get the first place prize, but didn't know what it would be.

After all of the events were over they had a big ceremony. We had to watch some of the smaller girls wrap long colored ribbons were tied at the top, around the May pole. A lot of people were there, including some parents who wanted to see how their kids were doing. There were sandwiches, casseroles, cakes, pies, and homemade ice cream, so everyone stood around and ate while the May pole was being wrapped, which for the most part was enter-taining, except for little Rosy with the thick glasses, who tripped over her own feet, fell, and lost hold of her ribbon. Mrs. Mayo picked her up and put her back in her place in the circle. I was wondering what kind of a prize we would get as they began calling out winners of all the games. As Benny and I went up to receive our prize, they handed each of us a blue ribbon with *"FIRST PLACE"* printed on it. I said to Benny, "This is nice but we practiced for two weeks, my hands are all cut up, and bleeding and all I got was a ribbon!" I told Benny, on the way to the spring house, "You can find another partner next year."

The next day at school Mrs. Pierce asked me to draw a picture of a log cabin. When she saw my hands, she asked, "What have you done to yourself?"

I explain that Benny had talked me into entering the wheelbarrow race on May Day.

"What in the world would you do that for?" she asked.

"I didn't think it would hurt that much," I replied.

"I'm going to rub some salt on your hands. It's going to hurt a little, at first, but it will help the healing."

And boy, did it ever burn.

She told me to put some mud on my hands as soon as I got the chance, to wash it off a short time later then rub on more salt. The next day I put on mud, washed, and then more salt. She wanted me to do this for about a week.

"The Indians do this to make their hands tough," she said. "It will do the same for you."

I thought, why would anyone want to do that? But she knew better than me, and I was sure that my hands couldn't get any worse so I gave it a try. After school I headed to the garden area and got my hands into some mud, and went back to Crawford House to wash then off. I met Buddy and Eddie along the way who wanted to know what the mud was for. I told them all about what Mrs. Pierce said about the Indian treatment.

"That must have hurt!" Buddy said.

"Like hell!" I agreed.

After a week my hands did get better and I could, at least, hold a pencil again, so, I guess Mrs. Pierce knew what she was talking about.

About a week or so later Eddie was playing marbles.

"It looks like Eddie has been hit on the head," Benny said to me. We saw a small spot where the hair wasn't growing. Eddie just laughed it off, saying we were nuts. A couple of days later when he got up we all noticed that the bald spot was a little larger and around his eye socket it was dark like he was getting a black eye. One of the guys from the house walked by.

"What happened, Eddie? Get in a fight?"

That upset him and he ran and looked in a mirror.

"Oh my God!"

I asked him what had happened and he told me that something must have bit him. Not knowing what it was, I said that he had better go and have the housemother have a look at it. He said it didn't hurt and would let her look at it this evening. That night at suppertime Mrs. Mayo saw his black eye, which had gotten worse. She told him to get to the infirmary right away, and for Buddy and me to go with him. She told us to hurry it along and we could make it up the hill before dark.

As we were going down the hill Eddie said that he felt alright and he didn't think it was anything for the nurse to get involved with. After we got there the nurse had Buddy and me wait outside so we went around the corner of the building to have a smoke. I guess we had been there about an hour and it was getting dark, so Buddy went in to tell the nurse we needed to start back to Crawford House.

"You two had better get started but Eddie is going to stay here for the night," she said. "Tell Mrs. Mayo that Eddie was bitten by a tick and that he will be spending the night here."

By the time all of the talking was done we walked out and it had gotten dark. Not only had it gotten dark but there was no moonlight to help us out and we had to walk up the hill to Crawford House, by ourselves.

"Jesus Christ, Buddy, what are we going to do now?"

Buddy and I had never been this far away at night so I think one of us was just about as much afraid as the other. We walked up the path, had to cross over the creek and then on the other side of the creek find the path again. In the dark that was hard to do.

As we stumbled around, Buddy stepped on my toe, and I yelled at him.

"Watch out, you asshole, you stepped on me!"

"How can I see your foot?" he answered. "I can't even see you!"

I told him to keep on talking so I could tell where he was. Just about then I fell on a large rock and when I stood up I didn't know which way to start walking.

"Let's just make sure we're going uphill," I told Buddy, since Crawford House was uphill. For the most part that worked out, because it wasn't long before we saw Crawford House and were able to walk toward the lights. When we finally got there the housemother met us at the back door and asked us, "What took you so long?"

"The nurse made us wait while she looked at Eddie and after that she said that she was going to keep him overnight, and to tell you that he had a tick bite," I said.

"Well, that's too bad. It's getting late and you two had better get to bed!" Mrs. Mayo said.

The next day at school, Mrs. Pierce wanted to know why Eddie wasn't there. We told her about the tick bite, and that Eddie had to spend the night in the infirmary. She took that opportunity to give us a lecture about the different type of bugs that live out in the woods, and that ticks are the worst of them.

"Especially for the boys who play in the woods a lot, and are around the creek catching frogs and crawdads", she said. "You have to be extra careful about all animals, large and small, because they hang around the creek for water."

I looked at Buddy and he looked at me, and I knew he was thinking, "Why did we even mention ticks?" I smiled at him to let him know that I felt the same way.

After class, after we carried laundry up the hill, Buddy and I went to the spring house for a smoke. We ran into Benny, who had a new kid with him. Benny introduced him to us as Harold Anderson, a good looking kid, about my size with blue eyes and brown hair. Buddy asked him where he was from.

He said he was from Kentucky, and added, "I just got in last night and they made me stay in the big house, at the bottom of the hill."

"I asked if I could take him around to meet some of the boys," Benny said. He and Harold turned to leave.

"Glad to meet you Harold," I said.

"Yeah, me too," added Buddy.

"See you guys around," Harold said, saving.

I turned to Buddy.

"I hope he isn't one that turns out to be an asshole!" I said.

"You can say that again!"

After school the next day, Buddy and I were walking up the hill when he turned to me.

"What do you think about Eddie? Should we go see him?"

"Let's wait until tomorrow and see how he is," I said. "We're half-way up the hill now. I don't want to go down and have to walk up again. Besides, he's probably back up in Crawford House by now."

"I guess you're right," Buddy said. "It would just be a waste of time."

We went straight to the spring house for a smoke and Daniel was there. I hadn't seen him for a while, as Daniel was older and mostly ran with a different group of boys that included my brother Jack. He said that he had some news. That got our attention, as news from the older boys was always a good thing.

"So, what's the news," I asked.

"Hold on to your shorts. Pat."

"Well, is it about Jack? Is he okay?"

"Pat, he's okay," and added, "if you'll give me a chance I'll explain!"

"Jack is running for the Student Council, and wants me ask you to vote for him," he said.

"Of course I will, he's my brother!"

"But that's not all."

"He wants all of your friends to vote for him too. Tonight after supper, the housefather is going to tell everyone all about it, and that four boys will be voted onto the Council."

That was good news. I was proud of Jack and was glad that Daniel let us know what was going on so we would make sure and go to the meeting.

When we sat down to eat we could hear whispers all around us. After we were done eating Mr. Mayo came in and told us to meet in the front room.

We all found a seat.

"Tonight you guys are going to vote four boys to be on the Student Council," he said. "It is important that you choose boys that are honest and fair because they will be representing you when you need help. They will also help decide what to do when boys get into trouble, such as what punishment to dish out. I'm going to give each one of you a piece of paper. I want you to write on it the name of four boys that you want to be councillors. I will be back in about thirty minutes and collect the ballots and count them in front of you. I will ask Benny Lambert to collect the ballots and to help me count them."

Of course I wrote down Jack's name, and then wrote down Benny Lambert, Daniel Anderson, and Earl Martin. When the housefather came back and counted the votes I was glad that the winners came out the way I had voted, and when I went to bed that night I slept well and was proud of my brother.

A few days later the council had us meet in the front room. Mr. Mayo came in and told us that the council had picked a new leader. Mr. Mayo turned to Jack.

"Okay, quiet everyone. I want you to meet the new head of the Coucil!"

Jack stepped forward and everybody clapped. Boy, did I like that!

Mr. Mayo said that the council would come up with a plan to deal with the penalty marks we had by our names on the bulletin board. He said that the council would meet and would tell us their decision tomorrow night.

After supper that night, we went out to the spring house. We all wondered what the council would do, but none of us ever imagined what they did come up with. I for one didn't like it at all. The next night we all met in the front room again. Mr. Mayo and Jack were there. Mr. Mayo said that the council had came up with a plan to work off our penalty marks.

"The council president would explain it to us, so I will give the floor to Jack Napier!"

"Hi, everyone, I'm new at this, so bear with me," Jack said. "The plan is to give each student a chance to work off his demerits and improve his health at the same time, so this is it: The school is going to build a round quarter-mile track. We don't know exactly where yet but we're thinking about putting it in the old pasture, out here next to Crawford House. It will be laid out in the next few days."

"You will be allowed to have eleven marks at one time, but any over eleven must be run off on the track. You will receive credit for one mark for each lap that you run. And one more thing, if you have over eleven marks they must all be ran off before you go on hikes, go frogging, or visit the local farms."

The only good thing that came out of all of that was, they were going to erase everybody's marks. We would all start all over with a clean slate, but none of that made up for the fact we were going to have to run. I thought Jack was turning into a little Hitler.

After the meeting my friends were looking at me as if I had done something wrong, and I didn't like that. That night Buddy asked me what was going on with my brother. I told him that I didn't like it any more than he did, but I couldn't do anything about it.

About a week later we watched some older boys and a man with a truck. The truck had a small grader attached to the front, which they used to clear a wide oval path through waist-high weeds in the old pasture. After they finished it a couple of weeks later, Buddy and I went over to check it out.

"Just how long is this thing, anyway?" I asked Buddy

"Well, your wonderful brother said it was to be a quarter mile."

"That don't tell me much", I said. "I've never ran a quarter mile before."

Buddy suggested we walk around it and count our steps, which we did, and kept losing our count. After three tries we finally decided it was around eighteen hundred steps, which we thought was almost two thousand yards. That meant we had to run that far just to work off one mark.

"Buddy," I said, "if we had twelve marks we'd have to run twenty-four thousand yards. We could be here all day!"

Boy was I getting pissed! Buddy's response wasn't much, either.

"I guess we'll have to watch what we do from now on."

Every day after school we would check the bulletin board to see if we had any new marks but that wasn't the end of it. Things got worse when we found out that council members had the right to give us marks, although the housefather had to approve them, but in most cases he went against us.

For a while we got by but mostly, I think, because we were being extra careful. One day when we had a smoke and sitting around down at the creek, Benny came by.

"You guys know that I will have to turn you in for smoking," Benny said.

"How can you do that? You're smoking yourself!" Buddy said.

Benny laughed.

"Calm down, I was just kidding. I wouldn't do that to you guys, but if a teacher was around I'd have to write you up."

Then we all laughed and thought, "Benny is still on our side."

Eddie had recovered from his tick bite. The housemother had restricted him to the house for the last couple of weeks, but he was back with us now. We could plan a hike if we could get permission to go, but none of that would do any good if we had accumulated too many marks.

After school, the next day, none of us had to tote the laundry up the hill so we decided to hang around the creek a little longer. Before long it clouded up and looked like rain, so we thought it was time to get back up the hill, except for Buddy and Harold who wanted to hang around the creek a little longer.

"Too bad for you guys, it looks like a storm is coming!" I said.

Boy was I ever right! Before we got half way to the top it started to pour, followed by a loud boom. We ran. By the time we got to the house the water was making its own little gully down the hill.

"Those guys are going to get soaked!" Eddie said.

"Soaked, nothing, they're gonna drown!" I said.

We went into the back door of Crawford House and tried to dry off before going into the front room where all of the other kids and the housemother were. As soon as she saw us she wanted to know where Buddy and Harold were. We told her that they were down at the school house, but we didn't say anything about the creek. Mr. Mayo said that he had better go get them so he left and we waited in the front room until suppertime. After supper Buddy and Harold still weren't back, so I just supposed that Mr. Mayo was having trouble finding them or was just waiting at the school house for the rain to let up.

Eddie said that he was going to check the bulletin board.

"Buddy has twenty marks and Harold has fourteen!" he said when he returned.

"Damn, we are planning to go hiking next Saturday and this is sure to mess things up! There is no point in going without them," I said. "I told you this would happen!"

The next morning it was still raining and the two still weren't back. I thought, "God only knows what they have gotten into."

Later on, we had our lunch and supper in the front room. We could see that water had completely flooded the back yard, and the rain was still coming down. As I lay in bed that night, I wondered why Mr. Mayo didn't bring Buddy and Harold back. I hoped that they were safe.

The next morning the sun was blasting through the window over my bed. I was so happy to see that the rain had stopped. After breakfast Buddy and Harold came walking into the front room looking like a couple bums. Mrs. Mayo asked, "What in God's name happened to you two?"

"Sorry, Mrs. Mayo, but we got caught on the other side of the creek and had to stay at the big boys building," Buddy said.

"Why did you stay on the other side when you could see a storm coming?"

"Sorry, Mrs. Mayo," added Harold.

"Yes, you two are sorry but you'll probably be sorrier when you see the bulletin board."

"How did you know, before we even got here?" asked Eddie.

"The housefather called the older boy's house, and I found out the whole story," said Mrs. Mayo.

They couldn't believe that something that they perceived as a misfortune would cause them to get demerits.

"And I hope that you two have learned something!" she added over her shoulder as she left.

———

Saturday, Buddy and Harold had to run track so we couldn't go on our planned hike. Eddie and I spent most of the day out near the woods. Buddy and Harold didn't get done running track until almost suppertime. After supper, Buddy and Harold, whose butts were both dragging, came into the front room.

"How did the running go, you guys?" I asked.

"How do you think it went?" grumbled Buddy.

"This is unfair punishment! I'm going to bed!" Harold said.

"Why so early?" Eddie asked.

"I hurt all over." Buddy was still grumbling as he walked back to his bed.

The next day after church Buddy and I headed over by the creek to have a smoke. We saw Eddie and Harold just coming down the hill and heading our way.

"What are you guys doing here? I thought you would be in bed recuperating today," Buddy joked.

"Oh, shut up!" retorted Eddie, "Your day will come, and it won't be so funny."

"I heard a rumor," Harold said.

"What kind of rumor?" Buddy and I both asked at the same time.

Eddie chimed in, "I think it's more than a rumor, I heard several of the boys talking about it at the house."

"Come on and let's have it!" I said. "The suspense is killing me!"

"Okay," said Harold, "but this crazy."

"Will you come out with it, already!"

"You know when you break a rule and they give you points against your name?" Harold said. "Well, the council has come up with another great idea. They're going to make us wear a sign on our back."

"What kind of sign?" Buddy asked.

"I don't know for sure but they're supposed to have a meeting about it tonight," said Eddie.

"Damn, I wish that I could get out of this God damned place!" I said, and kept on cussing while I walked over by the creek and lit up.

Later on that night after supper we were all sitting around the front room, all of the council members walked in. Needless to say, nobody applauded.

My brother Jack took the floor.

"I have some news for you guys," he said. "The council has been asked to help with some of the deportment problems here at the school, and here is what we've come up with: From now on if you are caught breaking a rule you will wear a sign indicating what you've done. For instance, if you steal something you will wear a cardboard sign that says: *I AM A THIEF.* It will actually be two signs, connected together at the top by two pieces of cloth, and it will be slipped over your head, so when you walk it will show both front and back. Do you guys have any questions?"

"Do we still get marks?" asked Buddy.

"Yes, everything will remain the same except the sign will have to be worn for more serious things."

"How long will we have to wear the sign?" asked Eddie.

"That will depend on how serious the infraction is, and how many times you've worn the sign."

"Do we have to wear it everywhere, even to school?" I asked.

"Yes, everywhere."

Then something just got all over me and I have no idea what made me do it but I said: "Who thought up this big pile of crap?"

All of a sudden you could have heard a pin drop, and I looked for a place to hide.

"You're lucky this isn't going into effect until Monday," Jack said, "but keep an eye on the bulletin board."

After the meeting, Buddy, Eddie, Harold, and I went down to the spring house for a smoke, and I was being treated like a rock star.

"Damn, where did you get the nerve to say that?" Buddy said.

"You're my hero!" Eddie said.

"You said what we were all thinking!"

"Maybe you guys are right," I said, "but I'll probably be running the track for the next year!"

The next day we checked the bulletin board to see if any of us had gotten any new marks. I was afraid to look so I had Buddy check for me—and much to my surprise none of us had any marks. For the next few days I waited for the other shoe to fall, and a bunch of marks would appear after my name.

By the time Sunday had rolled around, I had spent a week on the verge of a nervous breakdown. After church I walked into me bed area to change clothes and there sat Jack.

"Don't do that again!"

"Do what?" I acted dumb.

"You showed me up in front of everybody," he said.

"I'm sorry Jack, it just came out, but can I tell you that all of that stuff that has happened—the running of track and now wearing around signs—are the stupidest things that I and the others have ever heard of."

"Well, maybe so, but you must know that those things weren't my idea, and not even the council. They came from Mr. Mayo, so I'd suggest that you do the best that you can to stay out of trouble, and no more outbursts at meetings. Okay?"

"Okay," I agreed meekly, and added, "I'm not getting any marks?"

"Not this time brother. Not this time."

I felt as though a heavy burden had been lifted from my shoulders.

As Jack was leaving he turned.

"Do you think we could keep this conversation to ourselves?"

"Yes Jack."

The Wine Makers

A couple of weeks passed after the council imposed their famous penalty of carrying around a sign. For some reason we hadn't seen anyone carrying a sign, as of yet. Maybe everyone was on their good behavior or the powers that be were getting more lenient, but then again, I didn't think so. Sunday afternoon had rolled around again. Buddy was nagging at me to get my clothes changed so we could head down to the creek.

"What's the matter with you Buddy, you having a nicotine fit?" I asked.

"No, I just want to get out of here!"

"Me too, so give me a sec."

We practically ran down the hill and saw Eddie and Harold a ways in front of us. I yelled at them to wait up and the four of us headed on over to the creek.

Eddie was sitting at the edge of the creek with his feet in the water and smoking his corn-cob pipe with tobacco that he had stripped from butts, grumbling.

"You guys know that every time I think of that bullshit of wearing a sign around as a penalty, I just want to get out of here. What in the Hell do they think they're doing?"

That was just the beginning. He went on and on, about how unfair it was, and how they were turning this place into a prison camp. For the most part we agreed with him.

Out of the blue Harold said to me, "Pat, how come you never got any marks for sassing back to your brother?"

"It's nice to have a brother in high places," Eddie said.

"Come on you guys, you know I hate this as much as you do. Maybe it's slipped his mind," I said.

"We'll see," Harold said. "I hope you didn't make a deal with him."

"Maybe we'd better be careful what we say, we could have a spy right here among us," Eddie said.

I got upset and didn't know what to say. I had promised Jack that I wouldn't discuss our meeting, but these guys were the only friends that I had.

"I'll prove it to you!" I said.

That satisfied them, for the time being anyway.

———

Later Eddie was complaining about our lack of tobacco.

"Has anybody got a smoke? This pipe is making me sick!" he complained.

"Smoke, Hell! I'd like to have a drink!" Harold said, handing Eddie a cigarette.

"What kind of drink?" I asked.

"Wine," said Harold. "I like wine."

"Before I got shipped off to this dump, I used to sneak wine from my mom's bottle and replace it with grape juice."

"That sounds good, but there's no place around here to get wine," I said.

"Well, a couple of months ago I was talking to a kid from Kentucky who told me that he knew how to make wine. If you guys want to give it a try, I'll talk to him and see if he knows what he's talking about."

"What does he need to make the stuff," I asked.

"I dunno, I'll have to ask him."

Buddy said that he thought it wasn't a bad idea but we'd have to be extra careful for with all the penalties going around—marks, running track, and now carrying around signs. If we got caught we could find ourselves in a lot of trouble. We all agreed with that and decided to make a pact, not to discuss this with anyone outside of our group.

We told Harold to have the boy from Kentucky meet us at the spring house the following day after school.

———

After supper I walked down the hill by myself and crossed over to the big boy's house. When I walked in the front room I saw Jack playing checkers.

"Hi, little brother, what brings you here?"

"We need to talk!" I said, then added, "*not here.*"

We walked outside.

I couldn't wait to say, "You have to give me marks for smarting off at that meeting!"

"Now, that sounds stupid. Why would you *want* marks?"

"My friends think that you're protecting me, and they no longer trust me. They have even accused me of being a spy."

"That will be easy. I'll put five marks by your name tonight."

"That's not enough....I need fifteen!"

"Then fifteen it will be."

"Thanks Jack!"

———

The following day, after supper, Eddie, Buddy and I walked down to the spring house. Before long Harold and the kid from Kentucky came in and joined us. Harold introduced him as Bobby. He was sixteen but wasn't any taller than me, with bright red hair and a face full of freckles.

"I understand that you guys want to make some wine," he said.

"Yes," I said, "but we don't know where to start."

Bobby said that first you have to get a lot of grapes, a large container to put the juice in, and then some kind of cloth to strain it after it's made.

"You mean it's that simple?" asked Harold. "We could have been doing this all along!"

"It's not quite as simple as it sounds. You'll see. First you guys have to find a lot of grapes and something to put them in, then we have to crush the grapes and find a dark place to let it set while it turns into wine."

We knew where we could find wild grapes. Eddy said there was a large flower pot over by the victory garden that was filled with dirt. We could dump out the dirt, wash it and put it under the house.

"Okay, Bobby, is that all there is to it?" Harold asked.

"No, not quite. You'll need a lot of sugar and a clean white cloth to strain the wine after it's made."

The next day Buddy and I went out in the pasture to pick some grapes, but after a few hours we hadn't come up with too many bunches. Eddy and Harold had washed the flower pot and put it under the house. When Bobby saw our grapes he said it wasn't nearly enough. I told him that I thought we got them all.

"Why can't we use blackberries? I've heard of blackberry wine before," Harold said.

Bobby said that he thought it would work, so we decided to use blackberries along with the grapes. We all went out and picked blackberries, but we had to make sure that nobody saw us bring them in and put them under the house.

The next day, the five of us met under the house to begin the process of crushing the grapes and berries. I was the first one there, so I began picking the fruit off the bunches, when Eddie and Harold came up, stooping to get under the house.

"It looks like *someone has some running to do*," Eddie said.

"What's that supposed to mean, Eddie?" I asked, trying to act dumb.

"You just accumulated fifteen marks. What do you think of your big brother now?" Harold chimed in.

"He's an asshole, as usual!"

Buddy had just arrived, and asked what we talked about.

"It looks like you're still our hero, after all!" Harold said.

They all agreed with Buddy. It felt good to know that I was back in the good graces of my friends, but had no idea of how I was going to run all those laps.

With a passel of wild grapes and about the same amount of blackberries, we all picked the fruit off the bunches. When we were done we had about a half container of fruit. Bobby had to run track so he couldn't be there to guide us.

"What do we do now?" Buddy asked.

"According to Bobby, we crush it all up," said Harold.

"How do we do that?" asked Eddie.

"I have an old baseball bat that might work. I'll run and get it," I said.

That did the trick. Before long we had a bunch of grape skins, seeds, and a lot of juice. According to Bobby, all we needed now was a lot of sugar. Unfortunately, that proved to be the toughest problem. The only time we got sugar was at breakfast. Mrs. Mayo always ate with us, and she watched us like a hawk. The next morning all four of us decided to do the best we could to divert her attention while we tried to put a cup of sugar in our pockets. We made it back to our concoction and emptied our pockets, dirt and all. We had no way of measuring, so we decided that what we had would have to do.

Bobby came under the house just as we were finishing up with the sugar.

"You guys are looking good," he said. "Now all you have to do is put a board or something over the top and wait a couple of weeks for this to set up. Then you need to squeeze the juice from all the seeds and skins."

"And how do we do that?" I asked.

"A white cloth, like a handkerchief ," he said. "In your letter home this week have your mother send you some handkerchiefs."

"Now, just one of you do it because the housemother reads your letters. If all of you do it she'll get suspicious."

After I had written the letter Mrs. Mayo said that she was glad that I was going to start using a handkerchief *instead of my sleeve.*

———

During the next month, waiting for the grapes and blackberries to ferment was one of the hardest things that the four of us had done for awhile, so I tried to occupy my mind and also to run off some of my marks.

I had never done any running before and while I was huffing and puffing around the first lap, I'm thinking, "Asking Jack for those fifteen marks was just about the stupidest thing that I had ever done, but then again it got back the respect of my friends, so I guess it was worth it." During that month I ran off eleven of my marks, which made me proud of myself.

———

After a month of fermenting, we were finally ready to squeeze out that mess. We wound up with about three and a half quarts of wine, but now what would we do with it?

None of us could carry around a quart bottle of wine, which led Buddy to say, "We need some small bottles to put it in—small enough to put in our pockets."

"Sure," I said. "But there's nowhere around here to find small bottles."

A couple of days later, when we were playing down by the creek, Harold wandered off and snooped around behind the dispensary. He saw some small medicine bottles that had been discarded, so he picked up five of them. They held about six ounces each, which turned out to be just the right size to carry in our pockets, so we cleaned and filled them. Even so we still had about two and a half quarts left, so we stashed that away in a safe place to fill our bottles at a later day.

The next day was a Thursday. We were all chomping at the bit to get away from the school to try out our concoction, which we were calling wine.

After school we had to carry up laundry. While we were at the washhouse we saw a boy with a sign on, that read "I AM A THIEF". Buddy said that he didn't know the kid but he felt sorry for him.

"If that isn't bad enough I wonder how many marks he got," I said.

"That reminds me, we'd better check the bulletin board when we get back," Eddie said. "Tomorrow is Friday, and if we want to go on an overnight hike we have to make sure we can all go."

Buddy said he had checked it that morning and we were all okay. He had nine, Eddie had five, and I had four.

"That sounds good, but you know the housemother will probably be adding more to that by Friday," Harold said.

The first thing Friday morning we all ran and checked the bulletin board, and saw we were all still in good shape. No more marks had been added, but the day wasn't over yet. We all spent a nervous day, anxious to test our wine. The only way we could do that, we felt, was to go on a hike, so if we got drunk we would have time to sober up before returning to the school.

As we walked up the hill, after school Friday, we were all a little afraid to think we could have gotten more marks that would nave messed up the weekend, so the first thing we did was run to the bulletin board again, and breathed a collective sigh of relief when we found we were all clean. The second thing was getting permission to stay out overnight on our hike. Buddy and I was asked to do that.

"Mrs. Mayo, we would like permission to have an overnight hike," I said.

"Who all wants to go?"

"Harold, Eddie, and me and Buddy, here."

"You mean Buddy and I."

"Yes ma'am."

"You know that when you went overnight before, Benny went with you. Do you think that you will be okay?"

Buddy was quick to answer, "Oh, yes ma'am, we're only going to where Mike and Betty live. It's the closest farm. I know the way and we'll stay there and not go anywhere else."

"I know the way, too!" I chimed in.

"Alright, you boys, I'm going to trust you this time and give you my permission, but behave yourselves and be back here before noon tomorrow and not one minute later!"

After we went outside, and told Harold and Eddie, we jumped up and down with joy just to think we could finally go to the farm, drink our wine, have time to sober up, and no one at the school would know the difference.

———

I wasted no time getting ready, as we were traveling light. I had almost a whole pack of Marvel cigarettes (at ten cents a pack the cheapest I could buy), and my knife that was illegal at school. The blade was just a tad too long but you can't whittle with a two inch blade, and I had an empty front pocket for my small bottle of wine.

———

We got a good start. We got to the farm in about an hour. It was still light outside, and Mike and his wife were just getting ready to milk the cow. We told Mike we had to be back by noon the next day. He told us we could sleep in the barn and that he would awaken us in the morning. Betty, his wife, came in and said we could have breakfast in the morning with them.

We flattened out a big hay pile in the front of the barn and made a place to sleep. After Mike finished milking the cow he said if you boys smoke be sure to go outside because that's an easy way to lose the barn.

"With all the hay in here this place is a tinderbox," he said, then said goodnight and went on up to the house.

After he left, we couldn't wait to get a taste of our concoction. Buddy asked, "Who wants to be first?"

"You go ahead," I said, but he was a little hesitant. We just stood there.

"Go ahead!"

"I don't know," he said.

"*I'll do it,*" Eddie said, and he took a little sip.

"That's not bad," he said, so I took a sip and it tasted God-awful.

I watched as each other took a drink and they all made funny faces then we waited awhile and Eddie said that he had a funny feeling. I asked him, "Do you think that you are getting drunk?"

"I don't know, I've never been drunk before," he said.

I took another sip and surprisingly, it wasn't as bad this time. Then we all took sips. Soon we were all acting silly and laughing for no reason at all. When we talked it didn't make any sense. I don't know how the other three felt but I was actually starting to feel good, although I was a little dizzy.

We all four went outside for a smoke, and when the cool night air hit Buddy he vomited. I asked him how he felt

"*Better, now,*" he said. When we went back in to our straw beds, I don't even remember lying down.

Very early in the morning I was awakened by somebody over by the cow stall. It was still dark and hard to make out who it was. I thought at first it was one of the boys but when the lantern was put up on the stall, I could make out a girl starting to milk the cow.

I got up and found that I was still dizzy as I walked over to where she was. She said she was sorry for waking me up, but she had to get the milking done. I went back and lay down. A short time later she was done milking. She started to leave but then sat down the milk pail, walked to the closest corner, squatted down and started to pee just as I looked at her. I wondered if she was aware of me, but if she was, I guess it didn't matter. When she finished she stood up and got the milk bucket.

"My mother will have breakfast ready in about an hour, so why don't you guys come on up to the house," she said.

I awakened the others and told them that Betty was ready for us to come to breakfast. Buddy said that he felt sick. I said that he looked like he was as pale as a ghost. Eddie said he always looked that way and we all laughed.

"This ain't funny!" Buddy said.

"You just think that you're sick but you'll be okay after you eat something," Eddie said, so we left for breakfast. Betty had fixed pancakes and ham, and it was good. She said that she was glad we had a good night's sleep, and we were welcome to come back again.

"The next time you come maybe I can spend more time with you but right now I have a lot of work to do, and I need to get at it," Mike said.

We stayed around for awhile and talked to Betty and their daughter. When I saw her in the light of day I could tell that she was a little older than me; maybe thirteen. The dress that she was wearing was a little bit tight and made her small breasts stick out a little. She didn't say much but sat there and smiled a lot. Betty made up for it as she was talking all the time—asking us where we came from, how long we had been at the school, and just every-thing that crossed her mind.

We had to be back at the school by noon so we told Betty we had to get going before it got too late. She told us to be sure to come back again, and we said we would.

On the way back I told the others about the girl who was milking the cow and how she relieved herself in front of me. "You mean she just squatted down and took a piss?" asked Buddy.

"Just as if you wasn't there?" asked Eddie.

"I don't believe it!" Harold said.

"You either had too much wine or you're making it up."

We made it back before noon. The housemother said we had did well and the next time she wouldn't worry about us.

We still had time to kill before supper. I ran into Benny, and told him we went on an overnight hike. When he asked where we went I told him about the four of us and we went to Betty's farm.

"Did you have any trouble finding it?"

"No but we had a good time," I said. I didn't tell him about the wine because he was on the council, and I didn't want to take the chance that he might write us up even if he was a good friend. I did tell him about the girl peeing in the barn.

"Girls that live on the farms do that and that they don't think much about it," he said. "Sometimes when working out in the fields, and the outhouse would be too far to walk, they would just stop working, squat and piss right there on the spot. In the summertime when the outhouse smelled truly awful, they would hardly ever use it. I have noticed some of the mothers did it that way too, so it's more of a way of life than anything else."

Benny said that most of the girls didn't go to school as they were needed to worked on the farm but he still thought they were good people.

One day after school we had a little time to kill, so Daniel and I went down to the spring house just to get away from the other boys, and to talk about some of the things we planned to do the next day. Eddie and Buddy showed up and said we had to take a shower tonight after supper. The way the house was laid out the back door was right by the shower, which was about ten feet by three feet with a curb around the perimeter that was six inches deep. If someone walked in the back door they would walk right past the shower and on into the kitchen. Since there were only boys in the house, in most cases it wasn't a problem. The only females were the housemother and the cook, so taking a shower was nothing that bothered us. Sometimes the housemother would walk by on her way to the kitchen, but we got used to that and paid it no mind.

After supper we went upstairs to get our towel and house robe then went down to the shower, hung up our robe, and got in the shower. It was just Eddie, Buddy, and me, and as we were showering we heard what sounded like girl's voices.

"That must be the radio that the cook was listening to," Buddy said, so we went about our business.

Just about then the housemother came in, on her way to the kitchen and left the kitchen door open about six inches. As we got out of the shower to dry off we could see girls in the kitchen, and went over to get our robe. We had to walk past a spot where the girls could see us and we could hear the girls giggle. We got dried off.

"We should go right through the kitchen without our clothes on," Buddy said, but Eddie and I both told him that the cook was in the kitchen. We would get into a lot of trouble, so we donned our robes and walked through the kitchen. Awe got to the staircase, I looked back and here came Buddy as naked as a jaybird. He just walked across the dining room as pretty as you please, without a care in the world. I had an eye on the girls and could see that they were watching Buddy.

When we all got to the stair Eddie spoke up.

"You know, Buddy, the girls have been watching you!"

"I don't care, I hope they got an eye full. They shouldn't have been here in the first place. If the housemother says anything to me I'll just say that I didn't know that they were in the kitchen," Buddy said.

The next day at school I noticed that one of the girls was in the same class as Eddie and me. At recess we saw her with some of her girl friends. We couldn't hear her but we could tell that she was talking about what happened in the kitchen last night, because they kept looking at us and smiling. I had a feeling that by the end of the day, the whole school was going know about it.

Later on, after school we saw Buddy down at the creek. Eddie told him about the girls at recess that day and how they talked about him, and asked him if any of the girls were in his class. He said that he didn't look at the girls. He just walked by without noticing, so he didn't know what they looked like. I said to Buddy, "Well, just wait until tomorrow and you can see who's looking at you and laughing."

Buddy got a little nervous about going to school and he said that he might not go tomorrow. I told him that he had to or he would be in even more trouble.

"Maybe I'll be sick!" he said.

"We have to carry laundry up the hill today," Eddie said. We needed to get started or we wouldn't have time to go for a smoke before supper. After meeting Daniel at the wash house, we told him about what buddy had done

"Buddy doesn't act too bright sometimes," he said, then laughed. "He's always doing something stupid without thinking about what could happen to him."

After we got back from our laundry detail we had just enough time to wash up for supper. Buddy couldn't pass inspection by the housemother so he had to go back and rewash his hands. When he came back and passed inspection he had to hold his hands out in front while the rest of us ate. After we got done Buddy had to help clean up the dishes, and couldn't go with us to have our evening smoke.

The next day we had laundry detail again. Buddy had to stay after school again, and we were all wondering why he was in so much trouble lately. Almost every day something was causing him to rack up points by his name. We were all sitting around the spring house when Buddy walked up. Eddie asked him why he had to stay after school.

"One of the girls was teasing me about when I walked by them naked in the dining room the other night, and I got mad and threw a small book at her," he said.

"Did you hit her?" Eddie asked.

"No, but the teacher saw me, and I had to stay and help clean up the classroom."

"You know, Buddy, the way you've been acting lately, it won't be long before you won't be able to leave the area around Crawford House except to go to school or carry up the laundry, and you won't be able to go on hikes with us because you'll have so many marks," Daniel said.

"It's not my fault that she was teasing me!" Buddy said.

"You could have put on your robe like the rest of us did instead of making an ass out of yourself by running around and letting the girls see your naked body," Daniel said.

"What about the times we got caught swimming naked by the mountain girls at the swimming hole?" asked Buddy.

"That was different," explained Daniel, "The girls in the mountains are used to that. They will squat and pee right in front of you but the girls at school are from the city, and they are not used to seeing boys running around naked. Although some of them will giggle and not say anything. I guess you just did it in front of the wrong ones."

The next day was Saturday and we could go to the store, and buy stuff —we were glad as we had the whole day to do whatever we wanted. Besides, we just had to buy some real cigarettes. We had been smoking rabbit tobacco for so long that it tasted like shit.

We took our time getting to the store because we went by the creek and played around too long with a snake we caught. By the time we got to the store it was about one o'clock, and was surprised to find there were a couple of sheriff's cars and several men in uniforms standing in and around the store. They wouldn't let us in so we just hung around to see what had happened. After a while the police left and we got to go in. Eddie said that he heard one of the men say that someone had stolen something from the store and he thought it might have been one of the kids from the school.

"I wonder if it was one of the boys from Crawford House?" Buddy said.

"God, I hope not or we'll be spending some time in the front room tonight, for sure," I said.

That night most of us sat around waiting for Mr. Mayo to come into the front room and ask us questions about what happened at the store, but he never showed up, and boy was I relieved.

What usually happens with cases like this is: When they can't find the culprit, Mr. Mayo would just put it off limits for everyone. Maybe they found out who was guilty, but whatever the case, we heard no more about it.

The next day, being Sunday, we had our normal day at church and we spent some time around the front room.

"Let's play roll-to-the-bat," Eddie said.

"That sounds good to me," I said.

Buddy, Harold, Eddie, and I walked over to the old pasture where they had built our running track.

Roll-to-the-bat was a game with a ball and a bat where the person at bat would hit a fly ball to the others. If someone caught it, that person would come up to bat. If no one caught it, then the person that got the ball on a bounce could roll the ball to try and hit the bat, which the batter had laid down in front of himself. If the bat was hit then the "roller" would come up to bat, which was not so easy to do. Sometimes a person could stay up to bat for a long time.

On one occasion I wrote home and I asked my mother to send me a baseball glove. The glove that she sent was white and didn't have much of a pocket, with about an inch of leather between the finger and thumb. Not it wasn't a good glove, but it didn't work too well when catching a tennis ball…but it was a glove and everyone wanted to use it so I would let a boy use it all day for five marbles. Getting the marbles was more fun than playing the game.

While standing around waiting for Harold to hit a decent fly Eddie walked over.

"You know, this whole pile of crap is getting more boring every day!" he said.

"What do you have in mind?" I asked.

"Well, ole friend, to start with, remember the wine we made? There was a jar or two left. Do you remember what we did with it?"

"Yes, we hid it under the house but that's been a while, and who knows, I doubt if it's still there," I said.

"Well, let's go see," said Eddie. We snuck off from the other boys, walked over to Crawford House and crawled underneath, and sure enough, it was still there where we had dug a hole, covered it up, and put a concrete block over it.

I expressed my doubts about whether it was still good after all this time, and added, "We still have to be careful and not start drinking this until we can go on another hike,"

"Let's just taste it and see if it's still good," he said.

Since we didn't want to cart this stuff out to the farm and find it wasn't any good, that wasn't a bad idea. I opened the jar, which was only half full. I took a sip and handed it to Eddie.

"Was it any good?"

"You tell me."

Eddie took a sip.

"It's still good!"

"Well, not really *good* but It's better than before."

A Little Nip Goes a Long Way

Eddie and I walked back out to the pasture where Buddy tried his best to hit a decent fly ball to Harold. Several other boys that had joined the game.

"Come on over here, we need to talk! You too, Buddy, let someone else bat that can hit the ball." I joked.

"And you think you're so good?" he came back.

"If I wanted to," I said.

Eddie jumped in.

"You're both great, but we have some important business to talk about," he said.

"I'm all ears," Harold said.

"Okay, you guys, we've all been itching to take another overnight hike, right?" said Eddie.

"Gotta get outta here!" Harold mumbled.

"Me and Eddie just went under the house and found that our jars of wine are still there, so what do you say?" I said.

"I say let's do it!" said Harold with a little more enthusiasm.

"Well, Friday is coming up, and if we talk to Mrs. Mayo, maybe we can leave right after supper."

This time it was agreed that Harold and I would go in and ask the housemother for her permission to go on another overnight hike.

Thursday afternoon we went in and asked Mrs. Mayo, "Eddie, Buddy, Harold, and I would like to go on an overnight hike to Betty's farm. While we are there we can help her with some of the work around the house."

I knew I was saying things that she liked as I saw a rare smile when I put the "I" last when including my friends, and "Helping Betty," I knew she would like that.

"Helping her would be nice," she said. "I have some things that I would like for you to take and give to Betty. If you guys left right after supper tomorrow evening, you will have plenty of time to get there before dark."

"Thank you, Mrs. Mayo."

"You're welcome. Stop by here before you leave, and I will give you the package for Betty."

After supper the next day we went by and got the package for Betty while Buddy and Eddie went under Crawford House and got the wine. The four of us met at the spring house.

"You know, it's too bad we threw away the bottles we had for the wine, now we have to carry around this quart jar," said Buddy.

"Yeah," I agreed, "but we have the cloth sugar-sack that Mrs. Mayo wants us to take to Betty. Let's just put it in there."

"Just don't break it," said Buddy.

When we reached the farm it was almost dark. We said hi to Mike and went straight to the barn. We stashed our wine and flattened out a pile of hay for our beds. Then we then in to see Betty, who was fixing supper. She was surprised we had a gift from the house-mother, but she didn't open it.

"Monday is my birthday," she said.

I was glad we didn't spill wine on it.

She asked us if we wanted something to eat. We all declined, saying we had eaten just about an hour ago. Then I asked her if there was anything we could do to help. She said there were a couple buckets of slop by the back door. If we didn't mind we could carry them out to the hogs.

"Don't dare go in the pen, but pour the slop over the fence into the trough. Those hogs will run all over you!" she said.

"Yes ma'am," I said. "We have hogs at the school we have to slop."

Tired, we decided to go to bed early. We had planned a hike in the mountains tomorrow morning, and wanted to get an early start. Someone would be coming in before six in the morning to start milking the cow. Sometime close to sunup I looked toward where I heard a noise and someone was milking a cow. Whoever was doing it wasn't doing a very good job. Every time they touched the tit the cow tried to kick the pail. At closer look I saw that the would-be milker was Eddie.

Then I saw Doris, one of Betty's girls come in and said that she would milk the cow.

"I was going to do it but the darn cow kept trying to kick me!" Eddie said.

"Well, in the first place, she doesn't know you and secondly, your hands are cold. She doesn't like that," Doris said.

She got a hand full of hay and put it in front of the cow and that kept her occupied and easier to milk.

Then Betty came over and asked if someone would fill the tub with water so she could take a shower later. We got water from the well and filled the tub.

A large oak tree adjacent to the barn had a fork of a couple low branches. Mike secured an old bathtub on that fork, just about eight feet off the ground. Where the drain was, he put a pipe with a valve and a spray nozzle on it. This worked great in warm weather as the sun would warm the water in the tub, but in cold weather… not so much.

We got an early start and had planned to find one of the old cabins that Benny had taken us to, but before we got far we decided to take a drink of our wine. Buddy took the first drink and we followed him. Eddie and I didn't mention we had sampled it a couple of days before. We knew they would be jealous, so we took our turn and made the face as if it was bitter, which it was, but not as bad as before.

We only took one drink at first and just walked along, but after awhile I got a warm feeling inside.

"I think I will take another drink," Eddie said. We all followed suit, and this time we felt a little better about it. After a while we were giddy and we laughed at everything each other did. We had a good time, but walking got tricky.

Eddie got sick and vomited so we decided to stop and lie in the sun until some of our dizziness subsided. As we walked we drank more wine. This routine went on for most of the morning. Somehow we got turned around, got off the path, and found ourselves going up the hill when we were supposed to be going down.

Buddy said that he didn't remember this part of the mountain. I said we should start back down and find out where we were, so we did, and after awhile we saw the barn at Betty's farm.

"This has got to be a miracle!" Harold said.

We walked into a clump of trees and sat down to rest. Only about a hundred yards from the barn, we could walk down whenever we wanted. After awhile we left the trees and headed down. We saw the barn door open and out walked Betty, carrying a towel with a housecoat on.

"Let's go back into the trees so she won't see us!" Eddie said.

"Why?" Buddy asked.

"I think she's going to take a shower." Eddie said. Sure enough, she walked over to where the tub was in the tree. She pulled the sheet over to block the view from the house, but didn't block of the view from the side we were on. She took off her housecoat, hung it over a tree branch, and got in the shower. We were a football field away but there was no doubt as to what we were looking at. We walked around to the other side of the barn and just stayed there for a while. When we thought that she had gone into the house we went back to the barn.

I told Eddie that the woman in the shower didn't look like Betty.

"It wasn't one of Betty's girls, so it had to be her," Buddy said.

After we had a smoke we headed up to the house, but we were a little afraid to face Betty as we didn't know if she had seen us looking at her. When we got close to the house she came out.

"I hope you boys had a good time. Did you happen to find any arrow heads?"

"No ma'am, we weren't looking for any today, we just went up in the mountains to find old cabins, and found one we had seen before," Buddy said.

"Come on in and have a glass of milk," she said.

"We have to get back to the school pretty soon, but we would like to have the milk before we go," I said.

As we walked into the house, we saw a young woman sitting at the kitchen table.

"This is my cousin Mary, she has come to stay with us for a week," Betty said.

She appeared to be about twenty and was quite pretty. She just smiled at us.

I guess we blushed as we realized it was her we had seen in the shower. I couldn't help but wonder if she saw us. After we left I said to the other guys that I didn't think it was Betty we saw in the shower, not that I knew what she looked like with no clothes on, but she just didn't look like what I thought she would. They just looked at each other, wondering what I meant.

———

A few days after we returned from Betty's farm we were playing down by the creek at the area where the road crosses it. We had just finished with an egg race in the creek. While we were standing there we heard a car coming down the road. The water in the creek at that point was about ten inches deep. The only vehicles that came down the road were delivery trucks were built high enough that the engine wouldn't drown out.

The driver was Roy Hansel, who worked as an all around maintenance man for the school. Today he had his brother's older model car and was on his way to town. When he got to the creek he slowed down as the water was deeper today than usual, and he was worried about the motor drowning out. When he was almost stopped the four of us got around to the back of the car and lifted the rear end so the wheels would just spin. We couldn't hold it too long, but just long enough to get him to turn off the ignition, get out of the car, and try to catch us, but we were fast. After a warning and a few choice cuss words he got back in the car and restarted it. We went back to lift the rear again, but this time he put the car in reverse.

Now we were in a quandary. We had the rear end lifted but couldn't put it down lest the car would come backwards and hit us. He turned and looked at us and laughed, but he did kill the engine and let us put it down. He was still laughing as he drove off.

"I hope you guys learned a lesson!" he said.

Our arms were still aching. We continued down the hill to the country store where we bought our usual—cigarettes, a soda, and a Bit-0-Honey candy bar.

"We should get even with Roy for making us hold the car like that," Buddy said.

"We're the ones that screwed up. Why should we get even with Roy?" Eddie asked.

"Because I don't like him!" Buddy muttered. "And besides he could have hurt us, and he just drove off laughing!"

"Well, if it makes you feel any better, you figure out what we can do to get even with him, and we can all talk about it," Daniel said.

On the way back to the school we stopped by the spring house to have a smoke and decide what we were going to do after school tomorrow. Daniel said that for the last year or so he had been thinking about a very large boulder that was lodged on the hill above the creek.

"What are you doing that for?" I asked.

"Let's walk over to the hillside," Daniel said. When we got there pointed down. "Do you see how high and steep the creek banks are, and how it narrows just below the boulder?"

"Yeah, what about it?" I asked.

"Okay, here's the deal: If we can get that boulder to roll down the hill I think it would land right there in that narrow part of the creek," he said.

"Then what?" asked Buddy.

"Don't you see?" he said, excited now, "The water will back up, and we'll have a great swimming hole!"

"Daniel, you're talking crazy. That's a big rock and I don't see how we can possibly move it—and even if we do it's a way too dangerous," Harold said.

At that point, we all agreed that tomorrow after school we would look at the rock and see if we could do it.

The next day after school we went up the hill to take a look at the boulder. The hill was steep. The boulder was big, so big that if it rolled over one of us we would be crushed. Rolling it down in the right direction could present a problem. If it rolled too far to the right it could roll right through an old barn. Although the barn wasn't used anymore, the school still left it there so animals could use it to get out of the rain. The task required more ingenuity than most kids could be expected to have.

The rest of the day we spent trying to figure out how we could control the direction of the boulder once we got it rolling. We finally decided that the best way was to dig a path for the big rock to follow. Once we did we could start digging from under the boulder.

We had to get at least four shovels, which might be a problem as the only shovels we knew about were in the garden shed, and they were being used. The other problem was, this had to be done in secret, and the boulder was out in the open. We decided to go over to the spring house, have a smoke and try to figure this situation out.

Eddie suggested, "We would only work on it at night, so as not to be seen or maybe, or just on cloudy days."

Buddy added, "Maybe if only two of us worked at a time, then we wouldn't be noticed."

In the end we agreed with Buddy. Only two of us dug on it at a time.

Now this was one big rock. I guessed it to be about seven or eight feet in diameter and God only knows how much it weighed. I thought. This has got to be one of the stupidest things we have ever done, but I went along with it. These were my friends, and who knows, if this thing worked out and we didn't get enough marks to ground us for a year, this could be the makings of a darn nice swimming hole.

After a few days we began digging. We heard that rain was on the way, so we sneaked a couple of spade type shovels from the garden shed. We welcomed the rain because it would make the ground much easier for digging.

The first day, Daniel and Buddy dug on the path we had laid out from the boulder to the creek. They made good progress as the ground was soft and easy to dig. The next day Eddie and I took our turn, but didn't fare quite as well—it rained, and we got soaked. We still had a lot to do.

The next day we had to pick blackberries for the cannery, which took us away from our little project. We found it getting harder and harder to get back to digging, for what began as fun had turned into a lot of hard work. I for one couldn't help thinking of all the fun things that I could be doing. The others were thinking about the same as I was, and we stopped digging for awhile. We began planning another trip to one of the farms and also to do some frogging before it got too cold.

We were at the spring house taking a break and talking things over when Buddy talked about Roy again and how we had to get even with him.

"Damn, Buddy, what's wrong with you? Can't you get it out of your head?" Eddie said.

"What do you want to do?" Daniel asked.

"You know, I've been thinking about this ever since he tried to back over us that Saturday down by the creek. It's not going to be easy, and you guys are going to have to help me," Buddy said. "You guys all know how he gets up at around five, goes to the outhouse, empties the night pails, then goes to the maintenance shed to start up the school bus for his first pickup. If we go to his place and move the outhouse back a few feet, when he comes out to empty the night pails in the dark he might fall in."

"What the Hell," Eddie said. "Don't you know that he would catch us? On top of that he has a shotgun. Do you want us to get killed?"

"No, no, no, he won't take a shotgun with him to empty the night pails. Besides, he won't be able to run after us with shit all over him, and we will be long gone before he can go back in the house to get his gun. So, what's he gonna do?"

"he will have no clue who did it," Buddy added.

"This is crazy! Do you have any idea what will happen to us if we get caught?" I said.

My warning went over everyone's head.

"Okay, Buddy. I hope this satisfies your vendetta against Roy," Daniel said.

We decided to wait until a moonless night so we would not be recognized—and it was only a week in coming. After everyone was asleep the four of us slipped out of the dormitory and headed over to Roy's house, which was only about a half mile from the house. It was about one o'clock in the morning and very dark.

Eddie had brought along a rope. The plan was to tie it around the outhouse. The four of us would pull on the rope and move the outhouse back a couple of feet. Doing this in the dark was a little more difficult than we expected. After finally getting the rope secured, we tugged on it. It was difficult as the small outhouse was much heavier than we had anticipated. After about five attempts, with resting in between pulls, we finally moved it back about three feet.

After we got it moved we still had a lot of time left before Roy would come out of the house, so we hid behind some rocks about a hundred yards away. We had already planned out our escape route so we just sat and waited until five o'clock, and talked about what we had done. To tell the truth, it was quite funny. The wait was so long we nearly fell asleep, but then we heard something and we all sprang up to see what it was.

In the dark it was hard to make out what was happening, but then I could barely see that Roy was on his way to the outhouse.

Eddie whispered, "That doesn't look like Roy."

Daniel replied, "No wonder it don't look like Roy, it's *his wife, Edna!*"

She was just about to get to the outhouse. That meant that Roy was going to hear her scream and come running out of the house with his shotgun., so we took off running like a bat out of hell. We didn't look back even when we heard her scream. When we got back to the house we were all trembling with fear and completely out of breath.

I thought we would surely be in a lot of trouble now, but the next day at school we didn't hear anything. After school the four of us met at the spring house to have a smoke and talk over what we were going to do.

"First, we all have to remember to say we had nothing to do with what happened last night, no matter what anybody says," Daniel said, so we all swore an oath we would never admit it.

"We'd better not even act like we know what happened," Eddie said.

"Are you satisfied now? Or do you still want more revenge?" Daniel asked Buddy.

Buddy didn't bother to answer but you could tell that he was pretty sorry about the whole affair.

Daniel changed the subject.

"You guys know we haven't done any work on the boulder for a few days," he said.

Eddie added, "I agree with Dan. If we don't get going now, it won't be long before it will be too cold to dig. And we still want to go and visit the farm. Mrs. Mayo won't let us go if the weather gets too bad."

"Let's talk about it later. I'm hungry, and it must be getting close to suppertime!" I said.

We headed back to the house. By the time we got washed up and our hair combed, we barely made it to supper on time. While we stood around the table waiting to ask the blessing, I could see Donnie and Jonny—little tattle tale twins. They were always together; where you saw one you saw the other. They never left the area around the house. Donnie and Jonny always stayed close to the teachers because they were afraid we would kick their butts if we got the chance, and we would.

Mrs. Mayo told one of the boys to ask the blessing when we sat down to eat. After the blessing Donnie raised his hand.

"Mrs. Mayo, Jonny had his eyes open during the blessing," he said.

Without saying a word, Mrs. Mayo turned to the bulletin board and put five marks beside both of their names and then turned to him.

"Thank you, Donnie."

The next day at school Mrs. Pierce told us how the Indians would make fire, by taking two pieces of flint, striking them together to make a spark next to some dry grass, and then blowing on it to get a flame going. She made it sound so easy, the way she described it. We spent about an hour after school that day and couldn't get a flame, so we gave up and talked about the problem we had with the boulder.

We decided the best way to get the job done was to do a little work on it each day. Even when we went frogging, we could dig during the evening. The general idea was to continue doing the things we liked to do and still get the job done before it got too cold.

Since the next day was Saturday, we did our usual, going to the country store. After we bought our candy and cigarettes we decided to take another way back to the house. Heading off in a completely different direction, we planned to circle around the hill to get back. Though at first the terrain was what we were used to, after a while we came to an area where there were a lot of large rocks at the edge of the woods. We ran over and climbed on the rocks, exploring our new playground.

Eddie yelled out, "Hey you guys, come over here I found a cave!"

We all went over to where he was, and sure enough there was a cave that was about five foot wide and about the same in height. It looked like it went back a pretty good way.

"What do you suppose made this cave?" Buddy said.

"Maybe a bear lived in it!?" Earl said.

At that point, we were thinking that maybe going inside wasn't such a good idea, although Eddie wanted to. We sat down and had a smoke to think this over.

"We have to go in just to see what's in there," Buddy said.

"You go into the cave and tell us what you find," Earl replied.

"I'm not going in first, you found the cave, so you should go first," Buddy insisted.

"I'll go in," Daniel said.

We watched as he started in. After he had gone about ten feet he turned.

"Aren't you guys coming?" he asked.

I ran in and joined Daniel. After we had gone about twenty feet or so, it opened up to a rather large room. We both looked around and both had the same idea: This would be a great place to have as a shelter from the rain, and it wasn't far from the school. When we got out we told the others about what we had seen. They couldn't wait to see what we had found.

Everyone was checking out the echoes were created when we talked loud. We all figured this would make a great ready built fort that would be warm in the winter and cool in the summer. We could bring in broom sage and spread it on the floor to make it nice and cozy. On our way back to the school we talked about all the things we could do with our new fort.

"We still have to think about how we are going to finish getting the boulder to roll down the hill," Daniel said.

Instead of going back to the house we decided to go and do some work on digging around the rock. For once we all took part in the work. After about an hour, we stopped for a break and surveyed our progress.

"I don't see much dirt holding it in place. Let's all get behind it and give a push," I said.

We it a try but it wouldn't budge.

"Let's take the long split-rail from the fence and use it to try and pry it loose," Daniel said.

We rolled a large rock over to the boulder, used it to prop the rail, then pried on the back of the boulder. At first this didn't work, but we all got on the rail and pushed. The boulder moved a bit, then stopped.

"I think if we dig just a little bit more dirt from the front we might get it to start rolling," Earl said, so we spent another half hour digging. After we all got on the rail again but we still couldn't get it to move.

"It's almost time for supper. If we don't want more marks we should start towards the house," Buddy said. Before we got back the rain began soon soon turned into a downpour. We were totally drenched. Mrs. Mayo made us change into some dry clothes before we could eat, which made us late so we had to stand with our hands out in front for a while. The other boys looked at us as if we were some kind of bad boys. As we sat down to eat she put some marks by our names. After we finished, the four of us had to wash the dishes and clean up the kitchen, which didn't leave us much time to go to the spring house for a smoke.

While we were standing in the spring house looking at the rain, it had let up a bit.

"That damn boulder is sure is a lot of trouble. Just look at all the time we spent digging. It's made us miss out on frogging, and going on hikes in the woods," Buddy said.

"We almost have it done. We can't give up, now," Daniel answered.

"You say that every time we work on it!" Eddy said.

"We'd better get back to the house before we get into more trouble!" I said.

The rain continued to pour for another day or so. As a result we had to spend a lot of time in the front room, except when we went to school.

The weather was colder with each passing day.

———

One day after school when the rain had let up, Eddie and I stayed down the hill and played at the creek. We had a lot of time before supper so we looked for frogs, when it started raining again.

"Let's run before we get drenched again!" Eddie said.

As we crossed the bridge I looked up and saw the boulder. I said to Eddie, "You know, with all of this rain, I think the ground should be soft enough for that stupid rock to be pried loose."

"Well, the rain has slacked. Wanna give it a try?"

"I'm game." I replied.

We got the piece of timber, put it in place and the two of us pushed on our lever. At first all we saw was a slight movement and it kinda rocked, so we gave it another heavier push, and lo and behold the big boulder moved—slowly at first but as the terrain got a little steeper it picked up speed. At that point we both knew that nothing short of heaven or hell could stop this thing.

We could see that the direction was somewhat off to the right, but if it fell into the creek it still should be okay. We watched as the as boulder got to the creek but sadly, it went over the creek as if it wasn't there.

"Let's get outta here!" Eddie said.

We ran to the side of the woods and turned to look back at the rock—it had gone right through a barn. We waited at the spring house until suppertime, deciding not to say anything to the guys about what happened.

A few days later, walking down to school, we saw some men working on the barn, trying to patch the big hole that the boulder had made. I walked over and asked the man what had happened. He told us that the rain had loosened a big rock that came down and rolled through the barn.

A while later we told the other guys what we had done, but I don't think they believed us. That was okay.

———

A few days later, at school, Mrs. Pierce told us we had a piece of paper on our desk, and that she wanted us to read it. After we read for a while, she said that she would explain it.

"There is going to be an air raid system practiced at the school," She said.

Of course, we had no idea what she was talking about, so we waited for her to explain.

"The war has been going on for some time now, and we have to prepare for either the Germans or the Japs, and we have to be ready in case they fly over and bomb us," she said.

That scared the shit out of all of us, as we hadn't thought too much about the war here at school. War was happening far over the oceans and didn't concern us.

"There will be two short bell rings and one long one," she said, demonstrating with a small bell on her desk. "When you here this warning," she said, and she demonstrated with the small bell again, "you need to duck under the tables to protect yourselves and you need to stay that way until you hear the bell ring that the air raid is over." She demonstrated again with a lot of short rings. She also said there would be an air-raid test today at twelve noon.

I looked at some of the other boys and I could tell that they were scared. The thought of a plane dropping bombs on us stayed in our minds all day. At recess some of the kids, every now and then were looking up to the sky. For kids our age this was frightening.

For quite a while we couldn't leave the area of the school or Crawford House, which meant we couldn't go on hikes because of the fear of something happening from the war.

———

During that time we paid a lot more attention to the two dogs that stayed around the house. One of them was Peewee and the other was Princess. Peewee was as skinny as a rail—so much so that you could count his ribs. Princess, on the other hand, was as fat as could be. She would just lay around and eat anything that was available.

Peewee was very hyper and was always running, chasing rabbits, squirrels, quail, or anything else that moved.

One of the things we did for entertainment was to take a rubber tire, roll it down a hill, and watch him try to catch it. The tire was bigger than he was, so he would try to stop it by biting at it. The tire would knock him down, but he would always get up and try it again. Sometimes the tire would run over him, but he wouldn't give up. Peewee he would do this all day if we wanted to. Sometimes we had to tie him up just to let him rest and get his breath. At the same time Princess would just lay around and watch Peewee run up and down the hill.

One day while Peewee was providing our entertainment, one of the boys walked by with a partial loaf of stale bread that the cook said to give to the hogs. There was a katydid on the ground and the boy picked it up and saw Princess lying nearby, so he gave her a slice. Thinking it would be funny, he put the katydid between two slices of bread and gave it to her. Much to our amazement, she gobbled up the bread and spit out the bug, unharmed. The kid was so delighted that he gathered a few kids around and tried it again. Just like before, she ate the good and spit out the bad, unharmed.

For the next week or so we tried every bug we could find and camouflaged it with food, and there was no way we could get that dog to eat a bug or even sink her teeth into it, for that matter.

In the meantime Princess got fatter and lazier. Some of the guys thought that she was just getting too old and would soon have to be put down, but one day after school the cook came out.

"I think I know what's been ailing Princess," she said.

Several of us asked at the same time.

"What?"

"She's given birth to five little puppies!!"

That night after supper the housefather asked us about it.

"Do you boys want to keep the new puppies?"

We all answered.

"Yes!"

"Then you will have to care for them, but first of all; you will have to give them all names."

So we all went to the front room to decide on names and right off we could see that this was going to be a problem as everyone had their own set of names. Worse yet, all of the pups were solid white, but one had a black vee on its tail, and since the war going on we named him Victory, because we thought it was a sign that the war would be over. Needless to say, Victory was everyone's favorite.

As the pups got a little older we found the five of them getting into everything. Playing ball was almost impossible because they would get the ball and we would have to chase them to get it back. We had our hands full.

One day we came home from school and one of the dogs was missing. We looked all over the place but he was not to be found. At supper time we had to get washed up to eat. While we were getting ready and combing our hair we heard a whimper coming from the storage room. When we went to see what it was we found the little guy, lying there, barely able to move as his tummy was all bloated and swollen up, as tight as a drum. We got the housefather to take a look at him. Mr. Mayo said that he has eaten something but didn't know what it was. As we looked through the storeroom we saw a box with the top torn loose. In it was pig skins that people rubbed on their shoes to make them waterproof in the winter. These skins were about six inches long by two inches wide and a half inch thick.

According to Mr. Mayo, the little guy must have eaten about ten of them. He knew that something had to be done quick so he got a bottle of castor oil and forced a big dose down his throat. We nursed him the rest of the evening.

The next morning he shit all over the dormitory. Let me say, that was one Hell of a mess we had to clean up. At the time we wanted to kill him but we loved him so much, and as we tried to clean up he was dancing around and wanting to play.

———

After the pups got a little older and calmed down somewhat, we thought they were getting better about getting into things. One day after school, when we had to take the laundry up the hill, we heard the dogs barking but we didn't pay too much attention, since some of the boys were back at the house and were probably teasing the dogs.

Earl, Eddie, and I had stopped to take a break when one of the pups came down the hill to meet us. He looked like someone had taken a paint brush and painted him red. As he got closer we could see that he was covered with blood, so we looked to see if he had any cuts on him, but there was no way to tell where the blood was coming from. When we heard the other dogs barking, we went in that direction. Soon we came to the old apple orchard. We saw a large sheep standing out in the open field. The dogs were running by and taking a swipe at it; each time they did another wound was opened. The poor sheep just stood there, and didn't move while the dogs kept taking turns.

We had a terrible time trying to stop the dogs and getting them settled down, but we finally got them under control, and the housefather had us tie the dogs up.

After supper he was quite upset with us.

"Now, what happened today was a very bad thing. There is no doubt that the injured sheep will have to be killed. You guys may think it was just an accident and not your fault, but not really. It happened because you were not controlling the dogs. Do you remember that I told you boys that you had to take care of the pups? I realize now there are too many of them for you to properly control, so you're going to have to decide which dog you want to keep, and give away the other four. As far as the settling up for the sheep is concerned, I'll need to locate the owner and find out what will satisfy him."

Several days later we had to meet in the front room. Mr. Mayo had located the owner of the sheep, a man by the name of Mr. Langer, who had come to talk to us about his loss. He was a fairly young man, maybe in his middle twenties. We were all somewhat apprehensive about meeting him, but were quite surprised that he wasn't too upset. He told us that he had a small herd of sheep, about thirty, and that the one in question had wandered off, but our dogs did attack it, so he was willing to share half of the blame for the loss of his sheep.

"That seems fair," Mr. Mayo said. "What do you think your sheep was worth?"

"I paid ten dollars for the sheep, so to be fair, suppose we split that, and make the cost five dollars?" Mr. Langer said.

Mr. Mayo settled our debt by taking equal amounts from our personal accounts.

A week or so later we were able to give away four of the puppies and keep Victory. We kept him as our mascot for as long as I was in the school.

My Sore Toe

By July things had gotten back to normal. We planned hikes and frog hunting, though frogging wasn't as easy as it used to be, as we had caught most of them. One hot summer day I wandered off by myself. I don't know where the other boys were but I enjoyed just being away from Crawford House.

Most of the morning I spent following the creek, trying to find a concentration of crawdads or maybe hear the croaking of frogs for future hunting. After following the creek a couple of miles and circling up into the woods for a smoother walk back to the house, I ended up among rocks along the side of the creek. I noticed I had a sore toe, and it was slowing me down.

After entering the woods I soon came upon a hickory nut tree, where a lot of the nuts had fallen and were lying in large numbers on the ground. I loved hickory nuts, even though they were difficult to crack and the meat was hard to get out of the shell. I had this small hammer that I carried with me most of the time when hiking, just for this purpose. My mother had sent me a small toolbox that included a vise, a saw, a screwdriver, and this hammer, which was the only tool that had survived to this point. I had inserted it in a small loop on the side of my overhauls.

A few weeks before, I had stubbed my toe, causing it to get infected. I didn't want to tell the housefather about it because he would take a needle and open it up. Going barefoot all summer long, my feet had gotten tough and sticking a needle into one of them was a little difficult. I had seen what he did to other boys when they had infections. Everybody would be watching as he heated a needle over a fire and would stick it into the puss pocket and then squeeze it until he got the puss out. I had seen how the boys would scream in unbearable pain. I didn't want anyone to see me go through something like that, so I would try to walk as normal as possible around the teachers, although sometimes it hurt like hell.

By now, my big toe had gotten such a large puss pocket on it that I knew it wasn't getting any better. One day soon I would have to give in and go through that awful ordeal, but for now I had some hickory nuts to crack and eat. I got a large rock to crack them on, sat on the ground, took out my hammer, and cracked the nuts. I had the rock between my legs and must have been there a while enjoying eating nuts, forgetting about my sore toe. At one point when I had placed a nut on the rock and hit it with the hammer, I guess I wasn't holding it tight enough. The nut flew off the rock and hit my sore toe. I let out a scream that was so loud it must have echoed off the hills. Afraid to look at my toe, I just held it for a while. When I finally looked I saw it wasn't bleeding but it still hurt like hell.

With tears in my eyes I sat there for a few minutes, waiting for the hurting to stop. Finally I picked up another nut, put it on the rock, and tried cracking it as well. On the second nut, the same thing happened again, and this time I got so mad that, even though it hut like hell, I took the hammer and hit my toe before I knew what I was doing. After that I grabbed and held on to my toe and through tears I saw it was bleeding. I sat there crying, holding my toe and cussing myself for being so stupid for several minutes. Eventually it felt somewhat better, so I walked down to the creek and washed off the blood. I saw that I had broken open the puss pocket and had split my toe nail, but for the most part, it didn't hurt at all. As I walked back to Crawford House I noticed that I could walk normally with no pain.

That night, after supper we went to the spring house for a smoke and I told the other boys what I had done.

"Pat, you're crazier than a bedbug!" Buddy said.

"It beats having the housefather stick a needle in my foot," I answered.

"You've got that right!" Eddie said.

Not much later my toe nail came off, but a new one grew in its place. My toe felt a lot better and I no longer had to wear a bandage. Beth, the medic at the infirmary, warned me to keep it try, and for the most part I followed her advice as there was no way that I was going to let Mr. Mayo go sticking a needle in my toe if I could help it.

I was in the front room doing pencil shading when Buddy walked in.

"Whatcha say, wanna take a little hike down by the creek?"

"Who's all going?" I asked.

"Eddie, Earl, and us, if you think you can make it," he said a little sarcastically.

"I can walk circles around you, any day of the week!" I said.

"Let's do it then," he replied. "Eddie and Earl are down at the track. They had to run off a few marks, so we can meet them there."

The small creek ran by the main part of the school and also by one of the school's chicken coups. After meeting up with Eddie and Earl, we decided to take a smoke break before heading to the creek. Earl pulled a bag from his back pocket and headed over toward the chicken coup, saying, "I'll meet you guys at the first creek bend."

"What the hell is he up to?" I asked.

"God only knows!" muttered Buddy.

We finished our break and headed down to the creek. When we got there we didn't see Earl anywhere and decided to play around the water a while before looking for him. About twenty feet around the first bend, there sat Earl on a large rock by the water. As we got closer to him we could see that he was holding an egg.

"What in the hell are you doing with the egg, Earl?" Eddie said.

"I'm sucking out the yolk."

"Why?" I asked.

"I like it," he said. "When we get the eggs emptied we can have egg races in the creek." he pointed to the paper bag beside him.

"How do you get the yolk without swallowing the clear slime?" Buddy asked.

"I'm going to show you guys, and then you can do your own eggs so we can have a race," he said.

At that point he took another egg out of his sack, got a small rock and tapped the end of it until he got about a half an inch hole in the egg. He slung the egg around until the clear part was emptied out, and once again he sucked out the yolk.

"We now have an empty egg, perfect for an egg race," he said.

I told Earl that I wasn't doing that shit, but Earl said if we all did this we could put them in the creek and have a race. Every time one of the eggs got caught in an eddy current, that person would have to stay with his egg until it got free with no help.

"Oh, what the hell, we don't have anything else to do so let's give it a shot," Eddie said.

We all got an egg, put the small hole in it, and slung out the white crap. I slung out the yolk too, since I wasn't about to go sucking on an egg.

At the creek we put our empty eggs in the water at the same time; the current did the rest. Before long my egg got caught in a whirlpool, so I had a smoke while I just sat and waited. The other boys kept going down the creek, following their eggs while I waited for my egg to stop spinning around. Standing at water's edge I saw a small turtle and picked it up and played with it. In a few minutes I saw that my friends were past the creek's bend so I said to hell with the egg, put the turtle in my pocket and waded down to find them. As I got past the bend I saw them playing with something in a side pool. When I drew closer I realized it was a rather large snake, and they were trying to catch it.

I asked them, "What happened to the egg race?"

"I was winning when Earl saw this snake, and we all forgot about the race and followed it," Buddy said.

While we talked the snake slithered out of the water and into some tall grass. Since it was on my side of the creek I decided to give them a hand. I found a large stick and went into the tall grass. I couldn't see anything at first because of the grass, so I had put my foot on a small log to move it.

Buddy had gotten out of the water and followed me.

"Look out, it's right by your foot!" he warned, but I still didn't see it. Just about then the log moved, and as I jumped back, I came down with the stick as hard as I could.

I thought I had hit the snake hard enough to kill it but I was amazed to see the snake slither out of the grass and under some roots in the water, by the bank. Buddy and I waded over to where the others were.

"Did you see the size of the head on that thing? It's as big as my hand. I don't think we should mess around with it anymore," I said.

We saw come out of the water, and because it headed into some bushes, I thought I must have hit that thing pretty damn hard, because part of its insides were visible. As it glided along, those insides got caught on one of the bushes and he couldn't get it loose.

We wanted to help it get loose but after everyone saw how large it was, and we knew it must be madder than hell, so we looked for a longer stick. We had to walk over to the small woods, and when we got back, with a long forked stick, somehow the snake had got its innards untangled and was gone.

While the four of us looked in the bushes and the creek, I saw Eddie step into the water.

"Look out, Eddie, the snake is still around this area!" I warned him.

When we waded over to the area where we last saw the snake, Eddie let out a yell. He jumped out of the water and onto the bank, holding his foot.

Buddy yelled, "What happened, Eddie?"

"I dunno!"

Wading over to him, we got out of the creek and could see a quite a bit of blood on his foot. We helped him down to the water, washed the blood away, and saw a couple of small wounds on the bottom of his foot. *He had been bitten.*

We had to get him to the dispensary but had learned that if a person is snake bit, not to let him walk. With all of us helping him, we headed off to the nurse's office. After a struggle we made it. Poor Eddie thought that he would die, because we carried him over rough terrain, and almost dropped him several times.

Nearing the dispensary, Eddie spoke up.

"You guys think I'm gonna make it, don't you?"

Earl wasn't too much help.

"Don't worry about it, you're in good hands. But just in case, could I have your comic book collection?" he asked.

Eddie was half crying.

"Just shut up! Nobody's getting anything!"

The nurse made us wait outside while she took care of him. In about a half an hour she came out with Eddie and he was laughing. He said he had stepped on a sharp piece of glass and all he had was a small bandage on the bottom of his foot. We all noticed that he could walk just fine.

"Do you mean to tell me we broke our backs carrying you all the way up here when you could've walked?" Earl asked as we headed to the spring house.

"I guess so," Eddie said.

"You bastard!" Buddy said.

By this time Eddie was laughing and we couldn't help it, we all laughed too. As we neared the spring house Buddy jumped on Eddie's back.

"Now you can carry me for a while!" he said.

We laughed so hard we had trouble lighting up at the spring house.

———

Saturday night was radio night, the entire two years that I had been at the school. Joe Mayo, the housefather, would have all the boys sit around and listen to the programs were on the radio Saturday night. At the time this was entertainment at its finest. We all felt it was a real treat.

The first thing we did was to gather around the large table in the dining room. Mr. Mayo would ask one of the boys to turn off all the lights, making the room so dark that you couldn't see the person sitting next to you.

"Now the mood is set," he would say, "if anyone is afraid maybe you should leave now and go to bed."

Of course no one ever left. This was the highlight of the week.

Next Mr. Mayo turned on the radio and tuned in the program. Only the small green light on the radio dial was visible. A voice would come on and it would say, in an eerie voice, *"Welcome to the Inner Sanctum."*

Next we heard the sound of a squeaking door slowly opening, followed by some of the spookiest stories about murder and crime that you have ever heard. Some of them would scare us so bad it was like they were happening right then.

Each week the stories were different. Each one was better than the last, but there was one story that hit home because it reminded us of the twins in our house. They were nine or ten at the time. Both were tattle tales and afraid of their shadows.

When the program began, and the squeaking door and eerie voice had us all tense, the story continued about two little twin boys. One was very bad and the other was very nice, and when the bad one got in trouble he would blame the good one, who would get punished for the foul deed, and the bad one would just sit and laugh at the outcome.

When their grandmother figured out what was going on, she told the bad twin that some day he would be sorry for what he had been doing. He just laughed at her. One day the grandmother died. While the family attended her wake, the bad twin waited until nobody was watching and took the beautiful cameo brooch from around his dead grandmother's neck.

That night while his brother slept, he put the brooch around the good twin's neck and then went to bed, thinking that his brother would get in trouble the next day. As it came to pass, the next morning when the bad twin awoke he felt as though his neck was on fire. Even after drinking glass after glass of water it remained afire, seemingly.

The good twin dreamed about his dead grandmother that night. She told him she would talk to his brother and make sure that he was a better boy from now on. Then the bad one, looked at his brother and saw that the brooch was no longer on his neck. Returning to the living room where his grandmother lay in her casket, he was startled to see the brooch back on her neck, right where it belonged. While he watched, she opened her eyes and scared him so much that he didn't stop running until he reached his room and locked the door.

In bed that night, he couldn't sleep. After awhile it got very dark as if something covered his head. Terrified, he tried to get out of bed but couldn't, as if someone was holding him in place. He cried out in desperate fear.

"You'll be alright now, *you're with me!*" his grandmother said.

Soon after we knew the program was over because we heard the squeaking door slowly closing. When the lights were switched back on, we saw that Donny and Jonny were both crying.

Someone asked them, "Which one of you is the good twin and which is the bad one, because one of you is going to stay with your grandmother."

We all laughed until Mr. Mayo gave us a warning.

"The next boy that laughs or picks on the Johnson twins will get ten demerit marks!" he said.

When we were bored and had nothing to do, we could always tease the twins. We would make up a story about how the mountain people would come and kidnap little boys and take them to work on the farms. Of course this backfired on us because they would go to the housefather and we would get marks. Then we would have a reason to get even with them. They knew this would happen, so after they tattled we wouldn't see them out of the house for several days at least.

———

Every week the housemother had all of us memorize a verse from the Bible. After church on Sunday we would have to recite that verse to her before we could go out and play. On one Sunday everyone had their Bibles out, was reading and trying to remember John 3:16. The task turned out to be a little easier than I thought it would be, so I was the first of my group to get an okay from Mrs. Mayo. I garnered a few brownie points that day.

"I knew that you could do it Patrick, good work!" she said.

Since I had to wait almost an hour for my friends to get that simple verse recited, finishing early didn't do me much good. Around three o'clock we finally we got down to the spring house. At least it was cool, so we just stood around and planned some of the things we could do during the coming week.

I don't think that Buddy ever forgot anything. If someone did something to him, he would talk about it until some revenge was exacted.

"One of those damn twins tattled and caused me to get ten marks. We need to play a trick on them," he said.

"But you teased and teased, until you made them cry," I said.

"That doesn't matter. They still had no right to tattle!" he shot back.

"Okay," said Daniel, "what do you have got in mind?"

"Well, I don't know how we could pull it off, but it wouldn't be funny if we could find a way to get the two little tattle tales out to the swimming hole and have the mountain girls catch them naked," said Buddy.

Earl shook his head.

"I don't see how that's going to happen," he said. "First, there's no way that the twins are going anywhere with us. They would never trust us not to beat them up. And second, what would be the chances that those mountain girls would come along just when those two are in the swimming hole?"

Daniel was a couple years older than the rest of us. He got along with most everyone, especially the younger kids.

"If I ask Donny and Jonny to go on a hike with me I'm sure that they would go, but this thing has to be set up. I can get the twins there but what about the mountain girls?" Daniel said.

Earl spoke up.

"I know where two of them live, Jolene and Dora, it's not too far from Betty's farm," he said. "I could ask them. I'm sure that they would do it."

"Okay," Daniel said. "Let's do it a week from next Saturday at one o'clock."

"Why so long?" Buddy asked.

"This Saturday you guys have to hike out to ask the mountain girls…and tell them when to go to the swimming hole…right? We pull it off the following week."

I was a little nervous about this.

"If word gets out about this there will be hell to pay. The five of us will be running track for a year, and on top of that…our hiking days will be over, for sure!"

"You're probably right, so we need a secrecy pact, that no one tells a soul," Daniel said.

We all agreed.

———

A couple days later we saw Daniel at the spring house, where he told us that he and the twins agreed to go hiking.

Saturday, right after we went to the country store and got our cigarettes and candy, the four of us—Buddy, Earl, Eddie, and I—headed out toward Betty's farm. Right before we got there we turned off on a ridge which, according to Earl, led to where Jolene and Dora lived. After walking a couple hundred feet, Earl said he'd go on alone from there as their dad didn't cotton to too many boys showing up around the house.

After about thirty minutes Earl came back sporting a big grin.

"What's the deal Earl?" asked Eddie, adding, "are they gonna do it?"

"Jolene said that she wouldn't miss it for the world. They're getting a couple of their friends to go with them."

"Good job, Earl!" I said.

———

The following Saturday we got a good early start as we wanted to get off the trails before Daniel and the twins came along. The four of us got to the place on a hill overlooking the swimming hole, where the girls were waiting.

Before long we saw Daniel walking by the creek. Behind him were Donny and Jonny, but after them we saw another kid that looked to be about the same age as the twins. Daniel had told them that they should all go swimming because it was so hot. Just as if they were waiting for his signal, the twins and their friend stripped down and jumped into the water.

Daniel told the boys to stay in the water while he walked down the creek a little ways and looked for a good place to do some frogging. At that point the girls went down to the creek.

At the swimming hole the three were down to their necks in water, but when they saw the girls they were afraid to make a move.

"What are you little kids doing in our swimming hole? We want you out now! And we mean right now!" Jolene said.

That put the fear of God into the kids, and into a real Quandary as they surely weren't ready to go parading around naked. The twins shivered and cried.

One of the girls walked over and picked up all of their clothes.

"Okay, it looks like that you're staying in the water. That's fine with us...we're taking your clothes and you all can walk back to the school naked—if you want your clothes come and get them, now!" she said.

As we watched, they slowly got out of the pool. The girls pointed and laughed at their little wieners and teased them with their clothes until they came to get them. Then Daniel came back and acted like he was mad at the girls so the three kids wouldn't suspect him of being in on it.

We joined up with Daniel and the three kids on the way back, but made it look like it was just a coincidence. But even though the twins were afraid of their own shadow they weren't stupid; it was obvious they suspected us. All the way back we said we didn't know that the girls would be there. We told them we wouldn't say anything about what happened and they couldn't either because if the housemother found out about it they would be in a lot of trouble, not to mention how embarrassing it would be if this got around the school.

———

When we got to the house the twins and their friend went inside. The five of us went to the spring house for a smoke and to have a laugh, and boy did Buddy and Eddie laugh. I thought they would never stop laughing, and of course I laughed too.

After awhile we had to get ready for supper.

Eddie said. "You know, we spent a lot of time on this caper. We should think about going on a trip to the creek to do some serious frogging.

"Let's wait until next week, but for now, let's enjoy what we pulled off for a while," Buddy said.

Fort Construction 101

When I first met Harry Jamison he had golden blonde hair and was about a foot taller than the rest of us. Since he was older than me, I didn't pay too much attention to him. He was a quiet kid and always kept to himself. After that first year I saw him doing things that looked like something was wrong with him. Not understanding what, I just stayed away from him. One day after school I saw him putting tin cans on a large flat rock and flattening them with another rock. I thought this was weird, but I walked on by and didn't say anything. Later on that day Eddie and I were out in the woods, just fooling around.

"What do you think about Harry?" he asked me.

"I don't think much about him except I think he's strange," I said.

"Buddy told me that Harry was supposed to be pretty smart," Eddie said.

"Well, you couldn't prove it by me," I said.

"Did you ever talk to him?" Eddie asked.

"No, but if you want to, let's go see what he's doing, and why he's flattening those damn cans," I said.

When we got there he had a bunch of cans all beat out flat, so we asked him what he was doing. He said that he was making shingles, which kinda hit us as funny.

"Why would you want to do that?" Eddie asked.

"I'm making a fort and these shingles are going to be the roof," Harry said.

"What about the rest of the fort?" someone asked. He said he was thinking about it. A few days later we saw him again, with fifteen branches about eight feet long, nice and straight. I asked him if he needed any help.

"If you want to, you can help me with some string to tie the branches together. After that, we have to do a lot of digging," he said.

We told him we didn't have any string. He said he already had the string but it was inside of some burlap bags.

"I don't get it. What are you talking about?" I said.

"I'll show you," Harry said.

Using a small piece of wood that he had sharpened to a point, he separated one string at a time. Before long he had a piece of string about twelve feet long, so we did the same thing. With all three of us working, we wound up with a ball of twine long enough to fly a kite. By then it was time to go to supper, so we left Harry.

After supper Eddie, Harold, Buddy, and myself went down to the spring house for our evening smoke. When Eddie and I told Buddy and Harold about what Harry had told us, they looked at us as if we had lost our minds. After we explained to them how Harry wanted to build a fort, they got interested.

The next day after school we went over and asked Harry when he wanted to start digging. He said that he hadn't found a spot where he could build it yet, so we told him we knew a place where it would be hidden from the rest of the school, not too far from there. He said he would go with us to look at it.

"Do you guys have enough time to go, today?" he asked.

"Sure," I said, so we went over to the woods. On the other side of the woods was a nice rolling hill we could dig into. Harry took a look at the spot.

"This will take a lot of digging!" he said.

"This project will have to wait until Saturday so we will have the whole day to dig," I said.

"I like that idea," he agreed. "There's a lot of sage brush in the field around here. We could line the floor with it and make it nice and warm inside."

At first I thought that the digging would be fairly easy, but soon we found the ground was harder than we thought. Working with only one shovel and some flattened out tin cans, we didn't make much of a dent in the hill.

Harry laid out an area about ten feet across, with the idea we would go down about four feet at the top part. Wherever it ended up would be the area of the floor. With the dirt we dug out, we made a wall in front of the fort to hide the entrance.

"We need a large limb to make the roof," Harry said.

"I thought that you had those already cut," I said.

"Those were too short, and besides that, I have a better way to do it," Harry answered.

After we found a limb that would do the job it took all of us to carry it back to the fort. Harry dug a small trench to put the end of the branch in. It went back about four feet, and it got a little higher in the center. We put a pole in the ground to rest the limb on, and now we could see what he was trying to do, and it all made sense.

"Now it's time to put the roof on, but we left the flattened cans back at Crawford House," Harry said.

We decided we would have to wait for another day for that.

The next time we went to work on the fort we got the roof on. You could tell Harry was quite proud when we got the shingles all in place. He had worked so hard on them getting all the tin cans flattened out. Now our fort was completed and it was a good one!

———

All of a sudden Buddy started getting all kinds of marks we had to plan some things we could do without him. When Friday arrived he found out that he had twenty marks and would have to run off seven of them. He thought he would have that done before dark, but the housefather told him that he couldn't start running them off until Saturday morning. That killed our idea of going frogging that night.

I asked Harold, "What did Buddy do this time? I thought that he had run most of them off and had only five left."

"The housemother always goes on a rampage on Fridays," Harold said.

We decided to run down to the spring house, have a smoke and try to decide what to do tomorrow; when we got there Buddy was there. I was still pissed about Buddy getting all of the marks but didn't say much, because he was down on himself.

"What are you doing to keep getting those marks?" Harold asked Buddy.

"I guess I didn't make my bed. When the housefather came around it was all messed up and my towel and wash cloth were damp and lying on the floor—that's seven marks, right there," Buddy said.

"You mean, you didn't hang your towel and wash cloth on the end of the bed to dry?" I asked him.

"I did, but somebody must have come along and knocked them on the floor," and added, "It's almost suppertime. We'd better go before I get into more trouble," he said.

When Saturday morning rolled around we saw Buddy at the spring house.

"I'll probably be done running by noon and I can meet you guys then," he said.

"We'll be down at the creek, just below the new fort," I told him.

He took off to the track and we headed to the creek. We Harry already there. We asked why he didn't wait on us.

"I needed to get an early start because I wanted to redo the top a little. I thought it was kinda crooked," he said.

Harry was almost done reworking the top so we gathered up sage brush and put it on the floor. It was almost noon before we got it all done. When we did, Harry backed off about twenty feet.

"It looks pretty darn good from back here," he said. "Guys, I think we have a fort! I couldn't have done it without you!"

"It would just have taken you a little longer. You were the brains behind it," I said. For the first time, we saw a smile on Harry's face. We all smiled a little.

"The dirt we put in front of the fort camouflages the entrance," I said.

"If we scatter some sage brush on the top, you couldn't tell what it was, from the creek," Eddie said.

"We'll have to wait for another time…maybe Buddy can do that when he gets here," I said.

With our project completed we headed down to the creek. All of us looked back several times to admire our handiwork except maybe for Harold. He wasted no time stripping down and jumping in the water.

"This water is cold as hell!" he yelled.

We laughed.

"This water is always cold," I said. "If you want warmer swimming water we have to go to a swimming hole that Benny showed me. He and his friends made it, not too far down the river from here, but it's a little more in an open area so the sun warms up the water during the day."

We all agreed to go, since there weren't going to be too many more swimming days left this year. We had to wait for Buddy, so Harold got out, shivering, and put his clothes back on.

Unfortunately Buddy didn't get there until late. We didn't have time to go to the new swimming hole, so we just stayed down at the creek and played. Buddy said that the track was much harder than he thought it would be, and that he was going to have to find a way to stop this madness and find out who was sabotaging him.

"Any ideas, Buddy?" I asked.

"Of course I do, but I can't prove it—them stupid-ass twins, Donny and Jonny. They messed up my bed, and if I can find the proof, they're going to be so sorry!"

I asked Buddy why he thought that, and he told me, "A couple of weeks ago the twins tattled on me for cussing. When Mrs. Mayo asked me about it, I denied it. For some oddball reason she believed me and gave them marks for tattling. I guess it was more than they could take, and now this is their way of getting even with me."

I told Buddy we would have to watch his bed area. If we could catch them in the act, we could tell the housemother about it.

"I wouldn't tell the housemother about it," Buddy said. "I want to get even with them myself."

Harold and Eddie walked by and said that they were going up to the fort, so Buddy and I joined them. Buddy was pleased when he saw the finished job.

"I like it but I can't see anything, especially down be the creek," he said.

"That's because Harry wanted to put all of that dirt in front so no one could see in the door," Eddie said.

Harold said it was late and we had better get back to the house. We all agreed and headed back. On the way back we saw one of the boys from Crawford House. We didn't know his name but he knew us. He said that all of the boys had to meet in the front room after supper.

"God-damn, what did we do now?" Eddie said.

"It is probably another rule that the councilmen have made up," Buddy said.

"Shit, what can they do now that they haven't already done, and what could be worse than that?" Harry said.

That night after supper we all went to the front room. Mr. Mayo came in.

"The student council has a surprise for you!" he announced.

"Here it comes," I heard someone mutter.

Everybody heard that, and we snickered.

"I'll let them tell you what it is, so here's Benny Lambert, who I'm sure you all know by now," Mr. Mayo said.

Benny came up to the front of the room.

"I know it's been pretty hard on you guys. You've been real good following the rules that they've made and we think that you should be rewarded, so we've got a movie for everyone to watch," he said.

Then they brought out a screen and set it up.

I looked at Eddie.

"What are they going to do?"

"I dunno," he said.

But after awhile they turned on the movie, a story about the war with John Garfield. We enjoyed the picture: It gave us a good idea of how the war was going, since we had only heard bits and pieces from our teachers, but now we knew how bad war could be. After watching the movie we talked about how much we hated the Japs and Germans, but most of all we wanted fly fighter planes and become aces.

———

Not long after we saw a movie. Someone was sent a dartboard with Hitler's face on it. On days when we had to stay in the front room we could throw darts at him. I don't recall how points were scored, but it we always tried to hit him in the eye.

I guess that movie made us feel a little better about the council, that maybe they weren't as bad as we thought, but we still had to watch our butts around them.

One Thursday, Buddy hadn't received any new marks this week. Tomorrow being Friday, it wouldn't be unusual for the housemother to get into one of her moods and go wild with the marks. I told my friends, before we go to school tomorrow, let's be sure to look at Buddy's bed and see it's done right

———

When we go frogging it takes five of us. We needed Buddy, so it was important we find out what was going on.

Friday morning we got up and went down to breakfast. After we had to get ready for school. Most of the other guys had eaten and were starting to go down the hill. The last two to leave were Donny and Jonny. Just as I was about to leave, I thought I would go and have a look at Buddy's bed. When I went upstairs, just as we suspected, his bed was a total mess and his washcloth was on the floor. I made up his bed and hung up the washcloth and had to run like hell to keep from being late and getting marks myself.

At recess Buddy, Eddie, Earl, and I went to the creek for a smoke. Once there, I told Buddy what I had found out, and then I asked Eddie, "Did you guys check Buddy's bed before school this morning?"

"We sure did, and it was perfect," he said.

"Well, we have a couple of little bastards we need to take care of! I saw the twins leaving, and they were the last ones to go down the stairs, so I went up to check Buddy's bed and it was all messed up. I fixed it," I said.

Red faced, Buddy spoke up.

"I'm going to kick their asses!!" he said.

"But Buddy, I think the best way is to do nothing," I said.

"Why the hell not kick their asses?" asked Buddy, and added, "I hate those two little bastards!"

"Buddy, you get too carried away. On top of that, you will just get into more trouble. I have an idea: Let's wait until they have left for school and we'll give them a dose of their own medicine by messing up their beds. Let them get the marks," Eddie said

Earl who had been just listening until then.

"I agree with Eddie. Tell me, when did the two of them ever have to run off marks? Never! I say it's time they find out what it's like!"

Buddy was a lot calmer now. I could tell he was still pissed off, but he said that he liked our plan, and would try to go along with us.

After school that day, the first thing we did was check the bulletin board. We found we all had just a few marks. Since we stood a good chance of staying out after dark for our frogging, we got permission and headed down to the creek. It wasn't quite dark when we got there, so we just sat around talking.

"Donny and Jonny have a lot of marks," Harold said.

Buddy grinned from ear to ear.

"I'm glad, how many?"

"I don't remember the exact amount, but let's just say they'll be running track for the next few Saturdays."

Buddy's eyes lit up.

"That's music to my ears," he said, and we all laughed.

It was dark, but Eddie spoke up.

"Who wants to get in the water?"

"I will," I said.

Eddie and I got in and started looking for frogs. The water was ice cold, but after we caught a few frogs it didn't matter. Harold carried the frogs. Buddy and Earl did the spotting, so it didn't take us long to get ten.

"These are big ones!" Eddie said.

Benny had told us that the frogs should be plentiful since no one had been catching them for a while, and he turned out to be right.

When we back to the house we put our frogs in a small spring at the spring house until the next morning.

———

Saturday we got permission to go to the farm. We made an early start. Earl stayed behind to play in a marble tournament, and

Harry was busy as well, which made it just Buddy, Eddie, Harold, and me.

We walked along the creek because it was easier walking than taking the trails, and a lot more interesting. As we got farther up the creek we came across a swimming hole we were all familiar with. Harold wanted to go in but we talked him out of it, saying we wanted to get to the farm.

When we arrived we went straight to the barn. Betty was in the barnyard feeding the chickens. She was wearing bib overalls and a man's work shirt, and looked like a man except for the sunbonnet and her good sized breasts.

Saying she was glad to see us, she asked if we were going to spend the night.

"No, we have to get back before supper but we are going to wander around the woods. We just stopped by to see you and to say hello," I said.

"I'm going to take a nap. It's too hot for anything else!" she said.

"We'd like to stay overnight the next time we come," Harold said.

"That would be great!" she replied.

"We may go to the old swimming hole," I said.

"It's a good day for it," she said, and we left.

Soon we got to the widened place in the creek we usually used as our swimming hole.

"Are we going in now?" Harold asked.

"I know that you're anxious to go in, and so are we, but according to Benny, there is a much nicer one farther on down the creek, and I've been wanting to check it out. I don't think it's too far," I said.

"I heard about it too. We can't miss it if we follow the creek," Eddie said.

After about a half an hour we arrived, and couldn't wait to jump in. We left our clothes on the bank, far enough away that they wouldn't get wet when we splashed. We had a good time in this deeper, colder spot.

When Eddie got out to have a smoke, he stopped in his tracks. "Be quiet!"

Everyone stopped splashing and looked at Eddie, who was peeking over the creek bank.

"*There are two girls over there!*" he hissed, then slipped back into the water and swam back over to where we were.

"What are they doing, spying on us?" I asked.

"I dunno, it looks like they're picking some kind of berries. They're no more than thirty yards away."

"Maybe they don't know we're here. Let's just go and get our clothes and put them on before they see us," Harold said.

"Our clothes are out in the open, and I don't think we can get them without them seeing us," Eddie said.

We just stayed there with the water up to our chins, not knowing exactly what to do, except for Eddie who was at the bank keeping an eye on the girls. We waited a few minutes.

"They have moved farther away, and are behind some boulders," Eddie finally said.

We all had the same idea as we scampered out of the water and threw our clothes on. Once we were dressed we noticed that the girls had moved closer, so we went over and said hi. One of the girls was the girl I had seen milking the cow the last time we were at Betty's farm.

"What are you guys doing here?" She asked.

"We are just out on a hike, and decided to go swimming. When we saw you girls we came over to see what you were doing," I said.

She said that they were hiking also, when they came upon the blackberry vines and decided to fill their picnic basket. They would take them to Betty's and bake some pies. If we wanted some pie we were welcome.

I told her we didn't have time today but we would try to come back next week.

"What's your name?" I asked.

"I'm Doris and she's my sister," she said, pointing to the younger girl. "Her name is Sally. What's yours?"

"Pat," I said, then told her the other guys' names.

"When are you going to visit Betty again?"

"Maybe next week, if we can," I said.

Eddie said we should get back if we planned to stop at the spring house on the way, so we said goodbye to the girls and left.

———

Sunday after church we changed into our play clothes. It was too late to do much of anything, but the apple orchard wasn't too far, so we went over there.

At one time the school had built a sheep shed, but I don't believe they ever used it. We were just lying on the dirt floor and looking up at the rafters. It was a hot day, but here lying on the dirt it was cool.

Harold saw a hornet's nest up on a rafter and threw a rock at it. He didn't hit it but he came close enough to stir them up.

"What in the hell did you do that for?" Eddie asked.

We started running.

"Don't run or they will just go after you. Just stand still and they won't bother you," Buddy said.

"Are you crazy?" Eddie said. At the same time Harold got stung. Buddy broke his own rule and decided to run.

After awhile the hornets calmed down, so we went back and laid down. Buddy had another bright idea. He said if we all get a rock and threw them at the same time, we could run and get away before they could sting us. Being stupid kids with nothing else to do, we thought that would work.

Since dinner time was approaching and it was time to go anyway, we got our rocks and got ready. On the count of three we let our rocks fly and ran like hell, and wouldn't you know it, Buddy and Harold got stung.

"What happened to your idea of not running, Buddy?" Eddied asked when we got far enough away. We all laughed.

Back at the house while we were waiting for supper, the housemother noticed the stings. She put lotion on Buddy and Harold and they were okay.

At school the next day I had to draw some pictures of pilgrims for Thanksgiving. Mrs. Pierce wanted me to start now because the big day was a month away, but I took my time. At recess I went with the boys down to the creek to smoke. One of the girls in my class followed us, but we didn't see her until she came out from behind some bushes, after we had lit up.

"I've wondered why you guys always come down here to the creek, and now I know," she said.

Buddy knew the girl.

"Why are you spying on us?" he asked her.

"Are you going to tell on us?" I asked.

"I don't know, yet," she said, and left.

"Damn, now she will tell everyone!" Harold said. "We'd better get back to school!"

When we got back in class I looked around to see if anybody looked like they knew something, but it they all looked normal. The girl that spied on us just looked my way. The way she smiled at me, I knew she had something up her sleeve. After school I told Buddy and Eddie, "we'd better be more cautious when we smoke because I think that girl is planning something, and I don't think it's going to be good!"

———

A week later we got another chance to visit the farm. The fall weather had gotten cooler, but today was warm. The leaves were starting to turn, which made for a beautiful day to hike. We went by the spring house and out past the wooded area to a glade where you could see for miles. The fields were clear and the broom sage was about two feet high. It was a beautiful sight. We just had to stop and take it all in.

"It's great to look at all the things that you can see this time of year," Buddy said.

"I like it too," Eddie said, "but we can't stand here all day if we intend to get to the farm." We left and headed down the hill to the creek. The bushes hid the creek most places except where the grass came right up to the bank.

As we walked along we came to one of the swimming holes we normally used to cool off in when hiking on hot days. Buddy and Harold wanted to jump in.

"You guys must be crazy. This water is as cold as hell!" Eddie said.

We continued on. The farther we walked the more we felt like we were being followed. Every now and then I would look back and tell the guys to be quiet, then after awhile Eddie noticed it too. He looked at me.

"Did you hear something?" he asked.

"No, but I've had the feeling for awhile we're being followed," I said.

"Let's get away from the creek, and out in the open," Eddie said. We got on one of the trails, and continue to the farm that way.

When we got to the farm Betty was hanging clothes on the line to dry, Doris was drawing water from the well, and Mike was chopping wood for the fireplace. Mike had been at it for awhile. Wiping the sweat from his brow, he spoke to us.

"I'm glad you guys came by. I was needing a break. Why don't you come in to the house and join me in a glass of milk."

"Boy that would be great!" I said. I don't think there was anything I enjoyed more than a cold glass of milk after hiking for two hours on a hot day. After we had our milk, Mike said that he was going to have a smoke. As he got out his corncob pipe and lit up, Betty came in and started folding clothes. Doris walked in, got a bucket, and headed to the barn to do some milking. While I watched I thought to myself, "Damn, these people sure work hard, I wonder if someday, I'll have to do things that way."

Harold got me out of my revelry.

"Let's go help Mike," he said.

He and Buddy started carrying wood up to the house and stacking it on the porch. After that, Mike said we could help him feed the animals.

Mike had a mule that didn't want to eat hay. I said that I didn't think it was hungry.

"Let me show you something," Mike said.

He took an apple and gave it to the mule, who then started eating the hay.

"That's the way that mule is. He likes apples, and won't eat anything until you give him one. Betty says it's stubborn, just like me," Mike said.

When Doris finished milking I asked her if I could carry the milk up to the house. She looked at me and smiled.

"If you want to."

I grabbed the bucket to head for the house, but she stopped me.

"Do you remember when you and your friends were in the swimming hole, and you saw us picking blackberries?"

I felt embarrassed. I could feel my face starting to flush.

"Well, we didn't say anything when you guys came over and started talking to us. When we saw the four of you in the water, my sister Sally wanted to sneak up a little closer, so we went behind the bushes at the bank. After we got a good look, we went back to picking. She said it was fun and wanted to do it again."

"I suspected something like that," I said. "Wait until tell the others about this." I laughed.

"Don't tell them in front of me!" she said.

I promised to wait until we left.

"They probably won't believe me, anyway."

We stayed until almost four o'clock. When we said goodbye to the three of them, Doris looked at me.

"Remember," she said, and I smiled.

After we were well on our way, we stopped at the old swimming hole and had a smoke. As we sat on the bank Harold and Buddy said that they were going to get in the water. I thought let them, it will be a good time to tell them what Doris told me about sneaking upon us and seeing us naked.

"Are you guys crazy? It's too cold!" Eddie said.

"Let them," I said, nudging Eddie. He looked at me and got what I meant.

Harold already had his pants off and Buddy wasn't too far behind.

"Remember those girls that saw us a couple of weeks ago were picking blackberries?" I asked once they were in the water. "Well Doris told me that they sneaked over while we were swimming and they saw us before we saw them, and it was her sister's idea, who thought it was fun to see us naked."

"No they didn't. You just made that up!" Buddy said.

"I knew that you wouldn't believe me," I said, "so you can ask her next time you see her."

Eddie looked at me.

"Why didn't you tell us?"

"I just did. Listen… I think I hear something!" I said.

We got quiet and heard someone laughing, not too far away. Eddie and I went to see who it was. We parted the bushes and saw the girl from my class. She and two of her friends had followed us down to the creek to have a smoke. Before we could say anything they took off running.

Buddy and Harold got out of the water and asked me what we saw. I told them who I thought it was. It appeared that they had been back there watching us all along.

"How do you know that?" Harold asked.

"Why else would they be back there laughing when they almost never leave their house. I knew that she was planning something, that day she followed us down to the creek, and now we know," I said.

"We'd better get back before something else happens," Eddie said, so we got ready to leave.

Buddy wanted to know why they would do that. I said it's probably because they have nothing else to do, and now they can go back and tell the other girls how they sneaked up on us while we were naked.

"We ought to sneak up on them!" Harold said.

"How are we going to do that?" Buddy asked. "They wouldn't go in the creek naked. Girls just don't do that like boys do."

"How do you know what they do when nobody is around?" I asked. "They may be just as wild as we are."

Eddie laughed.

"Wouldn't that be something if we caught them. They'd probably start crying like little babies."

———

A few days later Eddie told us he had seen the girls going out to the pasture, sp he had followed them. He said they had found a way to get to the swimming hole from the other side.

"I don't know what good that will do us," I said. "They're probably just heading that way to spy on us."

"Maybe not," Eddie said. "Why don't we watch them. When they start to go their secret way, we can follow them. When they see we aren't there, we can see what they do."

"I don't think they will go swimming," I said. "They'll probably just go back and try to follow us later."

———

Come Saturday morning, we were just hanging around the house. Buddy, Harold, and Earl wanted to go and look for arrowheads. Eddie and I just wanted to stay at the house and take it easy, so they left. After awhile Eddie and I walked down to the school and watched the girls just to see if they might go on one of their little hikes down to the old swimming hole. As we waited, Before long we saw three of the girls sneak off from the others and head for the swimming hole.

We waited for a while before following them, and sure enough they headed straight for the creek. We hid behind some bushes while they just lay on the bank and talked. Eventually one of them got in the water, but didn't take off her clothes. The other two followed suit and played around for awhile, then got out. Their dresses were quite wet on the bottom.

"Let's go!" I told Eddie, but when we were started to leave, Eddie stopped us.

"Wait a minute!" he said. I looked back and saw one of the girls starting to take her dress off. Naked, she stood there and wrung the water from her dress. Eddie and I were so startled that speaking to them was the last thing on our minds.

As we turned to leave I said to Eddie, "Maybe we should have said something so they would know we can do the same thing to them that they did to us."

———

127

The next day wandered around out in the hills with nothing particular in mind. After messing around for an hour so, we stopped to take a break, sitting down on a large rock shelf. The shelf had about a ten foot drop off at the edge, and the mountain sloped down from there.

After we sat and talked for awhile, Eddie saw a vine hanging down from a tree. He and Daniel went over and pulled it away from the tree. Buddy watched as they kept pulling—soon they had it free except the point that was curled around the branches at the top of the tree.

Daniel was the first to go, swinging on the long vine, and gave a Tarzan yell as he swung out a little way and back again. After a few swings he would go back on the rock and get a running start, which increased his swinging distance a lot.

The rest of us could see how much fun he was having, so we joined in. Before long before we were swinging way out and having a ball.

The foliage on the trees hid the ground so we couldn't see how high we were, and we felt safe. We spent the rest of the day playing Tarzan, swinging on the vine. Eventually we had to get back for supper.

"Boy, did you see how far we were above the trees?" Buddy said. "When I looked down the mountain I could see the rest of the school."

"Yeah," said Eddie, "we'll have to remember where that vine was so we can go back and swing on it again."

I wanted to go back and swing again, too, but pointed out we would have to make it soon. Cold weather was on its way.

After we finished supper and was down at the spring house, Buddy remarked that this had been one of the most enjoyable days he'd had for a long time, and the rest of us agreed and planned to go back the next Saturday.

The following Monday at school, Mrs. Pierce talked about the Indians and how they lived all around the area of the school. If we looked we could find arrowheads that they used for hunting. She showed us some that she had collected. I was amazed that I looked at an arrowhead that might have killed an animal right around the school over a hundred years ago. That thought stayed with me for quite a while, and it every time I went out I looked for arrowheads.

Down at the creek for a smoke, Eddie reminded me about the girl that liked to follow us.

"I don't think that she will do too much following, what with the weather getting colder. Girls don't like being out in the cold."

"She isn't like other girls!!" Eddie argued. Then the bell rang, and we had to get back.

Girls Will Be Girls

Colder mornings and leaves starting to fall meant we might see a little snow soon. Halloween wasn't too far away, and I would turn nine. I had been at the school more than a year, which was quite a long spell to a boy my age. As I reflected on my stay there, I couldn't help but feel how lucky I was. I had learned so much, and had a lot of friends. Actually it was more than friendship; it was like a family.

Monday, on the walk down the hill to school, while the others talked about what to do at recess and after school, some things were eating on me: What was that girl up to, and why were her and her friends so hell-bent on seeing us naked. I asked Harold about that.

"Well, you see, girls think differently than we do. Number one and foremost, they want to embarrass us, and number two, they want to show us their smarts by being able to sneak up on us any time that they want to," he said.

"Well, maybe so, Harold," I said, "but I can't help thinking there's more to it than that."

At school everybody got ready for the holidays, even though they were a couple of months away. Some things, according to Mrs. Pierce, needed an early start, because in those days the students were expected to make all the Halloween and Thanksgiving decorations. She said that I had artistic talent, so when something needed to be drawn or painted she had me right in the middle of it.

At recess time Eddie and I went down to the creek for our usual smoke.

"Did you say anything to those girls about what we did to them, last week?" I asked him.

"I wanted to," he said, "but I didn't want to say anything to the girl we saw naked, and you see, if she hadn't been there, I would have said something to the other girl."

After recess I saw one of the other girls. She just looked at me and smiled, but I didn't get a chance to talk to her.

After school, Buddy, Harold, and I were walking up the hill.

"What did you and Eddie do when Harold and I went to look for arrowheads the other day?" Buddy asked.

I told him to wait until we went to the spring house, because I wanted everyone to be there. That night after supper, we all went to the spring house.

"Do you want to tell them, Eddie, or should I?" I asked.

"I give you the floor, Pat," he answered.

"Well, it started out innocently enough," I started. "Eddie and I were bored and walked down to the school, when we saw a group of girls that looked like they were going for a hike. When we saw the girl from my class head down towards the creek with two of her friends. We followed but they didn't go toward our swimming hole. Instead they crossed the bridge and headed up the hill. At that point we gave up and decided to go to the swimming hole ourselves. We headed up the creek. As we got near the swimming hole we heard laughter, so we sneaked over behind the bushes. We could see them lying on the bank talking and giggling."

"How did they get there without you seeing them?" Buddy asked.

"They found a trail went in from behind the creek, we never knew existed," I told him.

"Go ahead with what happened," Harold said.

"Okay, the girls laid there for awhile. Finally one of them decided to jump in with her dress on, and started swimming and splashing. Pretty soon the other two walked in and just started wading around. They got out after the bottom of their dresses wet. I was ready to leave before we got caught, but Eddie called me back and guess what? The first girl jumped in took off her dress, stood there naked and wrung the water out of her dress."

"What did you say to them?" Buddy asked. "Did you let them know we had gotten even?"

"We didn't say anything yet," I told him.

Buddy and Harold were both a little pissed off, because they wanted to get even with the girls. We wanted to do that too, but it was wintertime now and the girls wouldn't be going to the creek until summer.

———

As Halloween got closer, we got ready to have the Halloween carnival. All of us would be getting together with the girls at the party, so maybe we would get a chance to tell them what we did.

On the night of the party we all went down the hill to Mayo Hall where the main auditorium was. We couldn't wait to see what kind of cakes and pies that they would have, because that was all we cared about. The other stuff didn't matter to us, especially the dancing and some of the stupid games. We hadn't been there very long when I got a piece of pie. I was sitting by myself eating it when this girl came over and sat beside me.

I knew that she had something to tell me, but before she could say anything I spoke up.

"I know how you and your girlfriends have spied on us," I said. "We did the same thing to you. By the way, who was the girl that took off her dress and stood there naked?"

"Did you guys see that?" she asked.

"It was just me and Eddie," I said, "but yes, we saw that."

"It was Sally," she answered. "She will be mad!"

"Who is Sally?" I asked.

"Sally lives up in the mountains," the girl said. "She's the one that told us that you and your friends go swimming all the time. She told us how to get to the swimming hole, and how she watched you a lot of times."

I asked her if Sally had a sister.

"I think so," she said, "but I never met her."

At that point I got up to get another piece of pie, and she went over to talk to one of the other girls.

After the party, back up the hill, I felt pretty good about myself, being able to talk to the girl and letting her know we knew what she and her friends were up to. I couldn't wait to tell the other boys what I had found out.

———

The next day I found time to tell the boys about what I found out. I grabbed Eddie at recess.

"Let's all get away from the other boys and girls because I have something to tell you guys," I said.

"What is it?" Eddie asked when we were all together.

"Do you know who that girl was that took off her dress at the swimming hole?" I asked them.

"Was it Doris's sister, Sally?" Buddy answered. Everyone was surprised.

"Do you believe me now?" I asked him. "Remember what I told you at the farm about Doris telling me that she saw us at the swimming hole?"

"I thought you made that up," Buddy said.

"Well, I didn't. I think Sally is a bitch and Doris knows it!"

"I don't care," Harold said. "So what if they did see us, we would do the same thing to them and think nothing of it."

'It's not that they saw us, it's the way they went about it!" Eddie replied.

"The next time I won't try to hide," Buddy said. "What can they do, tell the teachers on us? They know we go swimming in the creek, naked, and most of the girls in the mountain do it too. Just wait until next summer!"

The next day the weather was cold, and when we went over the bridge at the creek there was ice on the bridge, and Eddie said it wouldn't be long before it snowed, and we could get out the sleds and have a ride.

———

Thanksgiving was fast approaching. I would miss it again, since I would be going home for the holidays. I was glad because I hadn't been home for the summer this year. I hadn't seen my mother for a whole year.

On the trip to Rome, Georgia, I slept most of the way. When we arrived a cold wind was blowing so hard that I had difficulty standing up. On top of that, it looked like it was going to rain. I remember thinking why not—it was always cold and wet at Christmas time, just so you couldn't go outside and play.

I got a pair of skates that year but never got a chance to use them because the weather was too bad. We had no place to skate back at school, so there was no use taking them with me. In the mountains it was all dirt, rocks, or grass. Anyway, it was nice to see all the relatives and my little brother Jerry. He was four years old now and was always tagging along and telling me everything that he had gotten for Christmas. I think that was the first time that I ever talked to him.

———

Christmas didn't last very long. In no time Jack and I had to return to the school. At first it was sad, leaving mom and the other relatives, but after I got to thinking about the boys at school, and wondering if they would all come back, I no longer thought about where I'd been, but where I was going.

Some boys would come to the school and only be there for the summer; he wouldn't come back after he went home for vacation. Just when you got to know someone he would be gone, and you would never see him again. I hoped that all of my friends would come back because we had had such a good time in the last year.

We didn't get back to the school until late at night. We stayed down at Mayo Hall until morning, then went up the hill to Crawford House. After I got my things unpacked I went out in the yard. The first person I ran into was Harold, who said he had seen Benny and Earl, but Eddie and Buddy hadn't made it back yet. Most of the other kids would probably be back the next day.

"I hope that Buddy and Eddie make it back!" I said.

———

Harold said the snow wasn't too deep, but he and Benny were going to take the sleds up on the hill anyway to see if there was enough snow for a ride. Benny said it might snow tonight, and if so there would be plenty for a good ride. I said that I didn't like the snow that much, but I would go with them.

"For now let's go in the front room, where it's nice and warm," I said.

The cook brought us cocoa and cookies in the front room. We sat around talking about our Christmas vacations and some of the things we had done the previous year.

After supper Mr. Mayo brought in his radio.

"It's Saturday night and you all know what that means!" he said.

"Inner sanctum!" Harold answered.

"If someone will set the mood by turning off the lights, we'll see what spooky tale is on tonight," Mr. Mayo said.

We all gathered around the radio. Again we heard the squeaking door open, sending shivers down our spines as always. Sometimes

I suspected Mr. Mayo kinda got a kick out scaring us to the point where we couldn't sleep. That night was no different.

When I tried to go to sleep, I laid there and wondered if Eddie and Buddy would be coming back. I did know one thing—it sure would different without them.

———

After breakfast the next morning, Harold and Benny wanted to get an early start. We got the sleds and started up the hill. I didn't want to go because it was so cold outside, but I didn't have anything else to do, so I went along with them. We had a hard climb up the hill. By the time we reached the top I was worn out, so I just sat there and watched them.

Benny went first, since he had done this before: He knew where to look for the old run. By the time he brought the sled up the hill I was frozen. Next turn went to Harold, who tried to follow the tracks set by Benny. He yelled most of the way.

"Okay Pat, it's your turn!" Benny said.

I was caught between not wanting to ride, but also not wanting them to think that I was afraid, so when Harold brought the sled back up, I took it and walked over to the edge of the hill and looked down.

"Damn, that's a long way!" I thought, but I gritted my teeth and did a belly flop on the sled. I had gone about fifty feet when I hit a big rock that threw me off course. Before I knew it I was airborne for about fifteen feet, then came down with a hell of a bang, but I held on for dear life. I had snow all over me and couldn't see anything; I came within inches of hitting a tree. Just when I gained my sight back I hit another rock and the sled went one way and I went the other. When I finally made it to the bottom the sled was on top of me, and I was wondering if I had broke anything. When I finally stood up the guys were running down the hill.

"That was one hell of a ride you made!" Benny said when they finally got to me.

"When you went airborne I thought sure that you were going to lose it, but you held in there!" Harold added.

"It's too late to go again," Benny said, so we went back to the house. Boy was I glad to go where I could get warm! After I got warm, I relived that sled ride over and over. I sure was proud of myself.

———

The next day we went out and walked around the hills. I was surprised at how many animal tracks we came upon. Without knowing what kind they were, I could see there were a lot of them. Benny identified them for us: most were either deer or rabbit tracks, but he also said that some of them were from either a mountain lion or a bobcat—both had big feet so he couldn't tell for sure.

I thought about all of the times we went out at night catching frogs. We never gave a thought there might be a mountain lion or bobcat just waiting to make a meal out of us.

"Maybe we'd better watch out the next time we go out at night!" I told Harold.

I guess we walked around for almost three hours until we were frozen, so we went back to the house and stayed in the front room until suppertime. The next day it was snowing; we stayed in until noon. While we were there Buddy and Eddie walked in. Boy were we glad to see them!

"I thought for awhile that you two weren't coming back. What happened?" I asked.

"We missed the train and had to stay another day in some small town," Eddie said.

"How did you miss the train?" I asked him.

"Buddy had to go to the bathroom, and when he got done, the train had left," he answered.

I looked at Buddy, who had this shit-eating grin on his face, and we all laughed.

"We can always count on Buddy," I said. "Don't you know you old fart, that you could have taken a shit on the train?"

"I think I need a cigarette," Harold said.

Down at the spring house, the little spring that ran through it was frozen but that didn't matter—we were all back together again in our favorite smoking place. And that was good. We were a year older and a little wiser as we talked and joked for an hour or two, then headed to the house.

On the way to the house we stayed outside and watched some of the kids having a snowball fight. As we stood there one of the boys hit the housemother just as she was going into the house. I thought, the shit is going to hit the fan now, but to my surprise she made a snowball, threw it back, and laughed.

"Did I just see what I thought I saw?" I asked Buddy.

"Well, I'll be damned, I thought that she would get mad about that," Buddy said.

After supper, sitting around in the front room, Harold asked me who the new kid was. I said, what new kid? He pointed to a big kid that would make about two of us. I said that I didn't know, but he sure is big.

Buddy and Eddie came over and sat down. I said we had a new kid. Eddie said yeah, he came in with us, so I asked what his name was.

"I'm not sure but it kinda sounded like Bobolinks or something like that," Eddied said, then added, "Let's keep an eye on him. He looks like he could kick all of our asses at one time."

After breakfast the next day we went outside. The sun was out; the air was a little warmer but there was still snow on the ground in spots, so we headed off to the creek just to see what changes had happened since we were here last. We had gone maybe fifty feet when we heard this voice yelling, "Where are you guys going?"

It was that big guy. I looked at Eddie.

"I guess we'll find out who the hell he is now."

We waited for him.

"I don't know anybody at the school yet, and you seem like the kind of guys that I could get along with," he said.

"What's your name?" Buddy asked him.

"Just call me Bobo," he answered. "I don't like my name."

"I guess it will be Bobo, then," I said.

After we told him our names he wanted to know where we were going. We told him we wanted to check out the creek.

"I like the water," he said. "Do you mind if I tag along?"

"Welcome aboard, Bobo!" Buddy said.

Later on Bobo told us that his dad had been killed fighting overseas, and his mother was too sick to take care of him, so she sent him up here to the school. He said that he didn't know if he would like it because he had never been away from home before.

"Bobo, most of us are in the same fix," I said, "but you'll get used to it after a while. One of the bad parts is all of the rules. We will explain them to you, and who to watch out for."

"You know, I feel better, already," he said. "I was hoping I would find some nice guys to hang out with to show me the ropes."

"Sometimes we're not all that nice," Buddy said, "because we do a lot of things that get us in trouble, but we do have fun."

After we got to the creek, there was ice out a couple feet from either bank but the current was running strong in the middle. The water was high, almost to the top of the banks.

"I bet our swimming hole is washed out!" I said to Buddy

"You guys have a swimming hole?" Bobo asked.

"It's not much of a swimming hole," I said. "It's only a couple of feet deep. We mostly just come and sit in it to cool off in the summer. There's a much nicer one, a couple of miles downstream."

"So, Bobo, do you smoke?" Buddy asked.

"I tried it once but I didn't like it," he said.

"We all smoke," I said, "but we can't let the teachers catch us or we'll get all kinds of demerit marks."

"Oh, I wouldn't tell on you. I want to be friends!"

Before long Bobo was saying things like: "excuse me", "I didn't mean to bump you", and "did I hurt you buddy, I didn't mean to".

"Why does he keep doing that?" Buddy asked me once.

"I think that he's just trying to be a good guy," I said. "Maybe in the past, because he's so big he was thought to be a bully, but I don't think he would step on a piss ant if he could avoid it."

After we got to know him he was just a big old boy that would do anything we asked him to. We had great fun with him around because he was very intimidating to the other kids.

With vacation over, it was time to start back to school. We would be coming into contact with the girls for the first time; we wanted to see if the same girls had come back, especially the girl that had spied on us before.

Mrs. Pierce was glad to see me. The first thing she said was, "Did you draw anything while you were away?"

"I was too busy with Christmas and all," I told her, "but I'm going to start drawing again as soon as the weather gets a little warmer."

"You have a lot of catching up to do," she said.

At recess we took Bobo with us down to the creek. While we were there Harold and Buddy said that they had seen the girl that spied on us in class. She smiled at them, then said something to the other girls, and they laughed at whatever she said.

"Did you find out her name?" I asked him.

"I didn't get a chance to," Buddy said. I thought, that don't make any difference, anyway.

After school we had to take the laundry up the hill. Bobo said that he was good at carrying things. I looked at Eddie and thought, I bet you are.

The trip up the hill went well until Buddy slipped and fell. The clothes he was carrying went into the mud.

"The housemother will like this!" I said.

"But I slipped!" Buddy said.

"I know that," I said, "but she will say that you were supposed to be careful!"

"I wonder how many marks I will get for this," he said.

"Why should she do anything to you?" Bobo asked, shaking his head. "It was an accident."

"You don't know our housemother!" I told him.

When we got back to Crawford House Buddy had to tell the housemother what happened, but to our surprise she was forgiving.

"I hope that you will be more careful the next time," was all she said.

———

Not much happened for the next couple of weeks, but with the weather getting warmer, the snow melted, and some of the trees started putting on a few leaves. Spring was just around the corner, but the weather wasn't quite warm enough to hike to the farms. While we waited we made plans for some of the things we wanted to do when the weather got warmer. One day Eddie came up with a bright idea.

"Hey you guys, let's go dig up our stash of vegetables we buried last year," he said, out of the blue.

"Do you know where we buried them?" Harold asked. "I have no idea!"

Eddie said that he knew exactly where the spot was. We went and got Buddy but we didn't have much time, so we hurried off. Sure enough, Eddie found the right spot. We dug them up the next day after school.

Each of us took some to school. The girls wondered where we got them, because there wasn't anything growing yet, but we just told them we found a place in the mountains where they grew all the time. They wanted to know where but we didn't tell them. They did everything they could think of to get us to tell. We said if we tell you, you'll just eat them all yourself and we wanted to keep it a secret, but that just made them madder at us.

———

As the weather warmed up and the trees were getting full of leaves, we knew it wouldn't be too long until we could go on a hike to the farms. After a few more weeks it got real hot.

"We should get permission to go on a hike to Betty's farm," Harold said, "and check out the old swimming hole, to see if it made it through the winter and the high water."

"That sounds like a great idea to me!" I agreed.

About two weeks passed before we were able to get permission to go, but it was Thursday and we couldn't leave until Friday so we kept a watch on the bulletin board. Eddie had eleven marks, Buddy had ten, and I had nine. At school we met at recess time and talked about it, wondering if any of us would be able to go, because the housemother would have a field day checking out all she could to give out marks.

When we got back to the house that afternoon, the first thing we did was check out the bulletin board. I was almost afraid to look, but we felt lucky, since the marks were the same as the morning.

Earl met us at the spring house and was down in the dumps

"What's eating on you, Earl?" I asked him.

"What's eating on me? I'll tell you what's eating on me. I, all of a sudden have seventeen marks. Just out of nowhere I have seventeen marks!!"

"Don't take it so hard Earl," I said. "We've all been in that boat. After we see the bulletin board tomorrow we'll probably be joining you on the track."

The truth was, we could still get a few more marks and still be alright, unless the housemother went wild out marks.

At breakfast Friday the housemother wasn't at the table, which we thought was strange. She was always there, but the housefather was sitting in her place. After breakfast, instead of running to school, we all went back to check our beds, just to be on the safe side. All day at school I worried about how many marks would be added to our names. This was to be our first trip of the year; I just knew we were going to mess it up, but we couldn't blame Buddy this time.

When Eddie and I went up the hill to Crawford House after school, neither one of us wanted to look at the bulletin board. At the back door we met Harold, who had already checked it out and had that know-it-all grin said,

"Guess what?" he said. "There are no more marks than yesterday!!"

"You've got to be kidding," I responded.

"I overheard someone say that the housemother is sick and has to stay in bed," he said.

I looked at Harold and Eddie.

"There *is* a God!"

"Boy, what a stroke of luck," Buddy said as he followed Harold out of the house. "I thought we would all have to run track and not get to go."

Harold, Buddy, Eddie, and I got permission to take our first trip of the year. We felt sorry for Earl, who had to run track and Bobo, who had a bad cold, but there was always next week.

Eddie wanted to follow the creek so we could check out the swimming hole on the way. Harold liked that idea, but as for me I couldn't care less.

The winter storms and snow had changed things around a little, especially at the creek. The runoff of the melting snow had made the creek a wild river, washing out some of the banks, but now it was back to normal. Now the creek and the old swimming hole were wider, but the water level was lower.

"We can make a better place to swim," Harold said, "if we dig down at the one area, and make it a little deeper."

"Well, you go ahead," I said, "but I ain't doing any digging in that cold water."

"Come on Pat, it will be fun!" Eddie laughed.

"I'll watch while you guys have all the fun." I said.

I sat on the bank while they got in the water. I could tell that they had forgotten how cold the water was this time of year, because it didn't take them long to give up on their little plan. They got out.

"Well did you guys have enough fun yet? And now can we go and visit Betty and Mike at the farm?" I asked.

"Damn, that water was cold!" Eddie said.

"Ask Harold, the Eskimo," I answered.

"Maybe it will get warmer later today," Buddy said, laughing.

We finally got restarted on the trail to the farm; it must have been eleven o'clock before we got there. Mike was busy down at the barn, and Betty and Doris were washing clothes. We said hello to them, went to see Mike, who was nailing boards on the side of the barn. Mike told us that the wind had done considerable damage to the place, but he was nearly done with the repairs. He asked us how we survived the winter.

"For the most part just fine," I told him, "except we had to stay in most of the time, when we weren't going to and from school."

"Let's go up to the house," Mike said. "I need a drink of water and a smoke."

When we walked to the house we saw that Betty and Doris were through with the laundry.

"I'm making vegetable soup," Betty said. "It will be done in a couple of hours. You're welcome to eat with us."

"That would be great!" I said.

"Have you seen Sally lately?" Doris asked me.

"No, where is she?" I said.

"She was here earlier but told me that she was going to visit a friend." Doris remarked.

———

Harold went off with Buddy, while Eddie and I went looking for arrowheads. While we were walking along, Eddie said that he wanted to go over to where we had built the fort, so we wandered over in that direction. We were happy to see that the winter hadn't hurt it much, but we had to put some dry broom sage on the floor, which made it a little better. A lot of the dirt had washed away, but that was alright. Looking over to the creek, we could see Buddy and Harold at the swimming hole. I guess we were about fifty yards away, but we could see the whole valley from where we stood.

"They must be crazy to get in that water, as cold as it is," Eddie said. "I thought they learned their lesson this morning."

"I don't know why they had to get naked to dig out that mud," I said, "but what the hell, Buddy is a little stupid and Harold isn't much better."

Eddie noticed some girls playing in the pasture, off to the right not too far from the swimming hole; after were oblivious to the boys digging. We watched the girls walk in the direction of the creek.

"I've got to see this," Eddie said.

One of the girls pointed toward the swimming hole. They walked behind some bushes on the creek bank. It was obvious that neither Buddy nor Harold knew they were there, because they kept on with what they were doing. The girls just hid behind the bushes and watched.

"Let's go down and act like we didn't see the girls," Eddie suggested, "just to see if the boys will come out."

We started down the hill. As we approached the swimming hole, Buddy noticed us.

"Come on in and give us a hand!" he called out.

"You're doing a good job without us," I told him. We watched for a little while, until I noticed the girls start to leave. I told Buddy we were going back to the farm, but he wanted to go with us. After we waited for them to get out and put their clothes on, the four of us headed back to the farm.

———

"You boys are just in time to have some soup," Betty said. Doris sat a place for us and we shared some delicious vegetable soup.

Mike asked us if we had found any arrowheads. Eddie told him that he had found one, and it was a good one. Most of the time we only found ones that had been broken. We also found looked like a bullet but they were broken too. Mike said that the only decent ones that he found were down by the creek because that's where the animals would go to get water. I said that makes sense.

"Don't you guys think it's about time we got started start back?" Harold said. We all agreed, so we said goodbye and got on our way. About a hundred yards away, we ran into Sally.

"I was over in the pasture with some of the other girls," she said. "I would have come back to Betty's if I had known that you were there."

"I'm sorry that I missed you," she said to Harold and Buddy, smiling. "When will you be coming back?"

"I don't know for sure," I told her, "but we hope it will be soon."
"Okay, bye now."

———

We walked back was fairly quickly because we wanted to be back for supper. We still found time to stop at the spring house to have a smoke, though. We told Harold and Buddy about going to the fort. Buddy asked how the fort made it through the winter. I told them it was in good shape.

"While we were up there at the fort we could see the whole valley, including you two down at the old swimming hole." I turned to Eddie.

"Tell them what else we saw." I laughed.

"What's so funny?" Buddy asked.

Eddie told them what we saw, while trying to contain his own laughter.

"Why didn't you warn us?" Harold asked. "Some friends!"

"I thought it was so funny," I told him, "Anyway we were too far away. If we tried to warn you when we got there, they would have heard us and run away."

Buddy asked we knew who they were.

"They were too far away to tell," I said, "but I think they were girls from the school."

Eddie, who was still laughing, said "They didn't see *much* so why worry about it?" then I laughed again.

We got back just in time for supper. Mr. Mayo was sitting at the table in the place of the housemother, which I thought was better for me because he wouldn't pay too much attention to what we ate, so I could get by without eating what I didn't like.

———

The next Monday at school we had to go through another air-raid warning. We all had to get under our desk and wait for the all-clear sign. I was under the desk with one of the girls that had spied on us last year, but I couldn't tell for sure which one because I hadn't seen her too well before.

"I wish we didn't have to do this," she said. "I don't like to get under the desk, especially with one of you guys."

After the all-clear bell rang and we were able to get up, I thought, "Why did she say that? I don't even know her."

After school I told Eddie what she had said.

"She was probably one of the girls that had spied on us last year," Eddie said. "It wouldn't surprise me if she was one of the girls were watching Harold and Buddy at the swimming hole the other day."

"More than likely," I agreed.

After school when we went back to Crawford House, sat in the front room, and made plans to go frog hunting next week.

The next day we hung around the playground, watching the girls, instead of going for our regular smoke. Harold asked me to go over to the swings with him. I told him to go ahead.

"I don't want to go by myself," he said.

"What are you afraid of, the girls?" I taunted.

Buddy came over to see what we talked about. I told him he should go with Harold over to the swings because he was afraid of the girls and needed a body guard.

"Maybe one of those girls has already *seen too much* of Harold," Buddy said. We both laughed, and Harold didn't like that at all. Then the bell rang: time to go back to class.

———

After school, we went back to Crawford House to check the bulletin board. Despite what we thought was good behavior week, we all had some new marks. Buddy had more than anybody else, but we were all right at the limit. Buddy had fifteen and the rest of us had twelve.

"This is only Thursday," Eddie said. "You know something, we can probably forget about doing anything this weekend. We're all going to be running track!"

"Oh what the hell, they say it's good for you," I said.

After that bit of bad news we headed to the spring house, but on the way we discovered that none of us had a cigarette.

"I have some rabbit tobacco," Buddy said, so we rolled one up. It was awful.

"We need to find something better than that! That shit will kill you!" I said, but we smoked it anyway.

"What are we going to do now if we have to run track Saturday?" Eddie asked.

"That depends on how many more marks we get on Friday," I said. "If it's just a few we could have them run off by noon, and still have enough time to go to the creek and play around." "We can go and catch frogs Friday night," Eddie said, "and it won't be so bad."

"I have another little bit of bad news," Harold said. "We're having liver for supper, so I guess we'd better go and get it!"

"Oh my God!" I said. "You know how I hate live. I hope you're kidding we us!"

"He's not kidding," Buddy said, "but I don't mind it. In fact I'll eat yours for twenty marbles."

"That's highway robbery," I told him.

Then Harold said that he would eat it for fifteen. Eddie said keep it going and maybe they will pay you for eating the liver, and laughed.

"What the hell are you trying to do," Benny said to Harold, "ruin a good thing?

At the supper table I let each of them split my liver for seven marbles each.

Friday we went back up the hill and checked the bulletin board, and there wasn't a one of us that wasn't pissed off. Buddy had twenty marks, I had seventeen, Eddie had fifteen, and Harold twenty-two, which led Harold to remark, "My God, the housemother must be mad at the world!"

It was settled, we would spend most of Saturday running track, but we still had Friday night to go frog hunting. Buddy got the burlap sack and we headed for the creek. We had a pretty good hike to get to the place where the frogs were. On the way Harold said that he had bought a pack of cigarettes from a kid at school.

"What in the hell are we waiting for," I said. "Let's have a smoke!"

When we got to a good frogging place, it still wasn't quite dark enough. While we waited, it started to rain, not too hard but just enough to get things good and muddy. Since we had waited too long to go frogging, we didn't let that stop us; we could put up with a little rain and mud.

Buddy and Harold got in the water anyway. Right off the bat, Buddy caught one. Moving along the creek, we had pretty good luck. I thought that I heard something then Eddie said that *he* thought that he heard something a little while back. We all looked around but didn't see anything, because it was pretty dark now. We concentrated on catching frogs, and didn't pay much attention to what was happening around us. We must have walked a mile when we decided to take a break and have a smoke.

I heard something for sure this time, but it was dark now and I couldn't see too far.

"There is something *in those bushes* over by the creek bank," Eddie said in a low whisper.

Taking the flashlight, I got closer to the bushes. I saw somebody move, and a girl came out.

"It's just me," Sally said.

"How long have you been following us?" I asked.

"Ever since you guys got in the creek," she confessed.

"Why?"

"I just wanted to see what you were doing."

"Why didn't you just come over and talk to us?" I asked.

"Just like the last time when we were digging in the swimming hole!" Buddy said.

She laughed.

"But we didn't know that you would be naked," she said, "and besides, how did you know we were there?"

I told her how Eddie and I were up on the hill, where we saw the whole thing, with her and her friends spying from behind the bushes.

"But that was an accident," she said.

"Why didn't you leave, then?" Eddie wanted know.

"Well, I thought it was fun," she giggled.

I said to her, "If we caught you and your friends out naked and spied on you, I bet that you wouldn't like it!"

"Well, I don't know if I would like it, or not, but I wouldn't make such a big fuss about it."

I told her that the next time we decide to be naked we'd look out for her. When I asked her what she was doing out here in the dark in the first place, she told us that she was on her way home when she saw us. Now, she said, it was late and she had to get home.

"Say hello to Doris," I said as she turned to leave. "Tell her we might go to the farm in a couple of weeks."

"Alright," she said, and left.

We continued up the creek for another hour, catching a bunch of frogs. As I stuffed a big bull frog in the sack, Eddie had a worried look on his face.

"I think we've come a lot farther away than we should've," he said. "It's going to be hard getting back in the rain."

I walked over to where Buddy and Harold were spotting for frogs.

"I think we'd better get back, it's getting late," I said.

As we got back, Buddy suggested it would be quicker to walk along the road, and certainly less muddy. We didn't realize how far we had come; we could make better time on the old dirt road, but it took us out of the way, making it longer. After awhile we had to stop and take a break. While we rested we noticed a church about twenty feet back from the road. Looking past it, we could see the lights from the school, at least a mile away.

"I knew it was a mistake to listen to Buddy about taking the road," Eddie said. "Now look how far we are away from the school. Damn, if we stay on this road it will take us at least an hour and a half to get there."

"Somebody take these frogs," Harold said. "I've been carrying them the whole way, and they're heavy!"

"Give them to Buddy," Eddie said. "he got us into this mess."

Since I didn't want to, I suggested we cut across the graveyard surrounding the church. As soon as I said it I knew was making a mistake. I should have just kept my mouth shut, but I had already opened my yap and the damage was done. They all agreed it was a good idea to cut through the graveyard, because it looked to be a lot closer. We were all getting tired.

"Before we go into that graveyard," Harold said, "let's not tell anybody we saw anything. Let's just go real quiet and make it through to the other side."

We all agreed to that, but you could tell that all of us were quite nervous, looking around a lot. We all had a cigarette and stepped across the split-rail fence.

We hadn't gone ten feet when someone said, *what was that?* That was all it took, and we started running. I just got startled when I stepped onto a fresh grave that couldn't have been there more than a couple days, and felt myself getting stuck.

My feet sunk down to the ankles. I was terrified at the thought of a dead person grabbing my foot. Somehow I put my feet in double time and I passed the other boys, was over the fence, and half way through the next field. Although that field was muddy too, it didn't slow me down a damn bit. By the time that the other boys caught me we were almost back to the school.

When we did stop and catch our breath, Eddie said, "You went by me so fast that I felt like I was standing still."

"Don't any of you ever take me through a graveyard again!" I said. "Especially at night!"

———

After we got back to the school, Harold said, "Where are the frogs?"

"When we ran I dropped them," Buddy said.

"Why?" I asked.

"I couldn't run fast enough carrying the frogs," he said.

"God-damn-it, Buddy," I said, "you mean you dropped all those frogs. We must have had fifteen to twenty, and after all that work! Why didn't you say something. I would have carried them."

"Pat, we were all running away from the same thing, and believe me, *those frogs were the last thing on my mind!*

"I had no idea about what you were doing, Buddy, but when I found that I had one foot in the grave, I didn't stick around to find out."

Then we all busted out laughing

"Well, we had fun though," Harold said.

———

Track day came the next morning. Since we didn't have anything else to do, we took our time and walked most of the laps, which gave us time to talk about the previous night's adventure and how Sally sneaked up on us.

"I think she was just waiting for us to take off our clothes," Eddie said.

"I think she gets a kick out of seeing us in the nude," Buddy said.

"You may be right," Harold said. "I wonder how many times those girls have spied on us we didn't know about. I don't know about Sally but one of the girls from school had been following us around. I know because we caught her, but I haven't seen her this year."

Crawford House is No More

That night I was lucky: we had a good meal and it didn't cost me any marbles. While we were eating a cow got into the victory garden, and started eating the corn.

"Boys, we'd better go and get the cow out before he tears up the whole darned place," the housefather said.

We all took off to get the cow. Let me tell you, that turned out to be a big mistake. Twenty boys trying to get the cow to do something was a big problem. One boy would go one way and the cow would go the other, and step into the tomatoes. Another boy would chase the cow from the tomatoes into the squash. Before long the poor cow had torn up half of the garden.

After we got the cow out of the garden we thought we had done a good job until we looked at all the damage it did.

"Well, you boys got the cow corralled, alright but look at the mess we've got!" the housefather said. "You boys will have to mend the fence, clean up this mess, and replant a few things."

"This ought to keep us busy for awhile," Buddy said, then added, "This is extra work. Maybe we can work off some of our marks."

After we cleaned ourselves up we went in to see the housefather. He agreed we would be able to work off our marks in the garden.

We started right after breakfast the next day and worked until supper, only taking time out for lunch. We repaired the fence repaired and replanted the vegetables.

"I don't think that I've put in a harder days' work since I've been here," I told Harold.

"At least we all have a clean slate on the bulletin board!" he said, grinning from ear to ear.

I put on a smile and felt better already.

Thursday afternoon we got up the hill early due to a teacher's meeting, so we had a lot of time to ourselves. Harry started making a bow so I went over to talk to him. He said that he had found a good piece of hickory and was carving a notch in it to hold the string. Hickory was the best wood to make a bow out of, he said. He planned to use that rabbit tobacco weed to make the arrows because it was straight, and just about the right length. I went and got a few of them and trimmed them up.

"They're still green but that's okay," Harry said. "They'll dry out in a day or so and it will take me that long to finish up the bow."

I stayed there talking with Harry. After a while Buddy and Eddie came over; they wanted to go have a smoke, so we went to the spring house. We talked about how Harry was making a bow and some arrows, and decided we should make some too.

"I would rather make a slingshot," Buddy said, and I agreed with him. A bow and arrow were hard to make. A slingshot was much easier and on top of that, it was easier to hit something with a slingshot.

"It's a lot easier to carry!" Buddy added.

"I don't care which one we make," Eddie said, "but we only have a small amount of inner tube, maybe enough to make two slingshots. I will give up mine."

"Let's just wait until we get more inner tube and then make them," Buddy said.

———

Spinach was served for supper, and that's something that I couldn't stand. Without Buddy sitting next to me I didn't have any way to get rid of it. After eating everything else on my plate, I just sat there waiting for a chance to dump it off. Since the kid next to me was talking to the kid on the other side, I waited for him to turn his head. When he did, I put my spinach on his plate. Before he got a chance to see the spinach I got up and went to the kitchen to wash my plate. Outside in the yard, Eddie came over, laughing. He saw what I had done.

"I couldn't help it," I said. "I thought that I was going to have to eat that God awful crap."

———

The next morning we were still laughing about it at breakfast, and the housemother overheard us, so we told her all about it. Mrs. Mayo thought it was funny too.

"I guess you boys will want to go out and get frogs again next week," she said.

"Probably so, Ma'am, it's a lot of fun," I said. "But I'll never go near that graveyard again!"

The day was so hot that I felt like going to sleep. When I nodded off Mrs. Pierce saw me.

"It's almost time for recess," she said. "Go out and get some fresh air."

"Let's go down by the creek and have a smoke," Buddy said when we got in the yard.

Down at the creek Eddie said that he saw one of the girls that had followed us that day, and we'd better watch out for her.

"I'll look around and see if she's here by the creek," Buddy said. After he returned we sat around and made plans for the weekend.

"You know, summer will soon be over," Earl said. "If we are going to visit Mike an Betty at the farm, we'd better plan to do it soon or it will be too late."

———

After school we had to carry laundry up the hill. Eddie wanted get there first so we would get the easy things to carry. We raced from the school to the laundry, and then we raced to Crawford House. As the first one there, I grabbed the first light load and took off. Eddie was right behind me. When we got to Crawford House we didn't see Buddy or Earl.

"I bet they took a short cut to try and beat us up the hill," Eddie said, "and something happened."

After several minutes we saw them. Buddy and his laundry were all wet.

"What in the hell happened to you?" I asked. "And what happened to the laundry?"

"Well, we were going to cross the creek and to the shorter way up the hill," Eddie said. "Then Buddy slipped and fell into the water."

"Why didn't you go over the bridge like everybody else does?" I asked Buddy.

"It was closer that way," he said. "We would have beaten you too, if I hadn't fell!"

I looked at him.

"The housemother is going to be pissed at you now."

"Maybe we can sneak past her and hide the clothes until they dry," Eddie said.

I looked at Buddy.

"Well, let's give it a try," I said.

After we got the clothes upstairs and hidden we got ready for supper.

"If she finds the laundry," I said to Eddie, "and you get caught, don't dare say we had anything to do with helping you. It will just make it worse."

That night we just sat around the front room waiting for something to go wrong, but all was quiet, so we went to bed. In the morning the bulletin board said we were all in good shape as far as marks were concerned; now we only had to worry about keeping our noses clean Thursday and Friday— that and the little thing about the housemother finding the wet clothes we hid.

By Thursday we had a few marks but well below the limit. Friday after school we took our time going back up the hill. At the bridge over the creek we stopped and looked in the water, where there appeared to be trash floating down the creek. Buddy got in the water, took hold of a wooden box, and pulled it over to the bank.

The box was about three feet square and quite heavy. We all helped carry it onto the grass, and managed to get the top off. Inside we found several books, some papers, and a dozen or more pictures.

The pictures were old and faded, but we could see that they were of a family. One was a man in an army uniform.

"Maybe we should take all of this to the housemother and see if she can find out who it belongs to," Eddie said.

We took it all to her, and explained how we got it. She said that she would look into it.

The next day we got permission to go visit Mike and Betty at the farm. We got an early start: We want to stop by the swimming hole to see if the summer rains had done any damage. The water level was up, which made it look inviting. Buddy and Harold wanted to go in, but we decided we would take a swim on the way back.

At the farm we discovered Mike had gone hunting with some of his friends and wouldn't be back until late, so we helped Betty with the milking and feeding the animals. After we went to the well to get water for the house, we told Betty we were going to walk around the woods until evening. She said that she would have supper ready at around five and invited us to eat with them.

Wandering off, we ended up at the old swimming hole. Eddie and I just lay around on the bank while Buddy, Earl, and Harold went in the water. After awhile Eddie and I got bored so we walked up the creek to look for frog eggs. We found quite a few. Since we hadn't been there for awhile, we decided to go frogging later on that night. Betty could cook them up for us; that way we could stay in the barn for the night and get an early start back to the school in the morning.

"Let's go back and tell the others what we plan to do," I said.

"Okay," Eddie said, "but in the meantime let's sneak back and see what they're doing."

As we approached the swimming hole we could see that they were still in the water.

"Let's see if we can get their clothes without them seeing us," Eddie said, so we got a little closer. They didn't notice when Eddie got their clothes. We took them up the creek a ways and came back, sat on the bank, and had a cigarette as if nothing had happened. After awhile Buddy told the other two that he was going out to have a smoke, and went to get his clothes. Seeing none, he looked at Eddie and me.

"Okay, you guys what did you do with our clothes?" he asked.

"We didn't touch your clothes," Eddie said. "All we did was walk up the creek."

"Where did you leave them?" I asked.

"We laid them right here by these rocks!" he said.

"I bet those girls were here while we were gone, and took them," Eddie suggested.

"Those God-damned little bitches," Buddy said, upset. "Just wait until I see them!"

Hearing Buddy's raving, Earl and Harold got out and were equally upset.

"I wonder what they could have done with them," Harold said.

"I'll bet if we all go looking for the clothes they'll probably jump out and catch one of us."

"I'm not going around naked looking for my clothes," Earl said, "so why don't we get back in the water, and you and Eddie try and find our clothes?"

When we got far enough away we both laughed.

"Let's not tell them what we did," Eddie said. "Just let them think it was the girls that took them."

When we brought the clothes back I said, "We had found them quite a ways up the creek but I bet they stuck around long enough to see you guys, naked in the water."

That just made them madder. Buddy pissed and moaned all the way back to the farm.

———

When we got back to the farm we told Betty we were going back to catch some frogs after it got dark. Betty fed us some vegetable soup and homemade biscuits were good. After eating we said we would be back in a couple of hours.

"That would be good," she said. "Mike should be home by then, and he likes frog legs."

As we turned to leave Sally came out of the house, wondering what we were going to do. When we told her we were going to get frogs after dark, she asked if she could go with us. Eddie said it was okay with him, but Buddy and Harold didn't like that idea at all. They didn't say anything, but Buddy just shrugged his shoulders and said okay.

Doris needed to milk the cow, so we all went to the barn. After we fed the animals it was almost dark, so we left, with Sally tagging along. Buddy was unhappy because he thought she was one of the girls that had taken his clothes that afternoon.

After we got started catching frogs in the water she said, "Do you guys mind if I give it a try?"

She got in the creek and before long we spotted one; she caught it on the first try.

"My God Pat, she's better than Buddy!" Eddie exclaimed. If Buddy wasn't pissed before, he sure was now.

After awhile we stopped for a smoke break.

"I'm tired and want to go back to the farm," Buddy said, so we caught a few more frogs and back. On the way Sally said she didn't think Buddy liked her. I told her he had caught some girls spying on him while he was naked in the swimming hole, so he was mad at all of the girls.

Sally laughed.

"I've been caught a few times myself," she said, "but I didn't let it bother me."

———

Back at the farm we had to clean the frogs and get the legs ready to fry. Doris took the legs back to Betty for frying. Mike was back; he had killed a deer, which they had already butchered and had hung in the smokehouse.

After Betty fried up the frog legs, we sat down and had a great meal. After we had a smoke with Mike, it was time to get to sleep.

Once again I was awakened before six by someone milking a cow. I got up for a closer look.

"Did you get a good night's sleep?" Doris asked.

"Hell no," I said. "That mule kept moving around."

"I need to get the cow milked," she said, "but maybe you can go back to sleep then."

I walked over to the milking stall.

It's amazing how you jerk on then little tits and get so much milk out," I said. "Doesn't it hurt the cow?"

"Not if you do it right," she said with a crooked smile, "and Pat, I've had a lot of practice."

Then I told her how Eddie and I made Buddy, Harold, and Earl think that the girls had caught them in the swimming hole naked.

"So don't say anything if they bitch about it," I told her, "but they believe Sally was there, so they might say something."

"You boys are something! Don't you ever get into fights?" she said, laughing.

"Not really. We've known each other for a couple of years, and for the most part like each other, so we take whatever the others dish out, and try to get even later. Sometimes we just play jokes on each other in order to see how the others will react."

"Sally goes and spies on you boys just for the fun of it," she said, "and then comes back and tells me about it."

"Did you ever do that?" I asked her.

"I'd never tell you if I did!" she laughed.

After she finished milking and I carried her milk to the house.

"If you guys go to the swimming hole today, be very careful because I just might be watching," she warned.

As she entered the house, she looked over her shoulder and smiled. I thought to myself, "What in the holy hell did all of that mean?"

I woke up the other boys and we went to the house for breakfast.

"I liked those frog legs that you guys brought yesterday," Mike said. "Next time you come we'll have venison for supper."

"What's venison?" Buddy asked.

"That's the fancy name for deer meat after it's been butchered," Mike told him.

"Why don't they just call it deer meat?" Harold asked. Everybody just looked at each other.

Eddie said he wanted to get an early start so we could go by the fort on the way back. We said good bye to Mike and Betty, but Doris wasn't around.

The sun was high in the sky when we arrived at our homemade; things were heating up. Eddie, Earl, and I stayed at the fort, while Buddy and Harold went down to the swimming hole. Eddie and I put new broom sage on the floor, and Earl repaired the dirt in front washed away by the rains.

After a half an hour Earl said that he wanted to go cool off in the creek; Eddie and I went with him. At the creek we stripped down and jumped in a spot about fifty feet from the swimming hole. I guess we played around for awhile, but got out because the water was pretty cold. While we waited for the sun to dry us off, we smoked a couple of cigarettes Eddie had with him. That's when I remembered what Doris said, so I looked around.

"What are you looking for?" Eddie asked.

"Well, Doris wasn't there when we left and she told me that she might spy on us if we went to the swimming hole!" I said.

"Why didn't you tell us?" Eddie wanted to know.

"I didn't think about it til just now. But I don't see anybody so maybe she just said that that so we would worry about it."

"Don't say anything about it to Buddy or Harold," Eddie said. "They're already pissed off enough."

We went to find Buddy and Harold, because we had to get back by suppertime.

———

Monday was very warm at school. We could hardly wait for recess to go down to the creek and stick our feet in the water. Buddy said he had seen Sally at school.

"Well she might be looking at you right now," I said.

When Buddy jumped up and started looking around, Eddie laughed.

"Buddy, why are you so jumpy?" he asked.

"I don't like it when somebody does that!" Buddy told him.

About that time the bell rang and we all had to go back to class. After school, Eddie and I stayed down by the creek while the others went up the hill to the house.

"I wonder if Sally is still hanging around the creek," I said to him.

"I don't think so Pat," Eddie said. "She surely would have shown herself by now."

I agreed. We had a smoke and back up the hill to Crawford House. Before we got too far Eddie said, "Do you smell smoke?"

"Yeah but I don't know where it's coming from," I said. "Maybe someone's cooking outside."

We were surrounded by trees with thick leaves, so it was difficult to see any distance. As we continued up the hill, the smell of smoke got worse. We could hear the voices of kids about our age.

When we got closer we could see flames, so we ran in that direction. Not only was it a fire but it was *Crawford House*, and boy, was it burning!

The housemother had all the kids together, standing way back at the outhouse. Eddie and I had to go through the woods to get up the hill to where she was. After we got to her she was happy to see us. She pointed to each kid and counted to make sure we were all accounted for.

"I want all of you stay together and close to me," she said. "We're going down the hill to Mayo Hall!"

There were men trying to put out the fire, but it was useless. The dry wood had quickly turned the fire into an inferno and the house was too far gone.

That night after earting supper at Mayo Hall, we went spent the night in a classroom at the schoolhouse. The next day they put us in the recreation room at the schoolhouse, where they brought in some cots for us to sleep on.

The fire left us with only the clothes we were wearing. On top of that, most of us had been barefooted. The next day the school got some clothes from somewhere, but we had a hard time finding anything that fit, so we had to laugh at the way we looked. Some of the girls donated some things to us. Although it was too warm to wear it, I got a pretty nice leather jacket that fit pretty well.

The school wrote a letter to our parents about the fire, so Before long we got new clothes from home.

———

At least a month went by before things got back to some sort of normalcy. Now we had moved to the main school things changed. We didn't have to run track, we didn't have to carry laundry up the hill, and we were all expected to use our best manners when we ate at Mayo Hall with the other boys and girls.

We got a new housemother, because Mr. and Mrs. Mayo lived up the hill. Her room was downstairs and we lived upstairs.

Some of our jobs changed, and which we liked for the most part. We no longer had to bring in coal for the cooking and pot-belly stoves. We had indoor toilets with hot and cold running water, although that meant that sometimes we were put on the detail to clean them. Mrs. Mayo put it this way: You have to learn to take the bad with the good. We still had chores to do, like keeping the area clean around the schoolhouse. We still had to make our beds and keep our new dormitory clean. Aside from we had it easy compared to before.

One of the best things that the new housemother, who was older than Mrs. Mayo and not nearly as stern. She turned out to be easier to get along with.

Basically all we had to do was hang around the school. What we didn't like about that was the playground at the school, used by the girls. Their playground was maybe thirty-five yards from where we lived. That was too close because they would be watching everything we did. But the creek where we went for a smoke was also much closer than the spring house.

———

One night after supper we asked the new housemother for permission to go to the farms. We didn't know whether she knew about our trips to the farms. We considered telling her how we had gone before, how the people took care of us, and how they taught us things about the mountains. We thought maybe she would think it was good for us.

"Maybe we should just tell her about catching frogs at night," Earl said. "How it has to be dark to catch them, and try to go to the farms later."

"Maybe so," Buddy said, "but we had better do it soon. It's getting late in the summer, and we won't have much more time to go to the farms."

We waited until Friday to tell her about going to get frogs.

"Do they let you go out at night?" she asked.

"We've been doing it all year," I assured her.

"I'll have to look into this and let you know," she decided.

We walked over to the creek to have a smoke.

"I'm so disappointed!" Eddie said. "I don't know if we'll get to go frogging at all, and if we do, how long is it going take her to let us know?"

"Maybe we should have said something to her before Friday," Earl said.

"Well it's too late now," Eddie retorted. "We'll have to wait and see what happens."

Friday evening we asked her if she had made up her mind about the frogging. She said it would be alright but we would have to be back by ten o'clock.

We got to our best frogging spot and sat on the bank waiting for darkness. We talked about the fire, how we lost the things we had, and we hadn't even been over to see Doris, Mike, and Betty. We decided to the new housemother about visiting them as soon as we got back. The weather started to turn cold and soon would be too cold for sleeping in the barn.

"If we left early Saturday morning we could be back before supper," Harold said, "we wouldn't have to worry about sleeping in the barn."

"I guess we could do that," I said, "but it takes a lot of fun out of the hike, because we would only be there a couple of hours.

———

Once it was dark, Eddie and Earl got into the water.

"God damn its cold," Earl said.

"Don't worry about that, let's just catch some frogs!" Buddy said.

"Come over and give me a hand," Earl told him. When Buddy came over, Earl grabbed his hand and pulled him in the water. Buddy let out a stream of cuss words.

"Don't worry about it, Buddy *let's just catch some frogs,*" Earl responded.

Buddy was wet and cold. Eddie pushed Earl in the creek.

"That wasn't called for!" he said.

"If you don't like it you can go back to the House!" I told Earl.

After awhile we stopped to for a smoke break. Earl said we were right to push him in, but he was tired of Buddy smarting off all the time. He said he was sorry he lost his temper, and we went back to catching frogs.

———

When we were ready to leave the creek, we tied out gunny sack of frogs shut and left it lying in the water; we would return the next day to clean them. We made it back before ten; the housemother was watching for us.

"Well did you catch any frogs?" she asked.

"Sure did, we got a bunch of them!" I answered.

The next day after we cleaned the frogs, we took them to the cook, who would fry them for us.

———

That night it rained, and the weather turned cold, so we were glad we went frogging when we did. Week after week we had bad weather. Between the rain and the cold it was too miserable to go outside, so the housemother tried to entertain us by telling stories, but that got old after a while.

One night after we had gone to bed the wind was blowing so hard that the whole building shook. The noise sounded like a freight train was going by...very spooky. The next morning there was ice all over the ground. Walking to the main hall for breakfast we could see snow on the mountains in the distance. Soon it would be snowing down here.

———

Most of the time we stayed in the dormitory; every now and then we made up an excuse to go out for a smoke. The housemother didn't mind if we went out to have a snowball fight or maybe get some fresh air, so we would use that to sneak off for a smoke.

After Halloween the weather was a little nicer, though the ground was covered with snow: the wind wasn't as strong and we didn't have the bitter cold. Harold said it was perfect for a few rides down the hill, but I reminded him that our sleds had burned in the fire.

"God damn, we can't even do that!" he said.

Buddy overheard Harold's ranting.

"Last year some of the girls were using a sled," he remarked, "but I don't think they've been using it this year. Maybe we could borrow it."

Buddy and Eddie went to the girls' house, where they trades the use and for "a favor". Without asking what they meant, he just said, "Sure." At the time, I didn't know how Buddy got the sled, and I didn't care.

That night the weather turned colder, and the wind came whistling back. We got an early start because the sledding hill was a long way off. By the time we got to the top of the hill we were tired and had to stop and catch our breath, so we sat down and had a smoke.

Eddie ended up going first. Once he got going, due to some of the dips and rises, I lost sight of him.

"I don't see him at the bottom!" Buddy said. "Where did he go?"

Halfway down the hill we saw the sled, broken up. Eddie was lying between two big rocks with a cut on his head. He was alright but was just sitting there.

"I think I hit every damn rock there was to hit, maybe the big ones twice!" he said. "After I hit the first one I lost count."

"The sled is broken up," I said, "so we might as well go back to the house."

"What are we going to tell the girls?" Buddy asked.

"Tell them what happened, what's the problem?" I said. "We can't help it if we had an accident."

"Well, they said we would have to do them a favor when we borrowed the sled," Eddie said.

"A favor?" I asked, looking at him.

"Yeah, it looked like the only way we could borrow the sled."

"What kind of favor?" I asked him.

"I don't know...just a favor. How do I know what girls like that are thinking!"

"Let's hope it wasn't the girl that spies on us," I said. "God only knows what kind of favor she will want. Let's take the sled back to the house. Maybe we can fix it."

Away For The Holidays

When Christmas vacation approached, I wanted to stay at the school. I had heard of a lot of things that they did for Christmas. Somehow I felt I was missing out on something.

I wrote a letter to my mother and told her that I wanted to spend Christmas at the school. I explained there were kids here that didn't have families to go to, and I wanted to stay with them. I had the housemother help me write the letter, so I had hopes that my mother would say okay without getting too upset.

A couple of weeks later the housemother came and told me that my mother said it would be alright for me to stay, and boy was I happy.

―――

A new kid named Jackie got to be a real good friend. He was my age and about my same size, though a little stouter. Jackie didn't have any parents and would have to stay at school through vacation times. Although he was new at the school, he was familiar with the mountains and the people who lived there. Eddie, Buddy, and Harold left to go on vacation, so it was just Earl, Jackie, and me.

"I have never spent Christmas at the school before," I told Jackie, "but I've heard that they have a good time. We'll get to do things we wouldn't be able to do if all the kids were here." With the housemother on vacation, we had Mr. Mayo for our housefather. I told Jackie he was a good guy.

The first few days we just talked and got to know each other.

"I only have one relative," Jackie told me. "My uncle that lives in Washington, DC but I hardly know him."

I told him about my family and that I had a brother that was here at the school, but he had gone home for Christmas.

―――

A couple of weeks after vacation started, I saw Harold coming back into the dormitory with his suitcase.

"What in the hell are you doing back here so soon?" I asked him.

"My mother and father had a big fight and are planning to get a divorce," he said, "so they sent me back. I never did understand why. I guess neither one of them wanted me."

We felt sorry for him and tried cheering him up.

"I'm sure that you're wrong about that," I told him. "They probably didn't want you right in the middle of their troubles."

No matter how hard we tried, Harold stayed down in the dumps and didn't want to take part in anything. He just sat around and pouted.

———

Mr. Mayo asked if we would like to go to a movie. We all got excited because we couldn't do that when all the other kids were here. That night was colder than a witch's tit and we had to ride in the back of a pickup, but we took blankets and covered up, about eight of us all together. We had to snuggle up close together to get warmer. The trip was fifteen miles to the show, which wouldn't have been too bad except for first five miles of dirt road, but when we got to the gravel road it started to snow. We were so excited about going to the show we didn't care.

The picture was "My Wild Irish Rose"—a good movie but not the kind we liked. For the most part, we liked war movies or scary ones. Everyone enjoyed our night out, especially riding in the truck in the snow. After the show we had to clean the snow out of the truck bed, and I believe it was even colder on the way back.

Jackie announced that he would stand up all the way back, so I said I was going too also. We stood up and held on to the cab. When the truck got up to speed the wind cut into our faces, and

I had to shut my eyes; then it started to rain but not too hard. I looked over and could see that Jackie was determined to stand there as long as I did.

By the time we got back to the school we had ice in our hair. My ears felt like they would fall off if someone touched them. When we went to the bathroom and looked in the mirror, Jackie said, "That was a stupid thing to do!"

"Well, I guess I'm just as stupid as you are," I said, and we had a laugh.

"I wanted to stop but I could see you, and I didn't want to give up before you did," Jackie said.

———

I was glad I stayed at school this year. Christmas was just a week away, and I could hardly wait.

The next day after breakfast we were invited to a party that the girls had. We had to get dressed up, but that was alright. They set up a table with all kinds of food and pies they had cooked. I was surprised that the girls could cook—and the food was even good. After we all sang Christmas carols and drank hot chocolate.

A day or two later the housefather said we had to get a Christmas tree. We got an axe and went out to find one, which wasn't too hard because there were all kinds of trees to choose from. We picked out a big one, about ten feet tall, and it was all we could do to get it back to the House. The housefather made a stand for it. He told us we had to decorate it, but we had no clue how to get started. He said that the girls' house was just fifty yards away, and we should invite them over to help us. In the meantime he would have the cook make some cookies and hot chocolate.

Jackie and I went over and asked their housemother if the girls could come over and help us decorate our tree.

"I believe that they would be glad to," she said, "but I will ask just the same. You boys can go back and they should be over in a few minutes."

After about thirty minutes six girls came over carrying ornaments, colored paper, and ribbons to make decorations with.

The girls had all kinds of ideas on how to make decorations, so we sat around doing whatever they told us to. We had a great time, laughing, talking, and kidding with each other.

I found out that girls weren't so bad after all, and they knew how to do things that boys never thought of. After we finished the tree we sat and talked with the girls for a long time. Since it was dark, we had to make sure they got back to their house safely.

The next day was a fairly warm day for that time of year, so Buddy, Harold, Jackie and I sneaked off to the creek for a smoke.

"What did you think of all the girls coming to help us last night?" Buddy asked me.

"I hate to admit this," I said, "but it was a lot more fun than I than I thought it would be."

The others reluctantly agreed with me.

"One of the girls asked me, 'Where do you boys go swimming, when it gets warm?'" Buddy said.

He didn't know what to say, since he didn't expect her to just come out and ask that.

"What did you tell her?" I asked him.

"I didn't tell her anything."

Harold said that he had overheard one of the girls talking about seeing two boys swimming naked.

"I wonder if she is one of the girls that spied on us last summer," I said to him.

Jackie didn't know what we talked about, so I filled him in on what some of the girls did last year. He got a big kick out of Buddy and Harold being caught naked by the girls.

"I don't think that's so funny!" Harold protested.

"I don't know why you're so mad," Jackie said, "you've got nothing to show them, anyway." We all busted out laughing, but Harold got up and walked away. I don't think Buddy cared one way or the other.

———

On Christmas Eve some of the older girls went around singing carols. Since it was still fairly warm we sat outside and watched them. You couldn't ask for a better picture on a Christmas card, with the girls all bundled up in their coats and scarves standing in the snow, singing Christmas carols.

The next morning at breakfast Mayo Hall was all decorated, with a big tree and all kinds of presents under it. After we all had eaten, some of the teachers gave out presents. Everybody got one, but it was a luck of the draw type of thing. We lined up with girls on one side of the room and boys on the other. The teacher would get a gift and say, "boy" or "girl" and the next in line would come up and get his or her present. It didn't matter what you got, because everyone liked getting a gift. The food they had during the holidays was the best part. I can't begin to name all the different kinds of cookies, pies, and cakes they had. It was the first time that I ever had fruit cake and boy was it good. I can still taste it today.

Jackie and I went out for a smoke. When we got back to the house, Harold showed us two new sleds that the school had bought us. They were pretty bright and you could tell that they were brand new. They were a lot better than the ones that burned up at Crawford House.

Right after breakfast the next morning we started up the hill to try out the sleds. The sun was out but there was a lot of snow. We had to pass Crawford House and I showed him the shed where we kept all of the sports equipment, including our sleds and baseball stuff. There were still some of the boards on the shed but they were burnt pretty badly. The coal bin next to the shed still had some coal in it.

After we got to the top of the hill Jackie looked down.

"How far is it to the bottom?" he asked.

"I don't know," I said. "I've never measured it, but it must be several hundred feet. At the bottom it goes through an old apple orchard and on into a pasture. I'll go first and you can follow in my tracks."

I jumped on a sled and started down. At about the halfway point I did a quick glance back and saw that he had already started down. Passing the orchard, I was thankful I missed the trees. I was on my way into the pasture when I ran over a boulder, throwing me off the trail. Once again luck was on my side, and I slowly came to a stop in the pasture. When I looked back Jackie came whizzing by me, and came to a stop at the fence by the track we used to run on.

"That was great," he said when I walked over. "I didn't have any trouble at all!"

"Now we have to walk back up the hill," I said.

———

"I guess one ride a day is all you can hope for," Jackie said as we pulled the sleds back up the hill. "By the time four or five people take their turns and bringing the sleds back, I don't think we will have time for another ride!"

We left the other guys and went back to the house. Since it wasn't time for supper yet we decided to go and have a smoke. On the way down to the creek we saw Buddy getting out of a car with his bags, so we went to help him. I was glad to see that he made it back. While we walked to the house, he said he had a good time at home but he was anxious to get back to see all of us.

"I haven't seen Eddie yet," I said. "I hope he makes it back today."

By the time we got Buddy's belongings back at the house it was time to eat supper, so we went to Mayo Hall, where we saw quite a few new kids.

What caught Buddy's eye were the twins Donny and Jonnie.

"*There* are those little bastards!" he said.

"What's wrong with them?" Jackie asked.

We had to tell him about all the things they did, how Buddy hated the little turds, and how he wanted to get even with them for what they did.

"That would be easy," Jackie said. "We can take them snipe hunting."

"I ain't taking them little bastards out hunting unless I have a gun!" Buddy said.

Jackie explained about the snipe hunt, which we had never heard of before. We agreed it would be great.

"But," I said, "They won't go anywhere with Buddy or me."

"Since I'm new I can set the whole thing up," Jackie said, "but we will have to wait until spring when the bushes are all full of leaves."

"Well, that's a long way off!" I said.

"Yeah!" Buddy said. "I don't think that I can wait that long. They just piss me off every time I see them."

TAKING DRAWING SERIOUSLY

We spent the rest of the winter much like the last two—roaming around the mountains, riding the sleds, chasing rabbits, and mostly just trying to stay warm until spring.

We were well into April before we got permission to take our first trip to the farm with Jackie. The five of us—Jackie, Buddy, Harold, Eddie, and I—left early Saturday and were able to stop by the swimming hole. Like last spring, the runoff from the mountains had caused the banks to widen. Silt had also been deposited on the bottom, which had to be cleaned out. Buddy and Harold agreed that they wanted to stay and start cleaning out the silt. They would meet us later at the farm.

Jackie, Eddie, and I went on to Mike and Betty's farm. Mike and Betty were out in the back planting seeds so we went to help them.

"You have a new friend this year," Betty said. "What's his name?"

I introduced them to Jackie.

"What are you planting?" I asked.

"Corn," Mike answered. "We've already planted radishes, squash, and tomatoes."After we finished we saw Doris coming from the barn. She had milked the cow and had the bucket in her hand. I went to help her carry the milk.

"Who's your good looking new friend?" she asked me. "And where's Buddy and Harold?"

"They stayed at the old swimming hole to do some work on it," I said. "And this is Jackie. He came to the school at Christmas time."

"Glad to meetcha Jackie, I'm Doris."

"My God, those two love the water," she said. "I bet it's cold too. I know one thing: if they're in the water, Sally is probably watching them."

"We plan to wander over there after awhile and see how they're doing," I said. "We'll look around to see if she's there."

"Are you guys going to stay in the barn tonight?" she asked.

"Yeah."

"I'll be coming in to milk the cow in the morning. I'll wake you up to help me."

"We'd better get started if we're going to check on Harold and Buddy," Eddie said, so we left.

Back at the creek we could tell that Buddy and Harold had been working hard. They had used large coffee cans to dip out the silt in the deep end. Buddy stood there and announced that the water was up to his chin.

"That may even be safe to dive into," I said.

"We saw a big water snake but it got away," Buddy said. "I've had a hard time getting Harold back in the water."

"I never did like snakes and I'm not going to start liking them now!" Harold said.

"Those snakes won't bother you, they're harmless," I told him.

"I don't care, I still don't like 'em."

I asked Buddy if the water was cold. He said it was cold at first but he had gotten used to it. I saw that he had his pants on, and asked him why he wasn't naked.

"Sally was here," he said. "She said that she wanted to help us, but had to go back to her house first. I didn't believe her so I kept my pants on. You know how she sneaks around."

"Now we have to wait for your pants to dry before we go back to the barn," I said.

After Buddy checked the bushes, he and Harold wrung out their pants and laid them on the some bushes to dry. The sun was hot, so it didn't take too long before we were able to start back.

———

When Doris came in to milk I saw her get some hay for the cow first. She put her stool in place and pulled on the tits. Even in the dark I could make out it was Doris, wearing overalls and a work shirt. I was still half asleep and didn't want to get up. The others were still asleep and I thought I would sleep a little longer too, but Doris' movements kept me awake. After she finished milking the cow, she went over to the barn door, opened it, took the straps loose on her overalls, squatted and peed. It wasn't very light out yet but I could still see her.

I had walked over to her by then and just watched her until she was done. As she was putting her straps back in place she noticed me.

"I thought you were asleep."

"No, I was just watching you milk the cow," I said.

"Why didn't you come over and visit?"

"I was too tired to get up, and afterwards you seemed to be busy," I said, looking at her and smiling.

She smiled back.

"Betty will have breakfast ready in about an hour," she said, "so get the boys up and come on up the house."

———

After breakfast we back to the school. We wanted time to go by the fort, to see if it had survived the winter. Jackie hadn't seen it yet, and it was on our way back, so it wouldn't take long to get there.

The fort didn't fare as well as the previous winter: the roof had caved in and the rain had washed most of the dirt down the hill. We didn't have the time for repairs.

———

We had to warn Jackie about church day.

The new housemother was easier to get along with than Mrs. Mayo but she had a thing about the Ten Commandments. We had to sit and listen to her read them to us after church. She would explain them in great detail, but no matter how much she read and explained, most of us didn't understand what they meant.

What interested us the most was, all that Commandment stuff took away from our Sunday afternoon playing time. After it was too late to do anything, so the day was lost as far as we were concerned.

At recess the next day, Jackie and I found a baby water snake, about eighteen inches long, when we went to the creek for a smoke. We wanted to play with it but didn't have any time because the bell was about to ring. We decided to put the snake in my zippered pocket, so we could keep it until after school.

Later the teacher was reading us a story about a family that was shipwrecked on an island. Just as they were trying to kill a large snake, Jackie looked at me.

"Look at your coat!" he said.

My coat was hanging over a table where three girls were sitting. The pocket was open and the snake was just about to fall on the table. Just as the bell rang, the snake fell, and the girls screamed. I took off and headed for the dormitory with Jackie right behind me. When we got to the stairs we both busted out laughing. A few seconds later Eddie, Buddy, and Harold caught up with us.

"All the girls were screaming," Eddie said. "One of them started crying."

"One of them even peed in her pants," Buddy laughed.

None of us could stop laughing for awhile.

"The teacher won't be able to tell where the snake came from," I finally said, "but I'm sure she'll be asking about it."

A week or so later we went back to visit Mike and Betty.

"Mike had to go help a friend," Betty told us when we arrived. "His sheep was killed, maybe by a bear. They're getting together with some more men to try to find it. Mike was quite worried when he left. He said you guys better be extra careful when you go back to school, and be sure to leave before dark."

Buddy's eyes got a little bigger when Betty was telling us about the bear, and maybe rightly so. In all the time I had been at the school, we had never thought about bears. Even when w were out at night catching frogs, and we would go for miles out in the country, we never gave a thought to anything that could harm us.

After visiting with Betty for a half an hour or so, Harold got restless and was anxious to take a hike, so we told Betty we might be back later on.

"Let's go in the opposite direction, follow the creek, and see where it goes," I said.

Everyone agreed, since we had never explored that part of the creek before. We walked maybe a hundred feet or so along the creek bank and came upon a wide place about twenty feet across.

"This has got to be a good place to take a swim!" Buddy exclaimed, and began to strip.

"Get out in the middle, Buddy, and see how deep it is!" Harold said.

Within a minute we all followed Buddy into the new spot to cool off. We put our clothes on some rocks, went through some bushes at the edge of the creek and jumped in. We had a great time splashing and trying to dunk one another. We were in the water for quite a spell. After we cooled off, we just sat and talked about all the things we had done this year.

"Listen!" Buddy said.

We stopped talking, and we heard giggling. At first we couldn't see anyone, but a few seconds later, over on the side of the creek, by some bushes, there were some kids watching us.

We saw two little boys that appeared to be four or five, and three girls. Two of them were about ten, but the other one had to be fifteen or even older. The two younger girls were the ones were giggling, but the older girl was just smiling. She had on a skirt went down below her knees and a shirt that was too small for her.

"We have your clothes over here when you get ready to get out," she said, then held up a pair of pants and waved them around. The smaller kids walked away but the one with the pants stood there watching us. When the older girl saw we were staying in the water, she picked up the rest of our clothes and walked away.

"What in the hell are we going to do now?" Jackie asked.

Then we saw that every four or five steps she dropped a piece of clothing. We stayed in the water for a spell. Finally Harold spoke up.

"I think they've gone, Buddy, why don't you go and get our clothes?" he said.

"I have a better idea," Buddy said. "Why don't you go get our clothes?"

We waited for a while longer and didn't hear anything, so we started out into the field to retrieve our clothes. We didn't get more than twenty feet when the tall girl jumped out and laughed at us while we were picking up our clothes and trying to cover up our privates.

She was still laughing as she ran away.

"You know," I said to Eddie, "we've been at the school for over two years and we've been to just about all of the farms, but I've never seen those kids."

"They must be visiting one of the farms," Eddie said. "We'll probably never see them again."

"I hope not!" I said.

———

Our relief was short-lived, because a week later while hiking out across one of the pastures, we saw one of the girls that had pestered us at the new swimming hole, picking blackberries. The smaller boys were with her, and an older lady was on the other side of the bushes. We figured that she must be their mother.

"Hi," she said, smiling and friendly.

The girl said, "That's the boys we saw in the water that didn't have any clothes on!"

The lady laughed.

"I guess you boys had a good time," she said.

"It was hot that day and we didn't know that anyone else was around," I told her.

"These girls have done seen all there is to see, so don't worry about it," she said, then added, "If you boys like to swim, there's a bigger swimming hole up the creek a ways. That's where we go."

"Let's go and see that water hole," Harold said after we left them.

A week later we went to the new swimming hole, but since we had to return to school the same day, we got an early start. When we got there about ten people were in the water, so we sat on the bank, had a cigarette and watched them swimming in the creek. The same lady with her kids was there, and another lady and some kids we had never seen. She wore shorts and a bra, but the kids were small and had nothing on.

Looking kinda like a private affair, we just sat on the bank, watched and hoped that they would get out soon.

"Why don't you guys come on in?" the first lady said.

But we didn't have any swimming trunks and we didn't feel like going in naked with females around, so we just sat on the bank and bided our time. After awhile Buddy went in with his pants on.

"You know, we might be waiting here all day," Daniel said, "so we might as well all go in the water!"

We all jumped in with our pants on. After awhile the ladies got out, went behind some bushes, changed their clothes, then came back and told the kids it was time to go. We stayed and took off our pants, spread them out to dry on the bushes, and enjoyed our swim.

After about twenty minutes or so one of the ladies came back and stood by the bank.

"I forgot to take my wet clothes," she said, then walked behind the bushes and retrieved them. When she walked back by she stopped again.

"Why didn't you boys, just go in without your pants when we were here," she asked, smiling. "We don't mind."

"You know," Daniel said, "we've been caught swimming naked so many times it probably doesn't matter anymore!"

"She was a grown woman," Buddy said, "and I don't want her looking at me naked!"

———

We didn't get back that way for a week or two. When we did, Eddie saw a place he thought we might have some big frogs.

"We should plan to come back at night," he said. so we thought we would check it out in the daylight and see if there were any signs of frogs, tadpoles or eggs. We found that the tadpoles had already developed legs, and they were swimming around.

We were about fifty yards from the swimming hole. Buddy said there were probably frogs there too, so we decided to come back at night. We had been catching frogs for over a year, and one thing we had learned: Frogs stayed in the water during the day, and at night they came out and started croaking. That's when we could catch them.

We decided to get permission to come back at night. While we were standing there talking we heard someone coming down the path. Waiting, we saw the woman who told us about the new swimming hole. With her were a boy and a girl, about four or five. They had a basket with some blackberries in it.

"Hello. Are you guys going swimming?" she called.

"No, we just came over here to see if there were any frogs in this part of the creek," Buddy responded.

"Are you kidding me?" she asked. "At night, the frogs here croak so loud that you can hear them from a mile away! If you guys catch any, you can bring them to me and I'll fry up the legs."

"We always catch a lot of them," I said, "but we have to do it at night. We have to get permission from the school to stay out after dark."

"Tonight?" she asked.

"I don't know," I replied, "but if we get permission we'll probably go to Betty and Mike's farm, and spend the night."

"You should come to my place," she said. "It's a half of a mile closer than Betty's and you can stay in my barn. I'll fry up all the frog legs you can catch."

When I asked her where she lived, she got a stick and drew directions in the dirt. Daniel said he had been by there before, and agreed it was closer than Betty's farm. We told her we would ask for permission to stay out overnight, and if we did we would come to her place.

"Oh, by the way, my name is Lily," she said, so we introduced ourselves.

Back to the house, we left it to Daniel to ask for permission to stay out overnight, since he was the oldest.

"Okay, you can go," Mrs. Mayo said, "but I want you all back here by two p.m. sharp. I have a meeting tomorrow, and I want to see that you're all back safely before I leave."

We got to the area of the swimming hole a little before dark, then walked a little further to try and see Lily's place.

"It's just over the next ridge," Daniel said.

"I'll walk on over and tell her we will be over later tonight," I said.

I walked on over the ridge maybe a half mile when I came upon the farm. Lily was out in the yard throwing some grain to the chickens, and when she saw me. With a big smile she said, "Pat, I see that you came back! Where are the others?"

"They're over at the creek getting ready to catch frogs," I replied. "It'll be kinda late when we get here so we'll just go to the barn. We can clean the frogs in the morning."

When I got back to the creek it was dark enough to start frogging. Just as we suspected the place was loaded with large bullfrogs. In a couple of hours we had caught more than we needed, so we sat on the bank, had a smoke then headed over to Lily's farm.

It was rather early when we arrived, maybe nine or nine thirty, so we fixed the straw around for our beds and lay there joking and bragging about the haul we made getting the frogs. Lily came in and told us we could come up to the house and have something to eat.

"I Heard you come into the barn, and figured that you had to be hungry," she said. Up at the house she had cooked a stew, which we ate with a glass of milk.

"Thanks for the stew Lily," I said. "I was hungrier than I thought."

"You're all welcome, but call me 'Lil'. Everyone else does."

Daniel asked her about her husband. She said he was a logger and was away working for a few days, but would be back for the weekend.

"It's not too late. If you guys want to clean those frogs tonight I'll fry them for you in the morning," she said.

We started cleaning frogs while she got her kids ready for bed, and changed into her nightshirt. When she came back she got her pipe from a top shelf, tamped a few pinches of tobacco into the bowl and lit up.

"I always smoke my pipe before I go to bed, it relaxes me when he's away," she told us. "I'm glad that you all stopped by to visit, because it gets lonely here with him gone."

Daniel told her it was late, and we had to leave early tomorrow, so we probably should go get some sleep.

"Take the lantern so you can see to get to the barn," she said. When she held up the lantern it caught on her nightshirt and pulled it up past her knees. I thought to myself boy, she sure is pretty.

———

Early the next morning Lil came down to the barn to feed the cow and horse. I could see her outline even though it was still dark. She took the lantern we had use the night before, lit it and hung it on the post next to the cow stall.

I was lying on the barn floor when she stepped on a short ladder and reached up to the loft to get a handful of hay. What a sight to wake up to! She revealed her complete butt! I didn't know why at the time, but I wanted to see more of her.

She walked over.

"You boys can get up pretty soon and I'll fry up those frog legs."

I lay back down and she went about taking care of the animals. When she was finished, as she left the barn she walked by me.

"Would you mind helping me get some water from the well?" she asked.

I would have done anything she asked.

Taking Drawing Seriously

During wintertime we couldn't go too far from school. Although it hadn't snowed yet the weather was very cold. We had to stay in the front room most of the time, except when we went to school. Sometimes we would run to school just to get to the warm classroom. When we combed our hair with water, it would freeze before we got to school.

Since Mrs. Pierce had been told us about Indians burying fruit and vegetables to be eaten later, we would sometimes dig up the apples we had buried and put one of them on her desk in the winter. She was proud we did it like the Indians used to. Sometimes we would bribe the girls for favors with the apples; they all wanted to know where our special tree was. Mrs. Pierce would overhear us and smile but she never gave away our secret.

One cold, windy evening after we had all been shut-in for a couple of days, Mrs. Pearl said that she would break the monotony by telling us a wintertime story, when one of the boys looked out the window.

"It's snowing!"

We all scurried to the window to see the first snowflakes of the winter. In no time the snow was three or four inches deep. The snow was late in arriving this year but Mother Nature made up for it in a hurry.

"That reminds me of a story from a long time ago," Mrs. Pearl said, looking at the snow. "About an old man who lived in the mountains but didn't like snow. Kids would throw snowballs at him, which would make him very angry. He would brush off the snow from his coat, and with his thick German accent warned them that one day they would be sorry for their meanness. He proclaimed that he would come and get them while they were sleeping. He would carry them off and they would never come back.

"But nothing ever happened, and the kids all thought they were safe, until one winter day the old man died. A few days later a girl was sitting all alone with her mother when they heard the crunch of footsteps in the snow. They were scared, but it was dark outside and they had to wait until the next morning. When they went to milk the cow they saw footsteps in the snow, were made by something with very large bare feet. After they finished milking they went inside, locked all the doors and stayed in all day."

"Later on, that evening when the father came home, he told them that one of the boys from another farm was missing, and that they had been searching for him. He said the farmer told him that he saw some big bare footprints that led out in the field and simply disappeared. And said that tomorrow they were getting dogs and forming a search party to look for the little boy, but weeks past and the boy was never found."

"The girl asked her father, how could footprints just disappear? Did fresh snow cover them up? The father replied, no, it had stopped snowing. It was the strangest thing: the footprints just disappeared, as if someone flew away, taking the boy with him."

"For the next few years, on the day of the first snow, a child would be taken, never to be seen again. In each case barefoot prints would lead out in the field and simply disappear.

"And children, to this day, farmers in that small farming community will not allow their kids outside during the first snow!"

Mrs. Pearl ended her story by saying, in a low and ominous voice, *"And the footprints led out in a field and just disappeared."*

When we went upstairs to go to bed we were afraid to look out of the window, because tonight was the first snow. Every now and then one of the boys would say, "Did you hear that?" It got real quiet. You could almost hear the snow crunch. It was difficult getting to sleep that night. The next morning, we looked for footprints in the snow, but there were none.

Mrs. Pearl could tell a story and make you believe it!

Winter came and went. As the snow slowly melted, ending our sledding and snowball fights, another winter meant that I was a year older. Being nine now, I figured I knew just about all there was to know about hiking around the mountain. I got the urge to visit Mike and Betty at their farm again.

Since Daniel had turned twelve, he moved to the big boys' house, leaving Harold, Jackie, Buddy, Eddie and me. We were going to miss him, and I knew that Buddy would miss his swimming partner. I've never known two people who could swim in as cold water like they could, but at least we had enough guys left to go frogging. We spent a lot of time making plans for the warm weather that was coming.

Meanwhile, without much else to do, I started drawing more. I found that when I was alone and in no hurry to finish, I was able to produce some pretty good drawing, such as the "The Old Apple Shed" that was behind the school. I drew most of the other buildings at the school, including one of my favorites, an "Old Barn" that was ready to collapse. Mrs. Pierce made me proud when she hung these drawings on the classroom walls.

But with spring almost here, I lost interest in drawing.

After church the next day we left to visit the farm. As always we went to the creek to see what effect the winter and early spring had on it, especially our swimming holes. Once again we saw that the mountain runoff had turned our creek into a small river—too high and swift for us to cross.

At the farm, Betty was in bed with a cold.

"Mike had to go back to work," she said. "He was getting extra hours because he missed a lot of work in the winter due to the snow. Now I have to milk the cow, and the animals still have to be fed."

We fed them and brought in dry firewood. Soon we got a fire, which warmed up the house. After awhile she felt better but stayed in bed.

Buddy and Harold wanted to see if the swift spring currents had made the swimming hole any bigger; I stayed with Betty. When the others left she asked me to get her pipe, and we had a smoke together.

"I'm glad that you boys came by," she said. "Can you milk a cow?"

"I had a girl show me how to do it once but I wasn't too good at it," I said.

"I don't know if I can do it, I'm so weak," she said.

I said I would try. I told her about the time the girl was showing me how to milk, her shirt was unbuttoned, and she saw me looking at her breasts.

"What did you think of that?" Betty asked.

"It was the first time that I had seen a girl's breasts, but I still thought they were pretty."

"I'll heat up some stew that I made a couple of nights ago." She got out of bed and her robe came open. She looked at me and smiled when she reclosed it and tied the rope-belt.

That was the first time I had seen so much of a pretty woman. She looked out the window.

"The other boys are coming back from the creek," she said. "They're just in time for some hot stew."

Buddy and Harold said the strong currents in the creek had made the swimming hole bigger. The water had washed the banks away and some of the bushes were gone. I told them Betty was too weak to milk the cow, so we would have to do it.

"We could each grab a tit and get it done faster!" Buddy said. That struck Betty's funny-bone and made her laugh.

Down at the barn I showed them what the girl had taught me. At first we were only getting a few drops, but Before long we were getting a good solid stream splashing into the bucket. After a while we finally got the job done. I carried the milk into the house while Buddy and Harold fed the animals.

"Thank you," Betty said with a big hug. When she let me go she had a tear in her eye.

"I am so glad that you came by. It's good to have the company of such nice boys," she said.

When Buddy and Harold came into the house we sat and talked with Betty for awhile and had a smoke. Before leaving to sleep in the barn we told Betty we would milk the cow in the morning.

———

We slept a little later the next morning, since there was no one there milking the cow. We found out Betty was feeling much better, so much so that she decided to cook breakfast for us. I got a fire started and we all sat down to eat. We all had a smoke and sat around and talked for a while, until her two kids got up. We spent at least an hour playing with them, but all three of us were anxious to go wandering around the mountain.

Down at the creek, the day was nice and warm, so Buddy stripped down and jumped in. After awhile Harold and I decided to join him. We had hardly got in the water when Lily walked over with her two small girls, sat on the bank and watched us.

We didn't want to get out while the girls were watching us, so we just sat in the water hoping they would leave. To our surprise Lily told the girls they could go into the water, but we got a reprieve when she told them to go behind the bushes and change their clothes into sack dresses. While they were doing we put our pants back on. The girls were only nine or ten, so we didn't pay them much attention, but then the lady went behind the bushes and changed into a pair of bib overalls were cut off at the knees. She didn't have a shirt on with the overalls which meant that her breasts were visible from the side, but they were small and hardly noticeable.

Soon it was time to leave, so we got out of the water and lay in the sun just to let our pants dry a little. As we lay there the lady and kids got out and went to change their clothes— except for Lily, who didn't bother to go behind the bushes. She removed her overalls and put on her dress right there on the bank, and paid us no mind.

We walked back to the farm to see if Betty needed any more help before we back to the school.

The next day at the school, I told Mrs. Pierce we visited a farm and the lady there was sick, so we helped her with the chores by milking, feeding the animals and bring in firewood, so she could stay in bed.

"You boys should be glad that you helped her," Mrs. Pierce said. "I am very proud of all of you for doing such a good thing. How did you make out milking the cow?"

"We actually did okay, although it was difficult getting started the first couple of times," I answered.

I guess Mrs. Pierce told her about our experience on the farm, because later on that day Mrs. Mayo came over to our dormitory to tell us she was very happy with us.

"Pat, I will make sure that you and your buddies will have permission to go to the farms anytime that you wanted," she said, "as long as the weather permits it."

Eddie and Jackie got over their colds, so we planned another trip to see Betty and Mike. Just like Mrs. Mayo told us, all we had to do was say where we were going and when we would be back. The five of us left early Saturday and got to the farm at around noon. We found Mike sitting outside cleaning his shotgun.

"What are you aiming to do Mike?" I asked.

"I'm going rabbit hunting!" he said. "Like to go with me?"

"Sure, it sounds like fun," I said.

"Okay," he said, "but all of you have to listen to me, and be where I can see all of you all the time!"

He didn't have to tell me twice, since I had been there before and it didn't turn out too well. I almost declined his offer, but he was an adult and I assumed it would be okay.

After we agreed with his rules we went down to a large pasture.

"I'll wait on one side of the creek," Mike said. "I want you guys to go out in the pasture and scare up the rabbits. If you can, get them going toward the creek. When they cross the creek they will stop, so that will be when I shoot them."

We did as he instructed, making a lot of noise, and we could see several of them hopping around. We were able to get behind them and herd them toward the creek. Before long we heard his gun go off once, then several more times.

He called us over, laughing.

"You boys did a good job," he said. "Sometimes it takes me all day to get two rabbits. Today, with your help, I bagged four in just a couple of hours. Now all we have to do is get them home, dress them, and get Betty to fry them up for supper."

Once we got back to the farm, Mike showed us how to skin and clean the rabbits, which sickened me. After what I saw, I wasn't sure I wanted to eat it. After Betty got the rabbits fried up, Mike saw we were hesitant to eat it.

"I can see that you boys haven't eaten rabbit before but if you try it I think that you'll like it," he said. "To me it tastes a lot like chicken."

I took a bite and it was alright. After awhile it started tasting good, so we all ate our fill.

"Now, wasn't that good?" Mike asked. He left the room and came back with his banjo, and started playing. We were all surprised at how good he was. He played a lot of songs we were familiar with, like *The Old Gray Mare, Camp Town Races* and others. I could tell Betty was glad to have him back home.

We couldn't spend the night because of church the next day, but we told Mike that the next time we came we would spend the night. We wanted him him to play his banjo for us some more.

We started down to the creek.

"That's where he shot the first rabbit," Buddy said. We could see some pieces of fur and a splattering of blood. I was sorry we ate the rabbit. I didn't think I would do it again. That's when we heard someone in the swimming hole, so we wandered over to see who it was. We found a couple of small kids, two girls were eleven or twelve, and an older woman who asked us if we wanted to come in, but we didn't have the time. The girls had flour sack dresses on. Back in those days people used to make clothes out of actual flour sacks, which you could tell because the flour company's name was on the material. That kinda surprised us, because most of the time they didn't wear anything.

After sitting there for awhile we left and headed back to the school. While we were walking back, Buddy said that he had recognized one of the girls at the creek. He had seen her at the school, she was older, maybe fifteen.

"Buddy thinks all girls are older because he's so small," Harold said, and we all had a laugh.

———

The next day at school Mrs. Pierce had us doing history. We talked about the Civil War and the slave trade. None of us knew much about those things.

"Do you remember when I had you draw the picture of Abraham Lincoln?" she said, standing over me. "Well, he was the president of America during the Civil War. He freed the slaves and brought the war to an end, so that's why we are studying about him. A lot of the battles were fought in this area. Some of the old buildings you see out in the country have bullet holes in them from the war, so the next time that you see an old log cabin look for the bullet holes. If you can find an old bullet from the war bring it to the class and share it with us."

Back at the house I told the guys, "The next time we hike to the mountains and we come upon the old cabins, we should look for some bullets holes in the walls."

"The one we went to last summer was old enough and probably had bullets in the walls," Eddie said.

The following Saturday we got permission to go overnight to Mike and Betty's farm. Not too far from the farm was an old cabin we hadn't noticed before, so we decided to check it out. We found it was pretty well trashed. Only two walls were standing and most of the boards in the floor were rotten.

"This place looks old enough," I said, so we started looking for bullet holes. When we were about to leave Buddy found another one. We tried to dig out the bullet, if that's what it was. Since we didn't have a knife and couldn't go deep enough into the wall, we went on to the farm. Betty she told us about another cabin about a mile farther up the mountain.

She asked us about our plans for the day. We told her we were going for a swim. She said it was a nice day for it, but she had to mend some things down at the barn. Buddy, Harold and Eddie had already left for the creek, so I said I would help her with the barn.

"Alright, let me get a hammer and some nails," she said, "and we can get started."

At the barn we had to get a ladder and nail some boards on the side. I held the ladder and she did all of the nailing. After we got that done we had to stretch some barbed wire on the fence. She had some kind of apparatus that she used to pull the wire tight, and then she would nail it.

After she did two or three posts, the wire came loose, springing back and hitting her around her legs.

"Oh my God!" she said, and grabbed her leg, bleeding. I asked her what I could do.

"We have to go in the house and get the cuts cleaned up," she said. Inside, she got some water and iodine. She washed each cut and put iodine on them. The wire had cut her high in spots on each leg, so she had to pull up her dress to treated them. She asked me to look at the back of her legs, but I didn't see any.

"Pull my dress up and look higher," she instructed, and then I saw that she had a couple small cuts. She told me to put iodine on those too. That presented a little problem for me because she didn't have any panties on, which made it difficult to concentrate on what I was supposed to do, looking at her naked butt and all. I had never seen a woman in this state of undress before.

After I finally got some iodine on her cuts she looked at me. I must have looked embarrassed.

"You did a good job," she assured me. "I couldn't see my backside so you had to do it. Sometimes, when nobody's here I walk around the house with nothing on. What would you do if you saw me like that?"

I found it a little hard to speak but I got out an, "I don't know."

"Let's go down to the creek and see what the other boys are doing," she said.

At the swimming hole Eddie, Harold and Buddy were in the water having a good time. Betty turned her back so they could get out and get dressed, then we walked back to the farm. After we ate some biscuits and gravy Betty made for us, we headed to the barn and fixed ourselves places to sleep. Later on while I lay there trying to sleep, I couldn't get the image of Betty's naked butt out of my mind. I thought about how it embarrassed me but it didn't bother her at all.

The next morning we woke up to the sound of Betty milking the cow. We helped by feeding the animals and getting firewood into the house. When we finished we went back up to the house and she cooked breakfast for us.

"Since we helped you when you were sick, the housemother told us we could come back and visit whenever we wanted to," I told her. "We thought we would try and come back next week, maybe catch some more frogs for Mike."

"What a nice thought!" she said, then hugged us all and gave us a kiss on the forehead.

———

Monday we went to see Mrs. Pierce—Buddy wanted to give her an arrowhead he had found at the farm. I told her about looking at old cabins for bullet holes.

"We plan to go on a hike next week and look for arrowheads," I said.

"The Indians would hunt along the creeks because the animals would come to the creek looking for water, which would make it easier for them kill. I think you can find some pretty decent arrowheads along the creek banks," she told me.

Then Mrs. Pierce asked me, "Pat, are you still drawing? Don't forget to bring to me the latest things that you have drawn. In two more weeks school will start. I'm anxious to see how your vacation has affected your drawing."

"I have got to draw something before we start back to school," I told Buddy. "I haven't drawn anything this summer because we've been too busy hiking all over the place, and she thinks that I've been spending time drawing."

Buddy suggested that I take my pad and pencil with me when we went back to the farm, where I could do my drawing in the evening time, which I decided would be worth a try.

———

When we arrived at Betty's farm the next week, I decided to draw the barn. I sat down and began to draw even before I saw her. The other boys went up to see her while I sat outside drawing. After awhile she came over to me and was surprised to see that I had drawn her barn.

"I didn't know that you could do that," she said. "All the times you came to visit, and you never said that you could draw. I want to show this to Mike! He'll really be surprised."

"When we go on hikes, I'm too busy having fun to draw. I usually only draw when I have nothing else to do." I told her about Mrs. Pierce's encouragement

"You must draw me a picture," she said. "One day you and your friends will move on, but I could have the picture to remember you by."

"I'll draw you one after I finish this picture of your barn for Mrs. Pierce," I promised.

After finishing the barn I drew the meadow with the creek, and all the bushes and trees. I had never drawn a scene like this before and didn't know if I could, so I kept it hidden until I was done. It took me a lot longer than expected to complete, maybe a month, but when I gave the picture to Betty, she said Mike would make a frame for it and hang it on the wall.

A couple of weeks after I had drew the old barn and some other landscapes around the swimming hole, we back to school, Mrs. Pierce was surprised to see my drawings of scenes of the mountain, creek, and pastures, because I had never drawn this type of picture before. I knew she would expect more from me, but I also knew that scenic pictures would take a lot longer to draw, which in turn would take away from my play time and hiking.

———

I must have drawn hundreds of pictures that have been lost. More than sixty years have passed; the school has since been rebuilt and turned into an all-boys institution. All of my teachers passed away long ago.

I can still remember some of the drawings, like the "Spring House" and the "Apple Shed". I sometimes wonder if these pictures are still hanging on someone's wall, somewhere. Most of all I wish Mrs. Pierce, God rest her soul, could see what I have drawn in my later years.

———

Even though school had started, we were still in the dog days of summer: it was hot and we were lazy. On a Saturday afternoon with nothing to do, we wandered off toward the creek. We did just that: We walked past the creek and circled around a large clump of trees and decided to rest on a large rock, have a smoke and enjoy the terrific view of the valley below.

Eddie and Jackie started arguing over how to fix up the fort. Buddy wandered up the trail a ways. All of a sudden he came running back.

"I found the vine we swung on last summer!" he said. "It's up this small side trail. Come on you guys and maybe we could give it another swing!"

We didn't have anything else to do, so we followed him over to the vine. The vine looked the same, but in the last year it had somewhat dried out. I was wondering if it would still hold our weight and be safe to swing on.

"I'll give it a swing and see how strong it is," Buddy said, but he didn't give it a good test. He just pulled on the vine, but didn't go out over the trees.

"Swing out, Buddy!" Jackie said.

Buddy hesitated; we could see he was afraid.

"Buddy boy," I said, "you said that you wanted to do this, now you're backing out!"

Jackie had never been on the swing, but he was willing to give it a try.

"Let Buddy do it!" I told him.

"The only way we can swing is if somebody takes a chance," Eddie said.

That's when Buddy said, "Pat, I dare you!!" Now I would take a dare, but not from Buddy. Eddie looked at me.

"Pat, you don't need to take that dare," he said, but now I was pissed. I got a hold of the vine, pulled it back to the far ledge, and got a good running start. The vine held pretty well when I left the edge of the rock. The side of the mountain looked steeper than I remembered—not only steeper, but the trees weren't beneath me. That's when I realized that instead of swinging back to the rock, I was falling towards the ground, which was quickly coming up to meet me. The last thing that I remembered was flashes of red as my body and head impacted something hard.

The next thing that I remember was Eddie trying to awaken me.

"Wake up, Pat!" he was saying. "Are you alright?"

I was still was seeing flashes of red when the other boys came down the hill. I couldn't move my body because it was hurting all over. With my hand I felt my face and got a hand full of blood.

"Where do you hurt?" Jackie asked.

"Every part of me!" I said.

I didn't want them to move me because my arms and legs felt like they were broken. I told them to just let me lay there.

"We have to get him down the mountain and to the nurse's office!" Jackie said.

"Wait awhile and let me see if I can stand up," I told him. Jackie and Eddie got a hold of me and helped me up on my feet. I stood there trying to keep my balance. I didn't think my legs were going to hold me, but with Eddie under one shoulder and Jackie under the other, we started down the mountain.

We were at least a mile from the school, but I could only go about a hundred feet before I had to stop and rest awhile. When I asked Jackie for a cigarette, he gave me one but it didn't taste good.

"That tastes like shit!" I said.

"No wonder, it's got blood all over it," Eddie told me.

I tried to laugh, but even that hurt so we started off again. At that pace it would take us all night to get back, so Eddie asked Buddy to go and find the housefather.

"Wait a minute," I said, "we have to make up a story as to how I got hurt. If they find out we were swinging on a grapevine, we may not be able to go on our hikes. Let's just say I slipped and fell down the hill and hit my head on a rock."

We agreed on the story and Buddy left to get the housefather. We waited until it got dark; I was sleepy and just wanted to go to bed. We had waited almost three hours and still no sign of Buddy or the housefather. It was scary; we could hear the night sounds of animals in the woods.

"This is getting spooky," I said to Eddie.

"I think I see a light over in the direction of the school!" he said. Jackie looked.

"There are two lights and they're moving this way," he said. "They look to be quite a ways off, but it shouldn't be too long before they're here."

The housefather and two other men brought a stretcher to carry me up the side of the hill to the back of the truck. It was a long hard ride lying on that stretcher in the truck, but we finally got to the school. I was surprised to see my friends and some of the girls from my class waiting at the nurse's office. After the nurse checked me out I was finally able to go to sleep. The next morning she told me I didn't have any broken bones except a broken nose. A lot of the pain was from bruised ribs and strains in my legs and arms. She said it would take awhile for them to heal.

"Tomorrow they will be taking you to the hospital in Charlottesville, but you will be back the same day if they find nothing wrong. How do you feel?"

"I am very hungry!"

"They will bring you food in a little while," she told me.

The next day I was taken to Charlottesville. They took all kinds of X-rays, but, finding nothing broken, they brought me back to the school infirmary. The nurse made me walk around the ward at least three times a day to get my legs back to normal strength.

I was in the infirmary about three weeks. On my release my buddies had a lot to catch me up on. Jackie said they tore down the fort and were building a new one. He said he didn't know if I was coming back. Some of the other boys thought I wouldn't be able to walk.

My headaches continued but I never told the nurse about them, because I was sure she would keep me in the infirmary. The boys laughed at that.

"You're just in time to go on a hike with us," Eddie said.

"I don't want to go up there where the vine swing was," I told them. "I don't care if I ever see that thing again! If you ever dare me to do anything again," I told Buddy, "I will kick your ass into next week!"

They all laughed except Buddy who moved away from me, but I was kidding him.

"I guess I was the stupid one," I said.

Two For The Road

A couple of days after I returned, down by the creek, where Harold and Buddy showed me how they cleaned out the swimming hole: They made it deeper so it would be hard for anyone to sneak up on them. I had to laugh because they had been caught so many times, I didn't think it would make any difference now.

"No matter what they do the girls will find a way to sneak upon on them," Jackie agreed.

"It will be hard for them to see us," Buddy claimed, "the way me and Harold have it fixed up back in the bushes."

"You guys make so much noise when in the water," Eddied said, "that I don't think that you can tell when someone sneaks up on you."

While they got in the water, Eddie, Jackie and I sat on the bank and had a smoke. We talked about the fort we were going to build.

"I want us to go back up the hill to where Crawford House burned," Eddied said, "and salvage the lumber that didn't burn in the apple shed."

I thought that was a pretty good idea, but the lumber was a long way from where we planned to build the fort and we didn't have any way to move it.

———

The next day we walked up to the apple shed to see how much lumber we could get. The corrugated metal roof was in good shape.

"We can use that as a sled," Jackie said. "Load the boards on it, tie a rope to the front, and pull it down to where we plan to use it.

A few days later, armed with a hammer and a rope, we headed back up to the shed. We tore off boards and stacked them on our makeshift sled. In the process, we tried to save as many nails as we could, although many of them had rusted over the years.

We then bent up the front of the sled so it wouldn't get caught in the dirt while pulling, and tied on the rope. The whole setup gave us doubts as to whether we could make it all the way to our building site, but we had to give it a try.

At first it wasn't too bad but then the rope broke and that took us extra time to tie up and try to find a way to attach it to the sled without cutting it in two, and then of course we needed our smoking breaks. Eddie had cut his toe. We all had scrapes and bruises because the terrain was so uneven and rocky.

After fighting this ordeal for the better part of the day, we had to stop and get back to the school for supper. The next day Buddy found a better piece of rope. We could see it was going to be a hot day, but we were determined to finish it.

After we got to where we would start downhill, we stopped to take a break.

"Boys, this is what we've been waiting for," Eddie said. "It will be easy going now!"

Buddy pulled from the front while the rest of us pushed from the rear. Except for dodging rocks and trees it was going smooth, until we hit some loose dirt and the sled got away from us. The planks fell off, hitting Buddy as he tumbled down the hill.

We ran down to help but Eddie stumbled and slid down the hill behind Buddy. Jackie and I laughed so hard we weren't much help. After we saw they weren't hurt, we looked back and saw our lumber strewn all over the hill.

Buddy walked over to us. I saw that he had cuts and scrapes on his arms and legs.

"You know you will have a hard time hiding that from the housemother. She's going to put iodine on those, and boy, that is going to hurt!"

"Maybe I'll find a way that she won't see me!" he said, knowing it would be impossible.

After we picked up the lumber and got it back on the sled, we start out again. It took us another couple of hours to get all our stuff down to where we wanted to build the fort.

We had to work at the cannery for the next few days, so we had to delay building the fort, but when we did start we had a lot of help. Earl and Benny decided to help us, so in all that meant there would be seven of us. Buddy and Harold helped us for awhile, but we couldn't keep them away from the swimming hole. They weren't much help anyway and for the most part just got in the way.

We did a pretty good job on the fort. In the following weeks we just lay around in it and watched Buddy and Harold messing around in the swimming hole. At times we would wander off, looking for arrowheads or just enjoying the scenery.

One day I guess the water was pretty cold, because when they got out Jackie was laughing.

"What's so funny?" Harold asked.

"It looks like you guys have two navels," Jackie said, and we all laugh.

Buddy looked down.

"I can still pee," he said, which made us laugh even more.

"If the girls came by now," Jackie said, "you wouldn't have to hide, because they wouldn't see much."

They were so embarrassed that they went and put their pants back on, but we just kept on laughing.

The next day at school some girls planning a softball game invited us to play with them, over at the pasture on Saturday. Jackie said maybe we would join them, but Buddy spoke up and said that he didn't like softball.

"No wonder you don't like softball," Jackie said. "You have two navels!"

I busted out laughing.

"What do you mean, two navels?" one of the girls asked.

Jackie and I laughed even louder. When Harold asked what we were laughing about, Buddy answered.

"Jackie told the girls we have two navels," he said.

Harold got a little pissed but I didn't care. Soon the girls were spreading the story to some other girls. Within a couple days the whole school knew about it. Later on one of the girls asked to see both of Buddy's navels. Jackie and I howled with laughter; the more she looked at us the more we would laugh.

———

We met the girls at the pasture for the ballgame, but Buddy and Harold didn't want to go with us. Jackie, Earl and I played for an hour or so, but Jackie and I both got bored and wanted to do something else.

The swimming hole was about a hundred yards away from where we were playing.

"I wonder if Buddy and Harold are in the swimming hole," I said to Jackie.

He looked at me.

"You know what? I just bet they are. Let's go over and see."

To my surprise, he offered to show the the swimming hole to the girls.

"I hope you know what you're doing!" I told him.

He just smiled. There were only three girls with us. Jackie told them all about the fort we built. Soon we approached the swimming hole.

"It sounds like somebody is in the water," one of the girls said.

"That's just the sound of the water running in the creek," Jackie lied.

Then as we got to where we could see the creek over the small hill, the girl said, "It looks like two boys!"

When we could see the swimming hole, the girls turned their heads.

"They don't have any clothes on!" they said in unison.

"I didn't know there would be anybody here," Jackie said, lying again.

The girls looked again. They giggled and acted as if they weren't trying to look, but they didn't walk away either.

"I would never have brought you here if I had known that they were in the water," Jackie said.

"Alright, we believe you," one of the girls replied.

Back at the pasture I overheard the girls talking.

"That was fun," I heard one of them say.

"You are a devil!" I told Jackie later that day, but he was laughing so hard, I don't think he heard me

"Did you see how they acted when they saw Buddy and Harold standing up in the water?" Jackie said.

It was one hell of a joke!

———

After that Buddy and Harold didn't trust us anymore. We told them we didn't know they were there when the girls saw them, and besides the girls got to see your two navels. Buddy didn't like that at all. It made matters even worse.

Back at the house we heard Buddy and Harold arguing about something. Eddie told me that Harold was pissed off at Buddy, so I asked him why.

"Buddy had talked him into going swimming," Eddie said. "When the girls caught them naked he blamed Buddy for it."

"This is turning out better than I thought," Jackie said. "Now Buddy is catching all the blame."

———

For the next couple of weeks we didn't do much of anything together, since everyone was pissed: Harold was mad at Buddy, and Buddy was mad at Jackie, Eddie and me. Mostly Jackie and I just hung around the fort and talked.

"I have an uncle that lives in Washington, D.C.," he told me at one point, "and I want to go see him."

"How do you plan to do that?" I asked.

"Well," he said, "I don't have it all planned out yet. I want you to go with me. I think if we left say, on a Sunday evening, they wouldn't be miss us until sometime Monday morning. By that time we would already be in Washington enjoying ourselves."

"It sounds like fun, but what do you think would happen to us when we got back?"

"Pat. Pat. Pat, sometimes you seem so naïve. This is a school, not a prison," he said. "Don't you know that all we need is a note from a family member, and you always get excused? I'll just say I was sick and he came to pick me up."

"What about me?" I asked.

"We'll figure out something for you, but right now we need to think about getting out of here for a few days."

All week long Jackie kept talking about his uncle, all the fun we would have in Washington, visiting the monuments and the capital. As Sunday drew near, I was as excited as he was.

Sunday finally rolled around. We worried that plans would go awry, because Eddie's mother came to visit and insisted that she meet all of his friends. We got a reprieve when she had to leave in the afternoon.

When the other boys left for supper, Jackie and I stayed in the dormitory. Carrying the few clothes we packed, we sneaked out the back, over to the creek and through the woods. In an hour it would be dark. We knew we would be spotted on the road, so we stayed in the woods.

We made good time but Charlottesville was was twenty-five away. If we made it that far, we planned to hitchhike to Washington. After a few hours of walking we both got very tired. We looked for a place to lie down, but it was dark and difficult to see anything. We finally found a large boulder to sit on and rest awhile.

The spooky night noises got us thinking about the wild animals that lived in the mountains, especially the bears. Although we tried to get a little sleep, the least little sound would make us jump up and wonder what it was.

When the moon came out, we could see a little bit but it was still scary.

"We might as well start walking rather than trying to sleep." I said

"At least we'll be getting closer," Jackie agreed.

By the end of the night we made it to the outskirts of Charlottesville. You talk about being tired and hungry! We hadn't eaten since noon the day before.

"The next time we plan a trip, let's eat before we go and pack a lunch!" I told Jackie. About that time he spotted an apple tree. We each ate at least three apples. Boy, did they taste good! We took a few with us as well.

When we got to the middle of town, we had no idea which way to go. All the streets looked the same. I saw a bus station.

"Let's go in there and maybe somebody can tell us which way to go," I said.

Inside the station Jackie said, "Look over there on the bench. Isn't that Eddie's mom?"

"Let's tell her the school gave us tickets to go to Washington," I suggested, "but we lost them hiking, and spent the night out in the cold. She might even buy us tickets."

When we got close enough for her to recognize us, she asked us why we were there.

"The school gave us tickets to go to Washington to visit Jackie's uncle for a week," I said, "but we lost the tickets."

"I will call the school and let them know what happened," she said.

"Boy, I bet they won't let us go now!" I said to Jackie.

"They'll take us back to school and we'll be in trouble."

"They won't do that, will they?" she asked.

"Yes they will," Jackie told her. "And maybe even worse than that!"

"I'll just buy you new tickets. The school doesn't ever need to know," she said. After she got the tickets, as she handed them to us she said, "Now, don't lose these."

Jackie and I had to wait until our bus left for Washington, so we sat over in a corner where no one could see us. We both had a touch of paranoia, thinking that the school had people out looking for us.

When the bus finally came we dashed on board. For the first time since leaving the school we felt safe, and in no time we were fast asleep. In what seemed like a short time, the driver announced we were pulling into Washington.

I woke up Jackie and told him we were there.

"As soon as we get off the bus I'll call my uncle, and he'll come and pick us up," Jackie said.

When Jackie went to make the phone call, I waited back in a corner where no one would see me. While I waited I got the strange feeling that something was wrong, like someone would come and get m, but soon Jackie came back.

"My uncle is on the way," he said.

Jackie had ten cents, so we got an ice cream cone—the first thing we had to eat since the apples the night before.

His uncle arrived sooner than I expected. I guess he lived by himself, since he was the only one we saw there. After he and Jackie talked for awhile, he said he would go down the street and get a pizza. I didn't know what a pizza was, but to me it didn't matter, since I was hungry enough to eat most anything.

We sat, ate and talked. I didn't pay too much attention to what they were saying and I just dozed off. I woke up to the sound of someone knocking on the door. His uncle was talking to someone and then two men came in.

"Are these the two boys?" one of them asked.

"Yes," his uncle answered.

I didn't know what to think.

"I can't believe it...you told on us!" Jackie said to his uncle. He was crying.

The two officers took us to the police station, where they took all of our clothes and made us put on blue coveralls—then they put us in a cell and locked the door. We sat on a cot and Jackie cried some more. I didn't know how to cheer him up. When I heard someone talking, I looked over and saw a lady in a cell just like the one we were in. Everything was open with nothing but bars between us. When I looked closer I could see three women in the cell.

When they saw us they came over to our cell.

"What did you boys do to get locked up in here?" one of them asked.

"We ran away from a boarding school," I said.

"Why did they put you in the women's section?" another one asked.

Jackie had perked up by then. He asked the ladies if one of them might have a cigarette. One of them handed two cigarettes and a book of matches through the bars. We waited until no one was around and lit up. We hadn't smoked since sometime the day before, so it was really good.

After awhile Jackie and I started talking about our predicament. He was that his uncle had called the police, but there was nothing we could do about it now. We just sat around wondering what was going to happen next.

The ladies did try to keep us entertained. They laughed and joked with each other a lot, and sometimes they included us in their conversations. Misty, who was the youngest of the three, said they had been arrested for being drunk.

"Why don't we tell them the truth," said Lori, who was an older woman in her fifties. "We were picked up for soliciting."

"What's that?" I asked.

"When you get a little older you'll understand," she said, "but for right now, let's just say it's against the law."

We thought we would starve to death before they gave us any food. When they finally managed, it was awful, but we ate it anyway. With the tray was a cup with a folding handle that Jackie would play catch with, just to pass the time, but that didn't help much. After awhile it was terribly boring just sitting around that cell.

I looked out the small window, where I saw a bird sitting on a limb. I remember thinking how wonderful it would be to be like that little bird, I could fly anywhere in the world that I wanted, but for now I'd settle for being outside. I promised myself that if and when I ever got out of this mess, I'd never sit in one of these cells again.

That night I couldn't sleep because those three women talked all night long. Every now and then they would call us and ask if we were alright. I believe they must have been night people.

One time when they woke us up, Jackie asked them if we could bum another cigarette, and they handed two more through the bars.

———

The next day at about noon they took us into a small room and sat us down, and after a few minute wait Mr. Mayo and Mr. Davis walked in. They both had stern looks on their faces.

"You boys have really done it this time!" Mr. Mayo finally said. They walked us out to the car and we headed back to the school. All the way back, I don't believe a word was spoken until Jackie whispered to me.

"We have to tell the truth because we've been caught red-handed," he said.

Back at the school, he took us to Mrs. Mayo.

"These two boys will not be allowed to leave the school property for thirty days!" Mr. Mayo said. "Do you both understand that?' he asked us.

"Yes sir, Mr. Mayo!" I said.

"Yes sir, Mr. Mayo!" I said.

"Keep an eye on these two!" he told Mrs. Mayo, then left.

Mrs. Mayo just sat and looked at us for awhile.

"Why?" she asked. "I trusted you two. Why?"

Then Jackie nudged me with his elbow, and I caught on immediately.

"Mrs. Mayo, Jackie's uncle lives in Washington," I said. "We were going to visit him so we could see the Capitol and the Washington and Lincoln Monuments. And ma'am, we weren't going to stay away, we were going to come right back."

She must have believed me.

"Okay, you boys heard your punishment," she said. "Go and try to stay out of trouble!"

———

We had only been gone for three days, but it felt like at least three weeks. The boys were in class when we returned, so we didn't see them until after school was out. Earl was the first to come up to the dormitory, followed by Eddie and Harold. They wanted to know all about our escapade, so we told them all about it.

Jackie started off by telling them a lot of lies. Maybe they weren't complete lies, but he surely bent the hell out of the truth. After Jackie finished telling them all the bullshit, we finally told them how cold and hungry we got on the first night, how we were afraid of the wild animals in the mountain, and how tired and sleepy we were after walking all the way to Charlottesville. Then Jackie told them about his uncle calling the cops and ratting on us, and how the cops took us and put us in jail. Right away they wanted to know what jail was like.

I let Jackie do all the talking, since he could lie better than me. Boy, did he tell some whoppers. Listening to him, he might have been talking about two other boys.

He told them how the ladies would come over to our cell and play cards, and give us cigarettes and candy. I just sat, listened and smiled. He made it look like we had been on a vacation when in fact we had a horrible time. I didn't ever want to do that again.

Not only did we have a bad time on the trip, but now we had to miss all the fun the other boys were at the fort and the farm. Jackie and I had to stay close to the house; it was difficult just to go for a smoke.

Although our only punishment was staying close to the school, we kept thinking they were going to come and put us on extra work details. No doubt they figured we would worry about that, so our worry was a part of the punishment.

———

One day the housemother gave us permission to go with the other boys on an overnight hike to the farm on Saturday. We were beside ourselves with happiness.

Since the summer was coming to a close, this would probably be our last chance to spend the night at Mike and Betty's farm. We went to the fort first, but we stopped just long enough for a smoke break.

Eddie told us he had gone to the farm a couple weeks before, and that Betty wasn't feeling too well. She had stayed in bed while they were there.

"What was wrong with her?" I asked.

"I don't know, she was just sick."

———

Mike was putting the mule back in the stall when we returned. Since he had done all his plowing for the day, he was going to take a break. Betty was still in her house robe when we got to the house; I could see she didn't feel good. Betty said Doris had gone to the store and would be back soon.

Eddie, Earl, and Buddy were messing around in the barn. Jackie and I had planned to go looking for arrowheads, but instead we stayed to help Mike cut wood for the fireplace. He had a crosscut saw, so we cut the limbs and he split them. Cutting wood with a crosscut saw was a lot of work, so it didn't take us long to work up a sweat.

"That's enough for today!" Mike said after about an hour, when Betty came out with cold glasses of milk. Jackie and I headed out to the fort to see if the other boys were there. On the way we met Doris.

"I didn't expect to see you guys again," she said. "I heard about you running away from the school. Guess what? Sally really missed you."

We didn't go into any details about the trip. Doris went on to the farm, while Jackie and I went to the fort, which turned out to be in pretty good shape. We put some new broom sage inside, then sat there and had a smoke.

"You know what?" Jackie said. "I'm really glad to be back at the school and here among my buddies."

"I agree," I said. "It isn't much fun walking out in the night that far with nothing to eat and having the crap scared out of us."

Going to get frogs was different, because although there were night noises, there were five of us. We felt safety in numbers.

"You know what even made it worse?" Jackie said. "We didn't have a flashlight!"

"Where is everybody?" Harold asked, walking up.

"Maybe they went to the swimming hole," I said.

"It's too cold for that!" Harold replied.

I thought it really had to be cold for Harold to admit that.

"It's time to go back to the farm," I said, thinking that all the guys would be there tonight, which would be a lot of fun for the last trip of the summer. We were all exceptionally tired that night from all the hiking, but even so we almost never got to sleep, what with everyone asking about our runaway trip to Washington D.C. As usual I awoke to Doris milking the cow, but this time she was all bundled up. The morning was colder than a witches' tit and I didn't want to get out of my straw bed. none of us were dressed for cold weather, and it would be awhile before the sun came up.

When the sun did come up I walked on back of the barn to relieve myself. Looking out over the valley, I could see the leaves turning to shades of red, yellow, and brown—a sure sign that summer was over and we didn't have much more time for hiking.

As kids we didn't pay too much attention to the seasons, but we knew when summer was over. We turned our attention to winter fun, like Halloween, Christmas, and sled rides. Although it was a month before Halloween and my birthday, I was already thinking about being ten years old. That idea was a little hard for me to comprehend. I had come a long way and it didn't seem that long.

———

With the day heating, by noon we had our shirts off. Buddy, Harold, and Earl went down to the swimming hole, while Jackie, Eddie, and I stayed at the farm with Mike and Betty. We sat in the back yard under the shade of a big oak tree. Betty made a pitcher of lemonade. When Doris came to hang some things on the clothes line she was quite a sight, in a pair of bib overalls with no shirt underneath. Every time she bent down to pick up a piece of laundry her titties would show. I saw Jackie enjoying the show at the same time he caught me looking. We just smiled and didn't say a word.

"We'd better get back," Eddie said. "With all the trouble you and Jackie have been through, you don't want to be late getting back on your first hike."

I agreed.

"If the others show up," I told Mike, "tell them we went back to the school."

On the way back we checked the swimming hole for the other boys, but it was empty. When we got back to the dormitory, it was almost time for supper and the other boys hadn't showed up yet.

"If Buddy had anything to do with it they will probably be late," Jackie said.

After we had supper returned to the dormitory, there was nothing to do but sit around and wait for bedtime.

———

Halloween would be the next big event. I lay in bed that night and thought about my birthday and how I would be ten. I thought about my first birthday here at the school. How stupid I must have looked to the other kids! How much I had changed in the last couple of years. I remembered how I would wander off by myself. One day I came across an old comic book and it reminded of how my old friend Stinky, and how I would shine shoes to buy comic books and trade them back, before I was shot.

I remembered the old apple orchard, off to the side of Crawford House, before it burnt, where I went to look at the pictures in the comic book. I hadn't learned to read yet. The book was about The Lone Ranger; he had this big white horse. I had climbed up in this apple tree to look at the pictures. After awhile I looked down and saw a white horse not too far away. He stood there eating grass, so I got this idea: If he was just a little closer I could let myself down and ride him, just like had seen The Lone Ranger do.

I was just a kid and didn't give a thought about how dangerous it would. I saw the horse slowly moving in my direction. When it got right under me I slipped down on its back. To my surprise it didn't move, but kept on eating grass, so I reached up and broke a limb off of the tree, and started hitting it. At first he just kept on eating then, all of a sudden he took off and the branches of the tree hit me in the face and head. I've got to tell you, that was not only scary, but as bumpy as all hell, and after about thirty some odd feet I was thrown off and my head hit a rock.

I saw stars. I was all scratched up and dizzy. As I got up I looked around and saw the horse over by the rail fence, on the other side of the field. I walked back to the house, where I saw some of the boys sitting over on the fence. They were shouting something at me but I couldn't make out what it was. They were all excited and pointing at something behind me. After awhile I looked back and saw this big black bull coming my way. I ran to the fence and climbed over. The bull came to the fence and stopped. It wasn't mad; it just stood there and looked at me. One of the boys hit it with a stick and it just walked away. Someone threw an apple that hit him in the nuts, and he let out a bellow. The boys all laughed but the bull turned around and started snorting, and the boys scattered in every direction.

———

All those things were funny to look back on now. Even stranger was that how it seemed I had spent the most of my life here at the school, since most of the memory of my earlier childhood was lost when I got shot.

After my first year here at the school I started to recall everything that I did in great detail. I thought everybody could do that. One day one of the boys asked me about something we did the summer before. When I answered him I included every little detail, even word for word conversations we had on a particular day.

"I didn't mean all that!" he said.

"Well, you asked me what we did," I said.

He looked at me funny.

"Damn, can't you just tell me without all that bull-shit?" he asked.

After that, I thought he was nuts. As time went on I realized it was better not to give all the particulars because it caused a lot of funny looks and sometimes arguments.

———

Another incident happened back during the same year that I rode the white horse, something almost as stupid, at a time some of the boys and I were messing around down at the creek. When the creek would rise in the spring due to the mountain runoff it would naturally get wider, so when the water receded it left called side pools all along the side of the creek. Often small fish would be deposited in these side pools.

We would try to catch these fish by putting our hands in and corralling them against the bank. Most of the boys had done this, but I was new and a little stupid. On that particular occasion, I found one went under a rock. When I stuck my hand under the rock to try and catch it I felt a sharp pain; I jerked my hand back with a small water snake hanging on my little finger by one fang. Earl took the snake off of my finger.

"How did you do that?" he asked.

I tried to answer but everyone was laughing so hard they didn't pay any attention to me. A little while later my hand started swelling, so we went to the housemother and she sent me down to the big boy's house to see the housefather. Since it was dark she sent Eddie with me. While we were there Eddie went out in the front yard to play with some of the guys and broke his arm. They had to take him to Charlottesville, and since I couldn't go up the hill by myself, I had to go with them.

I thought, how stupid of me to stick my hand under a rock that way, but Eddie said that he didn't mind because he got to stay out of school for a few days. My hand got well in a few days but Eddie had to wear the cast for six weeks.

A Nice Day For Swimming

Unbelievably, I was turning ten and an old hand at that stuff by now. It wasn't something I cared about but I did like the pies and other sweets that they put out. Bobbing for apples didn't interest me much, since the last time I almost drowned, but I did kinda enjoy watching the other boys.

Once when Harold went for the apple Eddie pushed his head down and held it for awhile. Harold came up spitting and coughing, but he didn't see who did it so he went after Buddy. That ended the apple bobbing for that night.

The rest of the night we just sat around and discussed some of the things we planned to do that winter, mostly sledding. Eddie had found another hill that he wanted us to try.

"I think it would be a lot more fun to find our own hill that the other kids don't know about," he said.

The next day Eddie, Buddy, Jackie, Earl, Harold, and I went to the hill Eddie told us about. Since it was just our little group we could make more rides down the hill.

"There's one little draw back," Eddie said. "Since no one has gone down before, we don't know where all the rocks and other obstacles are."

The first ride down would definitely be a test of courage and could cause a little hurting.

"I think I'll let you go first," I told Eddie.

He was airborne before he got fifty feet, but he didn't hit a rock. He came to an immediate halt, but Eddie kept on going to the bottom of the hill. When we got to him we could see something sticking out of the snow. Buddy, the first one there, announced it was a large piece of a rail fence just under the snow. Eddie walked back and saw what tripped him up.

"You know guys," he said, "I think we need to find a better place to ride our sled."

"I know of a better hill," Buddy said. "It's almost as big and has only broom sage on it in the summer, and only a few rocks."

I thought right then that if Buddy had anything to do with this, it had disaster written all over it. But then again, who knows? He took us to a hill not too far away.

"I'll take the first ride," he said.

From the top of the hill we couldn't see the bottom because of a hump about halfway down. When Buddy got ready, Earl gave him a shove and away he went. After he crested the halfway hump he disappeared from sight. After a couple of minutes we decided to walk down and check on him. Buddy was nowhere in sight. We looked all over the place until Harold spoke up.

"I see him," he said, pointing way over to the left.

Buddy had gone way off the hill and was over in the woods. We ran over to see if he was alright, and saw him coming out of the woods dragging the sled, laughing.

"Damn, that was a good ride!" he said.

I looked at Jackie.

"I don't know how he made it through those trees," I said, "but I guess everybody gets lucky every now and then."

We all took rides but we didn't go in the woods. Once we got a path made it was a good ride. We spent most of our time sledding that winter, until the weather got bad, so we had to stay in the house.

At school we prepared for Thanksgiving. I had to draw most all of the things associated with the holiday...pilgrims, Indians, log cabins, wigwams, and all sorts of fruit. I didn't care too much about drawing those types of pictures but I didn't want Mrs. Pierce to know that. I didn't want to disappoint her. I was more into drawing old barns, pastures, and scenery. It's not that I couldn't do it, but there was no challenge, and in fact it was boring.

About a week before Thanksgiving the housemother said I would be staying at the school for Thanksgiving but Jack and I would go home for Christmas...well, not really home. Since my mother would be in Miami, that's where we would be going.

For Thanksgiving Day they decorated the main hall with the different shades of autumn; the girls did most of it. In the evening we had turkey and stuffing with cranberry sauce, sweet potatoes, string beans, and corn bread. I had my share of everything, but the best dish was the candied yams with marshmallows on top. Later I barely had room for the pumpkin pie.

That night in bed I thought about my coming vacation. I would find it hard to say good bye to my buddies. The truth was, I was conflicted between going home and staying at the school. I enjoyed myself here, but on the other hand, I hadn't seen my mother and the rest of the family for two years. I knew she would be disappointed if I didn't come home for the holidays, so that tipped the scales.

That night I had a hard time getting to sleep. It was ironic that I was the kid that was supposed to be careful but seemed to have an accident at every turn. I remember what the priest told me when I was in the hospital: "You must have had a guardian angel watching over you."

If that is true now, he must be working overtime.

———

The holiday vacation started the next morning, so we had a lot of time to roam around the hills. Whiles Jackie and I sat on a rock trying to get a little sun, Jackie turned to me.

"I remember last summer," he said. "Buddy dared you to swing on that vine and you took that dare, and it damn near killed you...right?"

"Yes, and I told Buddy to *never dare me again!*"

"Pat, the way I see it, that's not enough…I think he owes you a dare."

"Like what?" I asked, wondering where this was going.

"Well, we all know Buddy's penchant for swimming, sometimes even when the water is too cold for most normal humans."

"Yeah," I said.

"Okay, the water in the creek is colder than a witch's tit, as a matter of fact, it's damn near freezing. What I want you to do is, dare him to go in the water, and not just go in the water, but go in naked."

I thought about this for awhile until I saw Harold and Buddy walking over to where we were sitting.

"Buddy, you owe me a dare!" I said.

"What do you mean?" Buddy asked.

I reminded him of the time that he dared me to go on the vine swing, when I got hurt.

"Okay, dare me to do something," he said.

"Well since you and Harold like the water so much," I said, "I dare you to go in the water!"

Jackie laughed.

"And without your clothes on!" he added.

Buddy started stammering.

"It's in the middle of winter and that water is ice cold," he said. "I ain't going in there!"

"How long does he have to stay in there?" Harold asked.

"As long as it takes to get wet."

"Buddy, I'll go in if you will," Harold said.

Then Buddy got all pissed off.

"Why did you have to open your big mouth?" he asked Harold, who was already taking his clothes off. Not to be out done, Buddy undressed while grumbling the whole time. They jumped in on the count of three, and almost like a cork, they popped up and were out of the water in a flash and jerking their clothes on.

"That wasn't as bad as we thought it would be!" Harold said.

"Eskimos!" Jackie and I said.

Buddy grumbled all the way to the house.

When we got up the next morning snow had covered everything. The housemother made us stay in the house until we went to supper at the main hall, which was only about fifty yards away. On the way someone threw a snowball and the fight was on; we couldn't wait to get our hands in the snow. When Jackie got hit in the neck, the snow went down his back. He blamed everybody and swore to get even. By the time we got to the hall, all of us were covered with snow, and the housemother just laughed at us; for once she understood.

After supper it was back to the dormitory, where boredom set in. The classrooms were locked but we could play in the hallway. Some of the boys played catch in the hall until a light was hit and broken. They ran back to the dorm as if nothing had happened, and since no one wanted to be seen in the hallway after that, we all ended up in the dorm. Some of the boys played ping pong until a couple of the boys got into an argument over whether a ball was "out" or not, and one threw a pillow at the other. Before you knew it every kid in the dorm was involved in a full blown pillow fight. Wouldn't you know it, the housemother walked in when the pillows were flying, and barely missed getting hit. Everybody froze; it was like getting caught with your hand in the cookie jar. There was nothing we could say, and when I looked around, I could see feathers in every nook and cranny of the room.

For the most part, the housemother was fairly easy to get along with, but this crossed the line. The dormitory was a complete mess. She was so mad that her face turned red, and we knew that she had reached her limit. She said, I want everybody to start cleaning up this mess right now, and don't even think about any nighttime snacks tonight.

We took most of the night to clean up the feathers. We all learned the hard way just how hard it was to get them up, because when we tried to sweep them they would just fly up in the air. Jackie had an idea: he thought that if we wet them they would be heavier and easier to sweep, so we went and got a pail of water and a mop. It seemed like a good idea at the time, but when we mopped, the feathers just stuck to the floor, which made them harder to sweep. We all learned a little lesson about making a mess, especially when we had to clean it up.

A few days later the housemother came and told me to start packing my clothes, because it was time to go see my family. I had never packed my clothes before, but I thought that I could do it. After a couple failed attempts the housemother came in to give me a hand. Most of the stuff that I packed, she dumped out and started all over again.

"When do I leave?" I asked her.

"Well, you will be going with your brother Jack," she said. "he and Mr. Mayo will come over and pick you up the day after to-morrow. Mr. Mayo will take the two of you to the train station in Charlottesville."

I wondered if I would get a chance to do anything with my buddies before I left. Later on that day we all went out in the woods and had a smoke. It was quite emotional for me to leave these guys, because they felt like my only family.

"If I don't get back, I want you guys to know that I will always remember you," I said.

"You'll be back or I'll come and get you!" Jackie said.

We all laughed.

"I will be staying at the school," he said, "and will be waiting for all of you guys to come back."

When the day finally came, I had to say good bye. Jackie waved at me when I looked out of the train window. I was sad to leave.

The train ride was alright but it was crowded with soldiers, and they had a lot of their things in the aisles. Soon I tired of the scenery and fell asleep. I woke up to find that the train had stopped, but only to let off some passengers and take on some others. I stayed awake and watched the people put their things away. I asked Jack how long it would be before we got to Miami.

"I don't know but it should be pretty soon," he said, so I went back to sleep.

I had just gotten to sleep when Jack woke me up.

"This is Miami, little brother," he said. "Time to get up!"

My mother met us at the station and gave us both a hug and a kiss, then took us to get something to eat. After we ate, she looked us over.

"You'd think you were going to Alaska, dressed that way! Let's go and get you some Florida clothes!" she said. After we got to her home, we went to downtown Miami and got some lighter clothes.

The last time I had visited my mother we met some boys that lived nearby. I wondered if they were still living there; the next day I saw one of them, Raul. He was riding a motor scooter and I waved at him. I thought he didn't see me but he went up the street and turned around, then came back and parked the scooter. He said he was going over to the bay to watch them building a bridge. He invited me to get on the back and go with him.

I thought about what my mother had told me about not going anywhere without Jack, so I told him I had to stay close to the house. She had bought us these Indian moccasins because the streets were too hot to go barefooted. Even during the winter it was hot in Miami.

After only a few days I got into trouble, when some of the boys wanted me to go with them to downtown Miami. I told them I wasn't supposed to leave the area, but they said we could take the bus to get there, and we would be back before my parents got home from work. I thought, as long as I got back early enough, it would be alright, so I went with them.

One boy's father was the manager of a large department store, and he wanted to surprise his father. After we got there we wandered around the store. I was amazed at the size of this place; I had never been in a store this large. I was worried about getting home before my mother did, so we got on the bus headed back. When the bus got back to our stop, I was in a hurry to get off and make it back home, which was only a block away. I didn't watch where I was going, and ran in front of a car, which knocked me about ten feet. I hit the pavement pretty hard, but didn't hurt so I got up and ran, still worried about being late. By the time I got to the house next to my mom's, my foot hurt so bad that I had to stop and sit down on the grass.

By then the boys and some people in the area were standing there, looking at me. One lady looked at my elbows and knees, all scraped up and bloody, but my toe hurt worse than anything else. She took off my moccasin, which made it feel better. How my big toe got bent back inside my shoe, I don't know. When my mom got home and found out what had happened, I was in trouble again.

Sometimes I wonder how my mother put up with me, but I managed to make it through vacation, until it was time to go back to school.

SILLY GIRLS

The trip back to school was almost like the trip to Miami—crowded, hot and smoky, since everybody on the train smoked. Every now and then I would go visit the other cars to see what the other people were doing, which took some of the boredom out of the trip.

I sat and thought about the things my buddies and I did last year. I couldn't wait to get back to the school. I thought about the coming year. I decided I would try to be smarter and not get trapped in some of the dares that got me into trouble before.

The train pulled into the station at noontime, so I thought I would have enough time at school to see all the boys and go have a smoke before suppertime. After we got off the train Jack looked around.

"I don't see the car from the school," he said.

While we waited, I thought about this was going to make us late getting back to school, and I was pissed. It would be dark when we got back! While we waited, Buddy and two other kids came up from behind me.

"Are you waiting for us?" he asked.

And I was shocked to see them.

"Where did *you* come from?" I asked him.

"We came in on another train," Buddy said, "about the same time you did."

"I see the car to take us back to the school," Jack said.

The ride back to the school was less than an hour, so we had plenty of time to get unpacked. Buddy and I went straight to the woods for a smoke. Jackie and Eddie were already there.

We traded stories about what we had done the last month. Earl and Harold hadn't made it back yet.

"You guys are the first to get back," Jackie said, "but I'm not worried/ They'll make it back when we least expect them."

"What did you do while we were gone?" I asked him.

"There wasn't a whole lot to do but Christmas was nice. They had a lot of good food, and they gave us some cheap presents, but it would have been a lot more fun if you guys had been here."

"Is that all you did for a full month?" Buddy asked.

"No, Buddy that was just one day! On days were decent I walked over to the fort and laid around, but it was usually cold and I couldn't stay there too long."

"It was so hot in Miami that I had to wear shoes or the street would burn my feet," I told Jackie.

"Did you do anything interesting or fun?" he asked.

I told him how I ran out from the bus and got hit by a car.

"You did what?"

The other boys started laughing, so I had to tell them the whole story.

"With all the things that you get into it's a wonder that you're not dead!" Jackie said.

The other boys laughed again.

"I don't think that I should hang around with you anymore," Buddy said. "You're getting too dangerous."

———

"Today I'm going to show you all how to make a kite," Mrs. Pierce said the next day.

She had us gather around her desk and showed us a sketch of a kite.

"All you have to do is get small, straight limbs, make a cross, and tie them together in the center. Then cover the crossed limbs with paper and glue it around the sides."

We went to work on the kites. The girls made the paper cut-outs and some of us boys went to find the small limbs. Jackie and I found some rabbit tobacco twigs we used for arrows, and they worked out just fine. After we had to glue paper on them and laid them on the table to dry. By the end of the day we had made seven kites we left overnight so the glue would dry.

The next day at noon Mrs. Pierce took us out to the pasture to try our luck at flying the kites. The wind was blowing pretty good for flying kites. Buddy and I teamed up and gave it our best effort. The problem was, the kites were too heavy in front, so they would nose dive into the ground.

"Maybe we need a tail," Mrs. Pierce said.

Buddy got an old piece of cloth. We cut it into strips, tied the strips together, and tied that long piece to the point in the back of the kite.

"You hold the twine," Buddy said. "I'll take the kite and run with it, and give it a chance to get up."

Jackie stood with me while Buddy ran with the kite. Some of the other boys and girls watched. He got about thirty yards when all of a sudden he fell down. The grass was so high we couldn't see him, but we heard him cussing. When he stood up we walked over to where he was, laughing.

Buddy, in his attempt to get the kite air born, didn't watch where he was running: He slipped on a cow pile and slid right through it. He had cow shit all down his backside and even in his hair. The closer we got to him the more we laughed, which even made him madder.

We weren't so much laughing at Buddy as we were laughing at the girls who held their noses as he walked by. Even Mrs. Pierce had to laugh, but the girls laughing even made it worse. Needless to say, Buddy had to leave and get cleaned up but worse than that, he spent an hour cleaning the shower when he was through.

A week later we had another snow. It was a complete surprise, since the weather had been pretty nice. Our plans to go on a hike were on hold, since we had to stay in the house for at least a day or two. We were allowed to spend a little time outside, but had to stay close to the dormitory. On the way to a smoke break at the creek, Buddy saw some rabbit tracks, which we followed. Before long before a rabbit jumped up. Someone tried to catch it and then we all got in on the chase. Let me tell you, that was one of the dandiest chases that you ever saw. Every time someone lunged at the rabbit it would make a quick right turn and we would go head over heels in the snow or run in to one another and sometimes bump our heads. Soon we decided it was fruitless, but we did have a good time.

"I don't know about that damn rabbit," Eddie said, "but I couldn't take any more of that."

———

With the weather warming up over the next couple of days, we thought that winter was over, but a day later, when we woke up, we were surprised to see the entire area was covered with a fresh blanket of fresh snow; the temperature had dropped.

"You know, this could be the last snow of the winter," I said to my friends. "Before it melts, we should try and get at least one more sled ride in."

"That's a great idea," Eddie said. "I'm ready!"

"Me too but let's find another hill," Earl chipped in. "That last place was too close to the woods. I have nightmares about seeing my face flattened into tree."

We took the sled and went looking. On the other side of the last pasture there looked like a good sledding hill with no obstructions.

"I've got dibs on the first ride!" Eddie said.

"You can have it," I told him. You never know what's under fresh snow, but that first ride went pretty smooth so, we all had a go at it. For the first time in a long while we didn't have a problem.

We got cold and wet, but that didn't bother us until we walked back, against the wind. It got colder all of a sudden and Earl had to stop.

"I can't go any farther!" he said.

I watched him tremble. He appeared to be turning blue.

"Here, take my coat," Eddie said.

After awhile we got him to start walking and we finally got back to the house. We were all just about frozen. When we arrived the housemother was standing in the doorway.

"Do you boys know that the temperature is below twenty degrees?" she said. "You stayed out way too long and lost your body heat. That could be very dangerous. *Don't do it again!*"

———

Spring

A month later the weather started getting better and the snow melted. When the trees started putting on leaves, we knew spring was around the corner and it wouldn't be long before we could start going on hikes.

We were a year older this spring and we had gotten used to the mountains; I guess we had done just about everything that boys our age could do. We were smarter about the ways of the mountain people and although they acted strange at first, we came to realize that they were the nicest people we ever met, and that holds true to this day.

The other boys were starting to look up to Jackie and me, so we took the lead in most of the things we did, especially about going on hikes. They looked for our approval on new ideas.

One day Earl said he had heard of a new game that the big boys played, called "Fox and Hounds"

"The way it's played is," he explained, "two boys take off and get a head start, and the rest of the boys try and find them. The first two boys are the foxes. They have to leave clues so their trail can be followed by the hounds."

Jackie and I wanted to be the foxes. We tore up paper into small pieces and dropped them along our trail. There was a lot of open field before we could get to the woods, so we wanted a two hour head start. Jackie and I took off.

"Let's go to Betty's farm," Jackie said after we got out a ways, "and leave the trail so they think we're hiding out in her barn. We can double back and wind up over at the swimming hole. Before they find out what we did, we'll be back at the school. That way we can spend the whole day to ourselves while they wander around looking for us."

At the farm Betty was at the barn feeding the horses. We told her what we were doing and not to tell the other boys we were here. She asked how long it would be before they arrived. We told her about the two hour head start so it shouldn't be too long. She agreed to go along with our little game.

We hadn't seen Betty since last year, and she didn't seem to have changed at all. She wore the same man's shirt and skirt, except the old shirt was missing two more buttons, and when she turned a certain way you could see her well-rounded breast. I know she saw me looking at times, but it didn't bother her.

We went down to the pasture. Since the sun had warmed up we took off our shirts, then sat down on the bank of the creek to have a cigarette. We couldn't believe it but we heard the other boys coming, so we had to get in the creek to keep them from seeing us.

"I don't understand how they could be so far off the trail," Jackie said after they went by, "after the paper trail we left for them."

I saw a piece of paper floating in the creek.

"There's you answer," I told him. "The wind must have blown our pieces of paper all over the place." We had to laugh.

"They'll have one hell of a time trying to find us with that kind of a trail," Jackie said.

We lay there on the bank for awhile, trying to decide what we wanted to do.

"What was that?" Jackie said suddenly.

"What was what?" I asked him.

"I heard voices coming from over the hill," he said.

We stood up and saw some older people coming our way. After they went by Jackie said, "Let's get out of here!"

We went up the creek a ways before they could see us, but heard them talking about the swimming hole.

"I think they're going swimming," I said. "Let's wait until they get there, then sneak up and watch them."

Near the swimming hole was a large group of boulders, which we hid behind. From where we were we could see only a part of the swimming hole because the bushes hid the most of it. The only time we could see them was when they got out for a smoke. We had never seen these women before so we figured that they must be new to the area.

"They sure are fat!" I told Jackie.

"Yeah, I can't hardly see that patch of hair between their legs, and look at those tits, they just hang down," he said. "Wait a minute, there's a skinny one over there!"

She looked a lot younger than the others, with smaller breasts and long legs. I figured she was probably a daughter of one of the others. Jackie wanted to go over and talk to them, but I I didn't think that was a good idea.

"What if we just walk up the creek and come back down on the other side," he suggested. "That way it will look like we just happened by, and we'll act like we didn't know they were here?"

"I'll bet you that they won't even care if we see them naked in the water," I said. : After all, they're out in the open for anybody to see."

We went up one side of the creek, crossed over and came back on the other. When we came upon the swimming hole, only the skinny one tried to cover her breasts. One of the other two just smiled and asked what we were doing.

"We were just looking for something to do when we heard you talking," Jackie said, "so we walked over to see what was going on."

"We were just cooling off in the water," the other one said.

I couldn't think of anything to say, but Jackie just stood there and kept on talking. The one was talking to us never once tried to cover up, but the other two got out of the water, dried off and put their clothes on. The talker finally got out of the water and said that they had to go now, but it was nice talking to us.

"You were right, they didn't even try to cover up," Jackie said to me as they left. "That was fun!"

"I told you...they just look at us as kids and don't even care if we see them."

"Wait until I tell the other boys about this," Jackie said.

"You know, most of them have seen this before."

"Pat, I'm a little bit pissed. No one told me about this. Shit we could have been looking at naked girls all last summer!"

He sounded serious.

"Well, if you want to do it again," I told him, "I know of another swimming hole that some other people go to. I know for a fact that Doris and Sally like to swim there."

"Did you ever catch them swimming?" he asked.

"No but both Harold and Buddy have," I answered.

———

At that time of my life, I didn't have any sexual desires but I was curious about everything, and I guess like every young boy had. Jackie made it pretty clear we would do it this summer. We never paid too much attention to those things before but now, more or less out of curiosity, it was a lot of fun seeing their private parts, and also seeing how they reacted.

———

Soon our little group went on one of our outings. We weren't going anywhere in particular, just roaming around in the hills looking for something to do. Buddy and Harold, as usual, wanted to go to the swimming hole so we went along. We weren't going in the water, but would just lay around and maybe have a smoke. If anything else interesting happened we would be there, to be a part of it.

Buddy and Harold couldn't wait to get in the water. After they went in we sat on the bank and had a cigarette. Eddie and Earl wandered off up the creek. After awhile we got bored and went to look for Eddie and Earl; on the way we met Betty and Doris, who said they were going to the store. They had met Eddie and Earl back up the creek. I said good… that's where we're heading.

"Where are Buddy and Harold?" Betty asked.

"They're down at the swimming hole," I said.

"Let's go surprise them," Betty said, looking at Doris.

"Good, they'll be glad to see you," I said, elbowing Jackie; they left.

"Buddy and Harold are going to be pissed at us if they find out we sent the girls to see them," I said.

Wound Eddie and Earl, who said there were only some small kids at the swimming hole, so they left to get us. We told them about sending Betty and Doris to see Buddy and Harold so we went back to the swimming hole. Betty and Doris were standing on the bank talking to Buddy and Harold. Buddy didn't want to get out of the water.

"Do you want to have a cigarette?" I asked him, with the girls watching.

"I already had one," he said.

"How about you Harold?" I asked.

He started to get out but thought better of it when Betty laughed.

"We'd better go now," she said to Doris, "or we'll be late getting home."

After they left Buddy got out and put his clothes.

"I thought they would never leave!" he said.

"What were you guys doing when the girls got here?" Jackie asked Buddy.

Harold answered that.

"We were lying on the bank having a cigarette."

Jackie had to hold back his laughter.

"I guess you could say that they caught you guys with your pants down," he said.

"Well, if you must know, we jumped in the water and stayed there, and it's not as funny as you think it is!"

"We had better get back," I told the guys, "or we will be late for supper." That ended our escapade for the day.

———

After supper we all headed down to the creek for a smoke.

"We should make some bows and arrows, and see if we could hit some rabbits," I told the guys.

The others all thought that was a good idea. We planned to do it the next day, but we had to work in the cannery. Since it was still daylight after we finished, we went looking for a hickory tree, since hickory made the best bows. We found some good limbs and went about making the bows.

I found a limb about four and a half feet long and cut a notch in each end to hold the string. Before the day ended we had made enough bows so that everybody had one. Next we had to find some rabbit tobacco twigs for the arrows, which we all knew where to find.

"We still have one small little problem," Jackie said during a smoke break.

"What's that?" I asked.

"Finding and killing a rabbit," he laughed.

"That shouldn't be a big problem," I said. "Since we see them hopping around in the field on the other side of the school." Which is where we headed early the next morning. Sure enough, we saw them and we got off a lot of shots, but for the most part it was a lot of close misses. We actually hit a couple of rabbits but our arrows just bounced off.

After awhile we stopped for a smoke break. Harold went off by himself.

"I think that I could do better without everyone scaring them off," he said.

About thirty minutes later he came back holding a rabbit.

"Now that's how it's done!" he announced. Sure enough, it had an arrow right through it.

Now we didn't have any reason not to believe him, so we went about our hunt, believing he had made a good shot—until Jackie found a rabbit trap that had been tripped, but with no rabbit in it.

"I think I know where Harold got that rabbit and he didn't kill it either!" he said.

Harold and Buddy had gone up the creek and weren't there when we found the trap, but we had a pretty good idea of what they had done.

"We should kick their asses!" Earl said.

"Let's just let it go," Eddie said. "When we see them we'll keep talking about how good a shot it was, and see if they will own up to it."

"That would be a good idea for normal people," Jackie said, "but I don't think Buddy fits that category." We all laughed and headed for supper.

After supper we went down to the woods. Jackie started talking about the "kill" that Harold had made, and Eddie wanted to know how he did it. Buddy tried to come to his defense.

"We both shot at the same time," he said, "but it was his arrow that hit the rabbit."

After awhile it was becoming obvious that neither one of them wanted to discuss this, but we were relentless in our praise about their shooting.

"Okay, it wasn't such a great shot! We found a trap with a rabbit in it," Buddy finally admitted.

"Yeah, we saw that too!" Eddie said, adding, "I never saw one that got out of a trap, before. That must have been one hell of a rabbit!"

Later that night while we were lying in bed Buddy and I talked.

"We took the rabbit out of the trap," he told me. "I held it while Harold shot it with the arrow."

I said, "You were putting your life in Harold's hands!"

Those Silly, Silly Girls

The weather was warm enough we were back to going barefooted. At first it was hard on our feet, but after awhile our feet would always get tough. We could walk on rocks and not feel it, though over the course of the summer there would be stumped toes and stone bruises to contend with. When this happened we would find the nearest cow pile and stick our foot in it. I can't swear that this helped, but it was better than having the nurse put some stinging stuff on it.

———

"Who is this Rosie that I've heard so much about?" Jackie asked, out of the blue. We were walking to the creek at the time.

"That is Buddy's new sweetheart," I told him.

"I hate that girl," Buddy said, all pissed. "Jackie ain't heard anything about her and me, he's just lying."

"I don't understand why you would hate such a nice girl," Jackie said; he knew he was getting to Buddy. "What did she ever do to you?"

I told Jackie that Rosie was just about the ugliest girl in school, and we used to tease Buddy about her all the time.

"I've got to see this girl," Jackie said. "She couldn't possibly be *that* bad."

"Well, don't look at her too long," Buddy said, "or she will put a curse on you, and you won't be able to sleep at night!"

After we had a laugh at Buddy's expense, he eventually calmed down and we continued on our way to the creek. Once we got there Eddie found a long piece of rope. If we could find a place where the creek was wide enough and there were tree limbs over the water, we could swing over the creek, he said.

"Why don't we take it over to the swimming hole?" Harold suggested.

"There ain't any trees to tie the rope to over the swimming hole!" Jackie answered.

"But there are trees over the swimming hole that the mountain people use," I said, so we headed off in that direction.

When we got to the swimming hole nobody was in the water, so we had time to get the rope tied off to a branch fairly close to the center of the water. Jackie waded out and hung on.

"Now, that's one solid rope," he announced after yanking on it a few times.

Harold volunteered to take the first swing, and landed right in the center of the creek. I watched as the others took their turn. I didn't have any desire to swing on that rope because I remembered the last time I swung on a rope, and that didn't turn out so well. I took off my shirt and lay on the rocks. After awhile it got pretty hot.

"I think I'll go in the water to cool off," I said to Jackie.

"I'll join you."

The two of us hardly ever went in the water. Jackie went in first. Before I took off my pants, I lit up a cigarette, but the other guys called out, "chicken!", so I snuffed out my smoke and jumped in the water. With six of us in at the same time, we didn't have too much room at the deep end. We had all gravitated there since we didn't want to be caught naked in the water.

We were so busy splashing each other and playing around that no one noticed the two ladies from the mountain when they came up. Jackie was the first to see them. He told me they hadn't got close enough to see us, but hoped they would go on by.

"I told you it would be hard to see when someone came up," Buddy said.

They went on by and I don't think they even saw us, but after they left, we all got out and got dressed. Then we went up the mountain and to look for abandoned cabins and arrowheads. We did this for an hour or so without much luck. Eddie wanted to see if the girls from the mountain had gone back to the swimming hole. We had nothing else to do, so we all went with him.

On the way Earl stumped his toe, so we had to wait until he checked it out.

"There are some cow piles in the pasture," Jackie said, "on the way to the swimming hole."

After we located one Earl put his foot in it.

"That feels a lot better now," he said, but he had to walk with his toes up high in the air, making it hard for him to walk any distance without taking breaks. Buddy and Harold stayed with him, while Jackie, Eddie, and I continued on to the swimming hole.

We could hear girls talking and laughing before we ever got there. Eddie wanted to sneak up on them to see what they were doing, so we hid behind the bushes and watched. They were using our rope. One of them was a big lady wearing a dress. When she swung out on the rope her dress ballooned up and she was wearing no underwear. Boy, did we get an eyeful!. When she hit the water we thought it would empty the pool.

The two women we saw earlier had picked up another family. There were four kids with them—three young boys that looked to be four or five and a girl about our age.

I looked at Jackie.

"Wait until that girl gets her dress wet!" I said.

Eddie looked at the older woman standing on the bank.

"I don't think she has anything on under that dress," he said.

"*I know* she doesn't!" I told him.

The young girl got in the water. When the dress got wet it didn't do much to hide anything. Jackie asked Buddy and Harold if they were going to get in the water.

"I might after all those people leave," Harold said.

"Why don't you go in now," I suggested. "They don't care."

"I don't even know them," Buddy said.

"So what, everybody else in the mountains has seen you na-ked," Jackie said. "Are you going to let them be the only ones that haven't seen you?"

Buddy got mad.

"Maybe they're both chicken!" I said.

Buddy and Harold jumped in with their clothes on, and we laughed again because they were still being chicken.

Harold got out and took a swing on the rope. He close to the girl. To our surprise she dunked his head under the water.

"he doesn't know what to do, he's just standing there," Buddy said. The girl laughed.

"The next time I will pull your pants down!" she said.

Harold was a little nervous when he got out and stood with us on the bank. The older women were getting a kick out of the goings on and were laughing.

Jackie thought the whole routine was hilarious. He told Harold he should do it again just to see what the girl would do.

"I don't think so," Harold said. "She might go through with her threat."

We added ourselves to the dare but Harold wouldn't budge.

"I think I've just about had enough of the girls around here see-ing my private parts!" he said.

Buddy surprised everybody when he took the rope and swung out, landing next to the older women. The larger of the two grabbed Buddy by the leg and held him until the girl came over. As Buddy struggled to escape the iron grip of the big woman the girl pulled his pants down to his knees. All of us including the women were laughing, but not Buddy. He was pissed. He came up on the bank and sat with Jackie and me, sulking.

"Buddy, I don't know why you would be pissed," I told him. "You knew exactly what was going to happen."

"I thought she was bluffing. I hope they all enjoyed the free show!"

After everyone had a laugh at Buddy's expense, they all started climbing out of the water. The two women went behind the bushes and changed their clothes, but the girl just took off her wet dress and put on a pair overalls right there by the creek bank.

"You know, that girl looked small," I told Jackie, "but I have to say, she is older than we thought."

We stuck around for awhile until the mountain people left and Jackie was ready to leave. Buddy and Harold wanted to stay a little longer and go back in the creek

"We didn't get a chance to enjoy the rope-swing we tied up," Buddy said.

By now it had gotten quite hot, so Earl and Eddie had decided to go in the water too. Before long we were all in the water, enjoying the swing and trying to dunk one another.

Earl had brought his slingshot. He asked Eddie if he wanted to go look for rabbits. After they left Jackie and I got out, had a cigarette and lay on the bank, and I guess we both dozed off. I was rudely awakened by what felt like ice cubes hitting my body, but when I opened my eyes I saw someone splashing us with water. We both jumped up and everyone else stood around laughing. Neither one of us had put on our clothes so we were standing there buck naked.

At first we saw only our buddies, but then I saw Doris and Sally standing there laughing right along with our friends. They weren't embarrassed by our nakedness, but we hurried up and dressed, anyway. Jackie was pissed at the boys and wanted to know whose great idea this was, but no answer was forthcoming.

"I told you that I would catch you one day!" Doris said.

What made it bad was, all the other guys were fully dressed, which made us look like a couple of fools. Jackie calmed down by now, and even he had to smile.

"I like to come down to the creek when you guys are here," Sally said. "It's a lot more fun."

What that silly grin on her face, she just looked like a little bitch.

After the girls left Jackie got pissed again.

"Okay, who brought the girls?" he asked.

"We were out looking for rabbits when we saw Buddy and Harold walking toward the creek with the two girls," Earl said.

"Okay Harold, what's the deal? I guess you didn't know we were here!" snapped Jackie.

"I'm sorry but I couldn't keep them away. How could we know you two would be lying here, naked as a jaybird," Harold said. He couldn't help cracking a smile as he talked.

"I don't remember anything funnier than when you two jumped up as they splashed you," Buddy said.

"Hey, you little assholes, I know that two of you went after the girls. The way you love the water, I can't think of any other reason you would have gotten out!"

Buddy gave it away when he laughed.

"We will get even with them for this," I said to Jackie.

"You can damn well bet we will, and you can count on that!" Jackie promised.

All the way back to the house Jackie talked about how we would get even with Buddy and Harold. I didn't care about it that much, since we had played our share of tricks on them, but Jackie was adamant. I could see his point.

Jackie didn't know the mountain girls as well as I did, so he left it up to me to deal with them. I suggested it might be better to try and get some of the girls at the school to catch the two of them. Even though the mountain girls didn't care about seeing them, the girls at school would be embarrassed, because they would have to sit with them in class every day.

"Damn, that's a great idea. How in the hell are we going to pull it off?"

"I dunno, but I guess between the two of us, we can come up with something."

"You know this is going to be tricky," Jackie said. "They know we're laying for them. They'll be watching our every move."

"Well, maybe we'll just have to wait a little while until this all blows over," I offered.

———

We spent the next few weeks visiting the farms and roaming around the mountains, looking for arrowheads and lying around. We managed to get a little work done on one of the old forts from last year, the one that overlooked the swimming hole, because it fit into our plans for getting even with Buddy and Harold.

"I haven't gotten any girls to go along with our plan yet," I told Jackie.

"What's the problem?"

"Well, I didn't count on this, but this is not an easy subject to discuss with the girls at school."

"So, what now?"

"Okay, what do you think of this?" I said, "Let's see if we can get Sally to help us."

"I thought that you didn't like her!"

"I don't...sometimes she can be a little bitch, but I'll try and overlook that. I think that's the only way we can get the girls at school to go along with us. She knows some of those girls. I think that they would listen to her because they know how devious she is, and would probably get a kick out of the idea."

"Well let's ask her and see what she says," Jackie said.

———

About a week later some of us spent the night at the farm. Early the next morning Sally came out to milk the cow, which woke me up.

"Good morning Sally, you're up early," I said to her.

"Got work to do Pat, can't sleep all day!"

I didn't want to get involved with her but we had decided on our plan, so I asked her.

"How would you like to help me and Jackie play a trick on the other boys?"

Her eyes lit up with the word "trick".

"What kind of trick?"

I explained how I wanted her to get some of the girls at school to go to the swimming hole and catch the other boys in the water, bare-assed naked. She got this devilish grin on her face.

"I think that could be arranged," she said. "When shall I do my thing?"

"I guess as soon as you can get around to it," I told her. "Just let me know when and we'll get the boys over to the swimming hole before you get there."

"So, why are you doing this?" she asked.

"Well, remember when Buddy and Harold went and got Doris and you to come and splash water on me and Jackie when we were lying there asleep naked? We're going to make them pay… big time!"

"This sounds like a lot of fun! But there's something that you don't know."

"Yeah, what's that?" I asked.

"It wasn't Buddy and Harold that led us to your bare butts."

"Oh?" I said. "Then who?"

"Well, Doris and I were walking down by the creek when we came upon Eddie and Earl. That's when Eddie said to us, 'Wanna have some fun?' That's when they led us to where you and Jackie were putting on your little show."

"Oh my God!" I said. "Wait until Jackie hears this. He is going to be pissed. His good friend Eddie ain't such a good friend after all."

"But it was Doris that splashed you guys. I would have been just as happy to stand there and watch you guys a little longer. And that's what really happened."

At that point I asked Sally not to mention any of this to Doris.

Later on that day I told Jackie about my conversation with Sally.

"That's okay, they'll get what's coming to them!" he said.

Walking back to the school that afternoon, we met Sally. She pulled me over to the side and said that she had ran into some of the girls from the school. She had it all set up for next Saturday afternoon.

"Be there!" she said.

———

Saturday, at around noon, Buddy, Harold, Eddie, and Earl were all set to go to the creek, just waiting for Jackie and me.

"My stomach isn't feeling so good, so I think I will stick around the house today," Jackie said.

"I'll stay here with Jackie," I told the others. "If he starts feeling better we'll come down and join you."

They took off. Jackie and I waited at the pasture next to the dormitory until we saw Sally and four other girls on the path that led to the creek. Some older girls were playing ball in the lower pasture, not too far from the creek. That was our sign to hightail it to the fort overlooking the swimming hole.

"I knew we had a good reason for building this fort," Jackie said. "We can lie here in the comfort of the shade and watch everything that goes on in the swimming hole, while enjoying an occasional smoke."

"Yeah, Jackie, it doesn't get much better than this," I agreed.

Then we saw the girls come down the side of the creek. They ended up behind the swimming area, stopped and hid behind the bushes. I had told Sally to wait for us before they came out and surprised the boys. While they waited, a couple girls snuck over, picked up the boys clothing, and put it on a rock ledge. This would force them to get out and walk naked for about thirty feet.

When we got closer I could see the girls peeking through the bushes at the boys. I thought to myself, these girls are just as bad as we are. After we got there we stopped and sat on the rock on the bank.

"Having fun, you guys?" I said.

"Come on in!" Eddie invited.

At that moment the girls came out, one at a time, with Sally bringing up the rear

"What are you boys doing in our swimming hole?" the first girl asked.

We saw the older girls start walking toward the creek. You should have seen the guys try to cover up while! Jackie and I just about busted a gut laughing, and the girls enjoyed it even more.

"I think this is the best thing we have ever done!" I said to Jackie.

"Without a doubt!" he agreed.

"Okay girls, you've had your fun, now at least give us our clothes!" Buddy pleaded.

"You can go and get your clothes any time you want too," Sally said. "We won't look."

The girls turned their back, so the boys got out and went to dress,

"Where are the clothes?" Eddie wanted to know.

"They're over there on that rock ledge," Sally told him.

When the boys went to get their clothes, the girls all turned around to look. They laughed and pointed and said things like 'look at that one', and 'look at this one'. At the top of the ledge the boys were in plain sight of the older girls. To our surprise the P.E. instructor was with the older girls, so she got herself an eyeful. That's when Sally and the girls disappeared out the back way.

"We'd better get the hell out of here, too before we get into a world of trouble!" I said to Jackie.

Jackie said, "I think you have a point," and we headed back to the fort.

Back at the fort, we felt safe and relaxed with a cigarette.

"We'd better watch out now," I told Jackie, "because the guys will be out to get even."

"I don't care, they will never to get us the way we got them!" he said.

———

A few days later at school we saw some of the girls from the swimming hole. They would look at us and snicker a little. One of them even asked me when we planned to do it again.

"Those girls are nasty little bitches," Jackie said later.

"I know," I said. "We'd better watch out. We don't know what they might do next, now that they know where we go up in the mountain."

A week later we went to visit Mike and Betty.

"I heard about the trick you and Jackie played on your buddies," Betty said right off the bat.

"Well, they had it coming," I said.

We stayed in the barn that night. When Betty came down to do the milking, I was already up and out in the yard smoking with Buddy. We had planned to go up the mountain to a cabin that he knew about, but the other boys were still sleeping. When they got up we went to the house; Doris told us that Betty was a little mad at us for what we did to Buddy and the other boys. I asked her if Betty was mad at Sally and she said that Betty wasn't happy about any of it.

Betty didn't say anything but she was very quiet.

After we left and were on our way to the mountain, Jackie told me more.

"Doris told me that one of the girls from the school has been talking, and that one of them let it slip about going to the swimming hole, and now the group of them are in trouble," he said.

I looked at him.

"I knew those little bitches would mess things up. Now we're going to catch all kinds of hell!"

"I don't know, it's been over a week since our little adventure and no one has said anything to us about it," Jackie pointed out. "Maybe Doris doesn't know what she's talking about. I think we should just wait and see."

The next day we had to work at the cannery. I told Jackie that this would be a good time to talk to the girls and find out what they knew. I looked around and saw the P.E. instructor, Miss Hightower was there. She was easy to spot because she was the only teacher to wear short pants, and she was only about twenty-five. The thing that bothered me today was, she had never come to the cannery before.

"She must be here for a reason!" I told Jackie.

"I don't think she saw us at the swimming hole," Jackie said. "Unless one of the girls told on us, she won't even know what we look like."

I looked at Jackie.

"That's what I'm worried about. It wouldn't surprise me one little bit if one of them little bitches has squealed on us!"

We started canning tomatoes. I told Jackie about the last time we did this. He just laughed.

"Do you want to start up a fight again?"

"Hell no!" I said, "The last time it took us damn near the whole night to get this place cleaned up."

I thought that any minute he would bust somebody in the chops with a tomato, and the fight would be on. I was relieved at the end of the day that he had kept his tomatoes to himself. After supper we went down to the creek.

"I thought for sure that you were going to start a tomato fight," I told Jackie. He laughed.

"You know damn well that I wanted to, but I felt we were in enough trouble already."

Buddy walked up. We asked him what he found out, but he said that he didn't get a chance to talk to anybody.

"I guess we'll have to do it tomorrow at school," I said. "You know, guys, I just have to know why Miss Hightower was at the cannery. Something is going on!"

Later that evening I sat in the front room trying to finish up a drawing of the fort and the surrounding area. I began wondering whether we were in trouble at all. Jackie and I were punishing ourselves with worry for no reason. The only other person that knew we were involved was Sally, and for some reason I just couldn't believe that she would squeal on us—mainly because she had been in so many dubious schemes herself that telling on us didn't make any sense at all.

The next day I couldn't wait to tell Jackie why I thought we weren't in trouble, but he wasn't so sure.

"Let's go find her and see if she knows anything," he said. "After all she knows the girls went with her that day."

"I haven't seen her at school," I said. "Maybe she's the one that got in trouble."

It was a few days later while we were down by the creek fooling around with Buddy and Harold when I asked them if they had seen Sally lately and Harold said, "You really don't want to!"

"Why?" I asked.

"Well, I talked to her…and she's really pissed at you two."

"Why?" I asked again.

"She thinks that you guys told on her."

Jackie said, "That don't make no sense! We were all in that together, and that would be like telling on ourselves!"

I told Jackie, "Maybe we should go and talk to her before she gets mad enough to tell the whole school."

"What the hell could she say now? Everybody knows about it by now," he said.

"I'm not so sure if that's true," I said, "they probably know what happened but don't know who was behind it…it's been over two weeks and I don't think we're in trouble yet."

"I hope you're right."

A few days later we had to pick blackberries for canning, and this time the girls had to go and pick with us. I told Buddy and Earl that Eddie, Jackie, and I would meet them down by the creek, in the pasture as that is where the big berries are, and as soon as we got our cans full we were going to the store. Jackie and I got our cans full at about noon and went to the cannery and then back down to the creek to wait for the others to finish.

When Earl and Eddie walked over I said, "Where's Buddy?"

Eddie said, "When Buddy picks he eats so many it takes him a long time to fill his cans."

Earl said, "Let's go ahead and leave without him."

We're not in that big of a hurry," I said. "We don't have anything else to do, anyway."

While we were waiting for Buddy we decided to wander over and see how the girls were doing. When we saw two of the girls that appeared to be about ten, we got the laugh of a life time. It must have been the first time that they had picked blackberries, for their faces were covered with purple blackberry juice. I told Jackie, "This reminds me of the time that the girls saw us with slimy frogs and thought we were sickoes."

Eddie and Buddy walked up.

"Let's get started," Buddy said. "I need to get some cigarettes and I want us to go by the creek on the other side of the store. Remember last year when we caught all those frogs there?"

After we got our cigarettes we went over to the creek, down past the store and it did *ever* look like a good place to get frogs… there were several side pools and we saw a lot of tadpoles swimming around. And we decided that next Saturday would be a good time to give it a try.

Saturday was finally a nice warm day, and we got all the necessary things we needed to go frogging. All six of us were going. It was a long way to get there but there was no use hurrying for we had to wait until dark to catch the evasive little critters.

After we got there we still had time to kill so we sat on the bank, smoked and talked about other times we went frogging. There were a lot of them to talk about and Buddy, Eddie, and I were on most of them, as Jackie didn't get here until a year later, so we told him about all the other times and all the trouble we had. He got a bang out of the things we told him.

Then Eddie said, "Let's get started! I think it's dark enough."

We all agreed. We had been anticipating a frogging trip for some time and who cared if it wasn't pitch dark.

Buddy and Harold got in the creek, Earl and I did the spotting, and Eddie and Jackie carried the frogs. Harold wasn't worth a crap at catching, although he always bragged about his prowess at it, he was missing more than he caught. Buddy was good at it, and when he made fun of Harold, I thought it was a good time to relieve Harold. I didn't mind at all because it was a lot more fun than spotting.

Jackie was so right about the frogs here. Before I could hand over the one that I had just caught someone was spotting another one. I guess we had caught about twenty frogs in no time flat, and Buddy, breathing like he had ran a mile said, "Let's take a break!"

We got out and sat on the bank, and Jackie said, "It looks like we'll be getting more than we need."

Then Eddie said, "Why don't we just keep on catching and see if we can set a new record."

I told Eddie, "I think that will be easy, because I believe the most we ever caught was the time that Buddy lost them in the graveyard, and I think that was twenty-five."

Buddy was quick to remark, "That wasn't my fault!" and added, "Sure let's catch more, and take them to the creek over by the school, so we won't have to walk so far in the dark to catch them."

I asked Buddy, "How long do you think they will stay there?" but he didn't have an answer for that. Then I offered, "You know, we can always take a bunch of them to Betty and Mike, and maybe we can get back on Betty's good graces again. You know how Mike likes them."

After we had our smoke we went back to catching frogs and after a half an hour or so we had all the frogs we could carry, and headed back to the school. We put our two tow-sacks in the creek next to the dorm until after church the next day.

Sunday, after church we headed out to Mike and Betty's farm. Jackie had a bad cold and the other boys didn't want to go, so it was just Buddy, Eddie, and me.

We had to hurry because we had to get there and back in time for supper. We got there late in the day. Mike was glad to see us and asked where the other boys were.

I said, "They had other things to do and couldn't make it this time. We probably shouldn't have come, as we have to go right back, but we wanted to bring you the frogs we caught last night."

Mike said, "I want to thank you for that. Come up to the house and have a glass of milk and we'll get these babies cleaned."

When we got to the house Betty gave us milk and we started helping Mike clean the frogs. We were surprised to find that Doris wasn't there. I wondered why but didn't ask, as she had always been there before. As soon as we finished the frogs we back, and just barely made it in time for supper.

The following week was bad luck for most of my buddies... Jackie's cold got a lot worse and the housemother said that he had to stay in bed for a few days, Harold and Eddie both had stone bruises on their feet and couldn't walk too far...she told them to stay off their feet for awhile, and poor Earl tripped on his own feet and fell cracking the small bone in his arm.

By the weekend it was only Buddy and I that could go anywhere, Saturday morning Buddy told me that he had gotten permission for us to go to the farm and stay overnight. I was a little surprised at that because Buddy had never stepped up and did that before. The two of us started off. The day was warm and it felt good to get away from the school on a day we didn't have to hurry back.

Buddy and I had been to the school longer than anyone else in our group and we knew our way around the mountains. On our way to the farm we would always stop at the same places and to-day was no different. As we sat on a large flat rock, having a smoke, we heard a noise off in the direction we had to go, Buddy asked, "What was that?"

I said, "Probably a rock came loose and slid down the hill."

Buddy was a little nervous with that answer, but we got up and started out anyway. There were always noises in the hills we walked, whether it be birds, animals fighting or mating, rocks falling, or sometimes just the wind whistling through the trees, but whatever the sound, we had grown used to it until something different came along... But we didn't hear it again and it was soon forgotten.

At noon we got to the farm. We saw Betty out in the garden with a hoe in her hands and sweat running off of her brow. As we walked up she took a rag and wiped the sweat. Buddy said, "Give me the hoe and take a break!"

"Are you guys a welcome sight! I didn't realize how hot it was until I started working," and added, "I think I'll take a drink of water and just sit here and watch."

She asked, "Where are the other boys?"

I said, "They all have some type of ailment or other, and it was Just Buddy and me this time, and we thought we'd stay in the barn tonight and feed the animals for you."

She said, "That would be a big help as Mike has gone hunting with some other men and it's difficult getting everything done."

After we finished helping her we and flattened out some straw for a place to sleep in the barn, and went back in the house to keep Betty company and share a smoke. After a half hour or so she said, "I'll walk out and milk the cow," so, we went too and Buddy fed the horse while I started feeding the chickens. They had this old rooster that you had to keep your eye on, as he would, all of a sudden, come after you and start trying to peck your feet. That old bastard had done this to me before and trust me, it hurt like hell!

After I had finished with the chickens I went into the barn and Buddy was milking the cow. Betty watched him and laughed. I guess Buddy didn't do so well at it, but he didn't give up. Betty looked at me.

"This may take awhile," she said, and we both laughed.

After Betty took the milk up to the house Buddy and I played around in the barn awhile until it got dark.

"Let's go up to the house and see if Betty needs any help," Buddy said. By the time we got there Betty had already started supper, so Buddy and I went to get more firewood for the stove. She had made hoe cakes and we had some with black molasses.

"I am worried about Mike getting home in the dark," she said.

"What's the worry?" Buddy asked. "Mike has done this many times. I'm sure that he'll be alright."

Betty said, "It's different this time, he has gone with some other men to look for a bear that has been in the area for about a week, and did a lot of damage at a nearby farm."

All of a sudden I remembered the strange noise we heard on the way, and a cold chill went down my spine and when I looked at Buddy, I knew that he was feeling it too.

We stayed at the house awhile longer and had a smoke with Betty then she got the two small girls ready for bed, and she changed into this long nightgown with buttons down the front with half of the buttons missing. Buddy made a comment about the missing buttons and she said, "Most of the time I just wrap it around me and don't use the buttons at all, and it works out alright as long as I watch how I sit down while you guys are here," and she gave us a wink.

I told Betty, "I think we'd better go on out to the barn as morning comes pretty quick here on the farm," and added I hope Mike gets back soon."

She said, "That's thoughtful of you Pat," then said, "I want you to take this lantern with you so you guys can see your way, but don't forget to put it out when you're finished with it."

We had already fixed up our sleeping area, so all we had to do was lie down, but neither one of us were sleepy, and we started talking about all the things we had done and how it was strange not having the other guys here. Buddy said, "I feel a lot safer when all six of us are together."

I told him, "It probably wouldn't change anything."

I was a little sleepy.

"Let's get a little sleep," I said. "You know it won't be long until Betty is in here milking that damn cow, and if we can get an early enough of a start, in the morning, maybe we can find that old cabin that you heard about.

I guess it wasn't long after I had fallen to sleep that Buddy was waking me, saying that he heard something. I was still half asleep and told him, "It is probably the horse moving around or that damn cow kicking the side of the stall."

He insisted that the noise came from outside, saying, "It sounded like some kind of large animal."

I sat up and tried to hear something, but Buddy kept talking and trying to explain what he had heard that all I heard was him, and then all of a sudden we heard a loud sound from outside. We could tell it wasn't from close by and we jumped up and ran over to where there were some cracks in the barn and looked out. Far the most part it was too dark to see anything, but every now and then the clouds would let the moon give off enough light, and we could see the area around the farm. There were some trees about fifty yards from the barn and we saw something moving that looked like a man, but before we could make it out the clouds had covered the moon again.

By now our imaginations were running wild and we were thinking all sorts of things as to what it could be, but to say the least, it was scaring the shit out of us. Then the horse was moving around and I was afraid it would break down the stall and get loose. With the horse acting up that way we were getting more afraid by the minute, and I said to Buddy, "Let's get up in the loft, I think we will be a lot safer if we were off the ground and could watch if anything happens down here. I went to the ladder and started up with Buddy hot on my heels.

By now we both had tears in our eyes, and it was very hard not to bust out crying, for both of us were thinking that whatever it was; it was after us. From up in the loft we could see a lot better and whatever it was back in the trees making one hell of a noise, and by this time we were so afraid we couldn't move.

Then there was a big bang that sounded like a gun and I heard someone cuss, and as we were waiting, I could make out the sound of Mikes voice, and he was talking to some other men. As the voices got louder we could tell that they were coming toward the barn. I yelled out, "Mike we're in the barn!!"

A few minutes later we could hear Mike call for us from inside the barn, saying, "Where are you boys?"

Mike was at the bottom of the ladder as we were looking down from the loft and said, "You can come on down now, as I think everything will be okay."

"We've been chasing that bear all night and I finally got a shot off, but I don't know if I hit him or not."

Buddy and I slowly crept down the ladder, then mike said, "I didn't know that you boys were here until you called out, but I'm glad that you had sense enough to go up to the loft. You never know what's going to happen when you're dealing with bears!" Then added, "Why don't the two of you come on up to the house and have a glass of milk or you will never get back to sleep after all that excitement."

Buddy and I followed Mike up to the house but I know we were probably thinking the same thing…"I'm glad that Mike has that gun in his hand!" We sat at the table and took our own sweet time sipping down the milk.

Mike got out his pipe, and we joined him in a smoke then he told us, "I have been after that bear for a long time and tonight I must have walked ten miles tracking him, and I'm so tired that I'm about to drop."

Then Buddy asked, "If you didn't get him, don't you think he's still around?"

"Well Buddy, It's like this; I may, or may not have hit him but when that gun went off, he took off…lickity-split, and if I was a betting man; I'd bet that he's still running."

Betty came out of the bedroom.

"Thank God, you're home safe! Did you get that critter?"

"Don't know for sure, but I don't think we'll be seeing him again," Mike said, and gave her a kiss. "Let's go to bed!"

Buddy and I headed back to the barn but we didn't have the lantern, and it was hard to find our way. Buddy kept saying things like; "what was that?" and "did you hear that?"

"Buddy, let's just get to the damn barn!" I said.

I don't think I got more than a few winks that night, and before daylight Betty was milking that damn cow. I continued to lie there for a few minutes then got up and fed the animals. Betty was almost done with the milking, so I walked outside and had a smoke as the sun peeked over the horizon. It would be a nice day but I still got a chill when I looked over toward the trees where we had seen that bear. Was it still around? Betty came out.

"I understand that you and Buddy got quite a scare last night."

"Yeah, we felt really helpless and didn't know what to do," I told her.

"You should have come up to the house."

"We were too afraid to even move, let alone leave the barn and come up to the house," I said.

"All I can say is; I'm so glad that neither one of you were hurt."

"I'll go along with that!"

"I'd better get this milk up to the house," she said. As she bent over to pick up the bucket, you could see that the buttons didn't keep the night shirt together, and I wondered if she knew what kind of a show she was putting on, or if she even cared. Sometimes I had the feeling that Betty looked at us as a part of her family. I know we thought the world of her, and I guess she was the only lady that was like a mother to all of the boys. Most of us saw more of her than we did of our own mothers.

By that time buddy had gotten up and I went with him to the house, and Betty made us something to eat before we left.

"Now, I don't want you two walking around in fear of that bear thing," Mike told us. "I scared the hell out of it, and I wouldn't be surprised if he's in the next county, still running."

"God I hope so!" I said.

"Me too!" Buddy said. "I guess we'd better go."

Then Betty gave us a hug and told us to hurry back, and to bring more of them frog legs.

We said our good-byes and started off down the hill, and while we walked along Buddy made a nuisance of himself.

"What was that? Did you hear something?" he would ask, over and over again. I got a little pissed.

"If you don't stop that shit I'm going to run off and leave you behind," I told him.

"I can outrun your ass any day of the week!" he said with a retort.

1945: MY LAST YEAR AT SCHOOL

We didn't get a heavy snow until late this year, but then we had been in the house so long that when we did, it was a blessing. I don't think that anybody thought of it as being cold outside, we just went out and played around like it was summer. We didn't go on a sled ride that day, but the thought of just being outside gave us relief.

The next day was a school-day. Mrs. Pierce was preparing for the fall season, so I had to draw all sorts of things, which kept me quite busy. The girls were doing the decorating of the classroom walls with the pictures that I had drawn, and orange and brown leaves.

Most of the boys were outside at recess time, but the girls and I had stayed inside to finish up the decorating. When I was finishing with my last drawing I could hear some of the girls talking low to each other and looking in my direction. I didn't know what they were saying but from the way they were acting, I had a funny feeling that they were being nasty. Every now and then when I looked at them they would act like they were decorating, then someone would drop something and bend over to pick it up and show me her bloomers.

Then, out of nowhere, one of the girls lifted her dress and giggled, and my eyes got big when I saw that she had no underwear on. I never did figure out what was so funny.

Then I noticed that the one who lifted her dress was one of the girls went to the swimming hole the day we played that trick on the boys and made all the comments when they ran out to get their clothes.

After I was done with my drawings I took them to Mrs. Pierce, and she was impressed, and said that they would fit in perfect with the decorations that the girls had done.

It was almost time for the bell to ring for school to be let out, and I went to the back of the room to get my coat. Most of the girls had left the hall. As I was putting on my coat I saw that the same little nasty girl had pulled the back of her dress up past her butt. She had her back to me, and acted like she didn't know it was hiked up. I thought wait until I tell Jackie about this.

I didn't know if she was aware that her butt was showing but knowing how nasty she was, I just had a feeling that she did it on purpose.

After school was out I found Jackie and we went out in the woods to have a smoke, and he asked about my and Buddy's sighting of the bear at Mike and Betty's, saying, "Pat, did you really see a bear?"

I said, "Well, it was dark so naturally we couldn't see too well, but we did see something that completely scared the shit out of us, I know it wasn't a cow, it was too big to be a dog, and it sounded like it was pissed off at the world."

Jackie said, "Sometimes when I'm by myself, walking in the dark, I would hear a sound like something is walking behind me, but I would never see anything."

"What are you trying to say?"

"I'll just say, like it was told to me; sometimes when you're afraid your imagination will play tricks on you," then he added, "Pat, you know there are all kinds of animals in these mountains but most of them are just as afraid of us as we are of them, so far the most part, they will leave us alone if we leave them alone."

Then I said, "That's easy for you to say, but I'll tell you what; after our little ordeal, I think I'm going to be just a little more careful when walking in the mountains, especially at night."

Then I told Jackie, "Do you remember when we played that trick on the other boys and that nasty girl was laughing and pointing at their wieners when they got out of the water to get their clothes?"

"How could I forget...that was one of the funniest parts."

I said, "Well, she's still at it." Then I told him about what she did in class today, and I thought he would never stop laughing then he said, "You know what?"

"No... What?"

"Well, my boy, what you have here is a girl friend."

"That's bullshit and you know it! That girl is just plain nasty!"

That night we had a big snowstorm and in the morning everything was covered with snow. When we went to breakfast it was over a foot deep, and later the housemother made us stay in the dormitory because it was still coming down, and it didn't let up until suppertime. It was just another boring day for us.

The next day the sun came out but even though it was quite cold all of us wanted to go out and play, so the housemother said we had to stay close to the house. We had a snowball fight and some of the girls got involved, and that gave us a chance to rub snow in their face and hair. That got some of them a little mad, but all in all we had a good time.

After supper, Buddy and some of the rest of us went down to the creek to have a smoke. The creek was frozen over and we could skate along on it with our shoes on. I told Buddy, "This is more fun than riding on the sled."

He agreed, saying, "Sure, we don't have to drag anything up that damn hill!"

We still had enough time before bedtime to talk about what we wanted to do tomorrow and most of the boys wanted find a good safe hill and go sledding.

The next day was Saturday and it was still as cold as hell but we were determined not to let a little thing like that get in the way of our plans. Eddie said that he knew of another place we could get a good ride, but we had to do a little work first. So, not knowing where we were going, we followed Eddie. After awhile I was thinking that he didn't know where the hell he was going, so I said, "Wait a minute, God-damn-it, I don't want to spend the whole day just to get to this place, so where the hell is it?"

"It's just over the next hill," he said, somewhat defensively.

Then as we crested the hill, we could see that the long hill would probably make for a nice ride, but the catch was; we had to take out a few fence rails and those long pieces of split timber weren't easy to hoist around. We left the top rail, as we were huffing and puffing when we got the bottom ones moved. The object now was to head on down the hill, go under the fence and proceed on across the frozen creek.

Since it was Eddie's idea, he volunteered to take the first ride and made it down with no problem. After we had all taken a turn, Buddy wanted to take a ride, going double, so he asked Earl to ride with him, and went okay, also. We all decided that going double looked like a lot of fun, so that's how we finished up the day.

We were cold and tired when Earl said, "Let's go and get supper...I don't think I can feel my toes."

Then Buddy said, I want to take one more ride," and we mumbled, "*Okay.*"

Buddy asked me to go with him and I said, "Why not?"

We started off and everything went smooth until we got past the fence, and as we hit the creek, instead of gliding over it, the ice broke and we sank like a rock. Here's where a little bit of luck came in; the water was only about armpit deep, but you want to talk about cold, when we scampered out, the water on our clothes was turning to ice. I looked at Buddy and he actually had ice on his head.

We were soaked to the skin and freezing as the guys gave us their coats and tried to warm us up, but that didn't do a whole lot of good and we still had to hurry and get back to the house. I was so cold that I didn't think that I was going to make it.

We took an hour or more to get to the dormitory. When we did the housemother was quite upset with the whole bunch of us, as she put it, and had Buddy and me, after we put on dry clothes, sitting in front of the heater for about three hours. She acted upset but still had one of the girls that worked in the kitchen bring Buddy and me a big bowl of hot soup.

When Jackie got back from supper he said, "All the other kids were laughing about that exciting sled ride that you and Buddy took."

I said, "You know, that's a bunch of shit! Every time something happens the entire school has to know about it. So, who blabbed?"

"Dunno, it was probably Eddie or Earl as the laughter started over at their table, but it's better left forgotten because the good news is; that you and Buddy are alright."

As I sat there with the blanket wrapped around me I laughed too.

"You know Buddy, that last ride of ours could have been *our last ride*."

Buddy looked at me.

"When you look at a certain way, we did have one hell of an exciting ride."

It was about a week later that Mrs. Pierce took the class on a field trip. Although the sun was out, it was still cold as hell. She wanted us to gather up flora from around the school. As kids we thought that everything that grew wild was weeds, but as we came upon different plants, she would name it, give it to one of the students to carry then record it in her tablet.

After we got back to the classroom, Mrs. Pierce had us use thumbtacks and add the plants we had just picked to the Halloween decorations we had put on the walls.

"Now, doesn't that look like we are out in the woods?" she asked. "Now we're ready for Halloween."

That evening we were down at the creek.

"You know," Jackie said, "I don't give one little shit about Halloween, and I don't think I will go to that stupid Halloween carnival."

"I pretty much agree with you as they always try and embarrass me by making me stand up when they say it's my birthday," I said.

"When is Halloween, anyway?" Jackie asked.

"About a month away, I think."

"Well, we don't have to worry about that for awhile," he grumbled.

I looked at Jackie.

"You know Pal, we haven't been out to visit Mike and Betty since me and Buddy's little escapade with the bear," and added, I wonder if the housemother will give us permission to stay out overnight... it's been warmer and most of the snow has melted."

"Your guess is as good as mine on that. You know how she feels about us going out when it's cold," Jackie said.

"I thought about that," I said, "So, why don't we tell her that Betty has a spare room we could stay in?'

"But she doesn't have a spare room."

I said, I know that, God-damn-it, but she doesn't!"

"Okay, but I don't think it'll work."

"Well, it's worth a try," I said.

Friday night, after supper Jackie and I went to the housemother and told her how we wanted to go and visit Betty's farm. At first she didn't want to let us go but I told her that Betty had been sick and that Mike had to work so we thought we could cut and carry in firewood, and milk the cow. She said, "That would really be a good thing to do for her but it is still cold and I would worry if you weren't back before supper as it's too cold to sleep in the barn, so I want you boys to mind me and be back before supper."

After she said it was okay we went upstairs to the dormitory and the first thing that Jackie said was, "I thought you were going to tell her about Betty's spare bedroom."

"Well, I was but I thought that telling her that she was sick and we were going to help would sound better, and how can you turn somebody down that's going to help someone?"

"Why you bastard, you can lie as good as me!" he said.

"Anyway it worked. Didn't it?

That night before we went to bed I told Jackie, "We have to get an early start in the morning if we intend to get back by suppertime."

The next morning, right after breakfast, we hit the road before the other boys could even ask us where we were going. The sun was up but it was colder than we thought it would be so to keep a little warmer we kept up a fast pace. We made good time and as we passed the swimming hole, Jackie remarked, "If Buddy and Harold were with us they would want to go in the water."

I said, "It would be colder than hell, but I bet they would still want to."

"Pat, that water is as cold as hell, even on a warm day!"

I said to Jackie, "You know, sometimes I think it's just an excuse for getting naked, and I'll bet if he could, he'd walk around without his clothes all the time."

"I hear you, then why does he get so pissed when the girls catch him in the water?"

Jackie, "I don't think he get's pissed at all. It's just an act!"

As we walked along and the sun got higher it got a little warmer, and by the time we got to the farm, it didn't feel cold at all. Betty was down at the barn and was surprised to see us.

"I didn't expect to see you guys until next summer."

"It gets boring around the school this time of year," I said, "but we never need an excuse to come and see you."

She replied, "That is so sweet of you, and I'm glad that you did."

Then Jackie gave me the 'evil eye' when I explained, "We didn't get permission to spend the night. The housemother said we could come and help you with some chores, but be back before suppertime."

"I'm still glad you're here, and about the only thing that needs doing is; maybe bringing in some firewood."

I said, "That should be easy enough," as we started clearing the snow off of the stack of wood.

We carried in about five armloads each, until both wood boxes were overflowing, and she said, "You boys have outdone yourselves this time and that deserves a treat."

While we were working on the wood, she had been mixing up pancakes.

"I want you boys to sat down and eat these while they're hot."

We had worked up quite an appetite.

"You don't have to tell us twice," Jackie said, "and ma'am I can't wait to taste them molasses!"

We stayed until late afternoon and back as we seemed to have plenty of time. We sauntered along taking in some beautiful scenery. At one point Jackie was pointing to a snowcapped mountain when we heard a noise in some bushes over to the left of us. Jackie picked up a rock.

"That won't do any good," I said. At that point, I think we were both frozen in fear. Then it jumped out, and immediately we took off running. We must have made it about to about fifty feet.

"Shit, that's only a deer!" Jackie said.

Then Jackie laughed so hard that he had tears in his eyes, when I caught my breath.

"I almost shit in my pants back there!" I said. He kept laughing. "Okay smart ass, what did *you* think it was?"

"Well," he said, "Since you ask me, other than my life flashing in front of my eyes, I believe I was thinking about the so-called bear that you and Buddy saw that time," and added, "that's the first time that I was ever scared shitless by a deer."

As we walked along, we paid attention to every little sound we heard, and I believe we made it back to the school somewhat quicker than usual. And when we did return, the housemother said we had to get ready for supper, and we did real good getting back when we promised.

After supper we all congregated down at the creek and the first thing that Buddy wanted to know was; "Did you guys catch sight of the bear we saw when Pat and I were there?"

And I thought Jackie was going to choke on his own spit, and said, "Now that you mention it..." and continued to relate our experience with the deer, adding his own embellishments where needed.

"That must have been the monster deer," Eddie said, and we all laughed.

The next morning at school, Mrs. Pierce had me draw pictures about Halloween. My favorite was the black cat. I could make look like it had the fire of the devil in its eyes, but the rest of the things, I didn't care too much about.

"I think it's the devil in you coming out," Mrs. Pierce said.

Halloween and the carnival came the following week. I didn't care too much about the whole affair but Jackie and some of the boys planned to scare the girls after the carnival was over. I didn't know what they were planning but with Jackie, Buddy, and Earl involved, it would be something to talk about.

When the day of the big event arrived we all crowded into Mayo Hall. As usual we boys sat together. Every now and then some of the girls would come over and talk to us. As the night progressed the conversation was more and more about the bear that chased Buddy and me, or at least that's how the story had ended up. As the girls started talking about it you could see that they were scared.

"There has been a bear spotted close to the school so when you girls walk home tonight...be very careful!" Jackie told one of the girls. Later on I noticed that same girl telling a group of the others about what Jackie had told her. I don't believe there was a girl in the house who didn't have bears on her mind.

The girls' building was about fifty yards from Mayo Hall, which meant they would have to walk by the storage sheds along the way. Before they left Jackie came over to me.

"Buddy, Eddie, and I are going to leave before the girls do, so cover for me," he said. I I didn't know exactly what he meant by covering for him, but I agreed to. Mrs. Pierce came over.

"Pat, you did a great job with the decorations and oh, by-the-way, have a happy birthday."

"Thank you," I said, but my heart wasn't in it. I couldn't help but wonder what the boys were up to. Then I saw the girls putting on their coats and getting ready to leave, and I thought, Oh boy. Some of the boys and girls helped the teachers clean up, but I didn't want to get caught in that shit. Right on cue, Buddy and Harold came over.

"Let's get out of here before they have us cleaning up this mess," Harold said.

"Come with me," Jackie said when we got outside. The five of us - Buddy, Harold, Jackie, Earl, and me - walked over to the back of the storage sheds where they had this horn with some kind of a muffler in the end of it. When you blew the horn it sounded like an animal growling.

We waited until the girls got right up next to the shed. Jackie blew on that contraption of his, and I never heard such loud screams and saw girls running in all directions, but we didn't move, then he let out another loud noise. By now the girls had made it to their house, still screaming, and we were barely able to control our laughing. Eventually we straightened ourselves up. Buddy had been keeping watch at the corner of the shed.

"The coast is clear!" he shouted, and we headed back to our dorm.

"I have a plan," Jackie said as we trotted back. "I want to come back later after they have gone to bed."

After we had been back for about a half an hour Jackie and Buddy came over to my bed. Their plan was to take the horn and go over to under the girl's window and make those same growling noises. This was against my better judgment but I thought, what the hell, anything for a laugh. So we went over to the girl's dorm and saw there were bushes were grown up against one of the windows.

"This is perfect," Buddie said. He scraped the bushes along the window, and at the same time Jackie made the growling noises on the horn, then we heard the girls whispering...*that the bear was outside.*

Then Buddy almost gave it away when he laughed, but we managed to get away before we were heard, and when we got out of hearing range, we had the laugh of our lives. By now, we were all about to freeze, getting pretty sleepy, and couldn't wait to get into the warmth of our beds in the dorm.

As I lay in bed that night I got to thinking about all this bear stuff and how it got out of hand. The more I thought about it, the more I started to believe that Buddy and I had a problem with our bear story at the farm: Mike was a very good shot with a gun and I don't believe he would have missed a bear at that close of a range, and then too, he had been out with his friends and I remember Betty telling me that he often drinks too much cider. I convinced myself that *nobody saw a bear that night.*

The next day at school the classroom was all abuzz with the girls talking about what happened last night and how close they came to being attacked by a bear. Every now and then I would look at Jackie and Buddy, and they would be smiling. By the end of the day the teachers talked about something (none of them wanted to say the word 'bear') that had scared the girls.

I don't know how things got so far out of hand, but the way the girls were gabbing about it, I knew that by the end of the day it would spread all over the school. At recess time Jackie and all the other boys were involved in the "bear prank" went down to the creek to have a smoke, and it was crazy, because it appeared that they were still laughing. That's when I said to them all, "I think we have to make an oath; not to breathe a word to anyone about what we did last night."

Jackie said, "But it was just a joke."

"But, we all know the school won't look at it that way, especially the housemother, and I'm afraid that if she knows it was us, she might forbid us from ever going to the farm again."

They all agreed with me and we made an oath, never to say anything more about it. I guess the talk went on for a few more days and each of us were walking on eggshells, expecting someone would let it slip.

In a week or so, things got back to normal, and Thanksgiving was approaching. As usual we were back to decorating the classroom, and I was asked to draw pictures of turkeys, pilgrims, Indians, and all the other stuff went along with the holiday. I didn't mind doing those tasks for Mrs. Pierce because she was always extra nice to me. No sooner would I get started than the girls would watch me and ask what I was going to draw next.

One of the girls wanted to draw, so I gave her one of the pictures that I had drawn and told her to draw it. I thought it would keep her busy, and so she would leave me alone, but I was mistaken. She kept asking me questions about what to do, sitting sit next to me and talking about how she wanted to draw people. I told her to go on and draw them, and went on about what I was doing.

Later on she showed me the people she had drawn, and they weren't too bad. Not that they were good by any account but they did look like people, as crude as they were. I told her it wasn't a bad job and to keep on trying until she got better.

"I have a lot of other pictures that I have drawn," she said, "but I keep them locked up so the other girls won't take them. If you want to see them, I will bring them to school tomorrow."

"I would like to look at them," I said.

I thought that would get rid of her, and I could get some drawing done. It worked for a little while, but at suppertime I couldn't believe this girl came over and sat next to me.

"My name is Jolene," she said. "I already know your name is Pat."

After we ate Jackie and I went down to the creek for our usual smoke.

"Who was your new eating partner?" he asked with a sly grin. I was immediately on the defensive.

"She's said her name was Jolene and she's not my partner! She's the girl that bugged me all day about my drawing."

"Well if you asked me, I would say that she likes you."

"Honestly, she is kinda cute but I don't trust her. I don't know exactly why, but the way she acts, I can't help but think that she may be nasty," I said.

Jackie gave me that sarcastic laugh again.

"All the more the reason to look out for when she tries to kiss you!"

Buddy overheard Jackie's warning and wanted to know what we talked about.

"Our good buddy Pat really gets around," Jackie said. "He has another girlfriend."

All I needed was having Buddy spreading it all over the school.

"If you say anything about this to anyone," I warned him, "I'm going to kick your ass up between your shoulders."

"Look out Buddy!" Jackie said, and they both laughed.

The next day Mrs. Pierce told us it was only two days until Thanksgiving, and asked us if we were ready. Everybody said, "Yes!" I was especially ready for that was when we could eat to our hearts content, and believe me I was ready for that. It looked like my buddies all had the same idea for when the day came we all made ourselves sick from eating.

We had a long four day weekend and after we recuperated from stuffing our stomachs we spent most of our time sledding, and luckily none of us were injured. Monday when we returned to school, it was a lazy day and we had very little to do. Mrs. Pierce said it was too cold to go out for recess, and when Jolene walked over to my desk, I wasn't surprised at all, because I knew by now that she was going to be hard to shake. She said, "I've got some pictures to show you," and added, *"Don't let anybody else see them!"*

I didn't know what was so great about keeping them a secret, and as she walked back to her seat, I opened folder. At first it kinda looked like something that a five- year old would draw. They were stick-people but the odd thing was; she had added wieners to the drawings of boys.

I just knew there was something nasty about her, and it didn't take long for my suspicions to be confirmed. After I had looked at her drawings I glanced over at her and she was just sitting there smiling as if nothing was wrong.

That afternoon as I walked with Buddy back to the dorm I told him about her drawings, and he laughed.

"She likes you!"

"I don't know why nobody will take me serious about this girl," I said. "She's as nasty-minded as you are, and you'd better not make a big deal out of this!"

I didn't hear anymore about it so I guess he kept his mouth shut.

A couple of days later the house mother came and told me that I would be leaving to go home for Christmas, and that my brother, Jack would be coming over to help me pack. Then I would stay at the big boy's house tonight and would leave from there the next day.

Later on that evening I met all my buddies and told them, "I will be leaving tomorrow and I will see you guys when I get back. And Jack came over later and helped me pack the things that I was taking with me, and the next morning early, Jack, me, and eight other boys were driven to the train station in Charlottesville. At first it was exciting to go on the train ride, but it got boring real fast.

When we got to Miami my mother met us and later we went to get something to eat. Miami was hot, not cold like at school, and we weren't dressed for that. When we got to her house Jack and I changed into the lighter clothes that mom had bought for us the last time we were here.

One of the reasons that I wasn't too crazy about going home for the holidays was; there was very little to do. Mom would say, "I want you boys to stick close to the house...the big city can get quite dangerous, particularly when you don't know your way around."

In the afternoon while she was at work Jack and I would listen to the radio which wasn't too bad as we didn't have a radio at school since Crawford House burned down. In those days it most of the afternoon programs on the radio were for kids. We would listen to "Jack Armstrong the All-American Boy", "Sky King", and so many others.

Jack and I didn't know anybody in Miami as we had been there for a short time and the boys we had met last year had either moved away or we just couldn't locate them, so we did a lot of radio listening.

Christmas to us seemed just like any other holiday and we couldn't wait to get back to the school, which was now more like home to me. The day finally came to go back...now, I loved my mother but I had gotten used to the school and that's where I wanted to be.

When we got back to Charlottesville we had to wait for the car that was to take us back and I thought I was going to freeze my ass off. When it finally arrived I thought I would warm up, but to my dismay, there was no heater in the car and that turned out to be the coldest damn ride since Jack and I stood up in the back of that pickup the year before.

It was late that night and they had me stay in the big boy's house, and the next morning I went back to the dormitory and was glad to be back with my friends. Buddy and Eddie were there but Harold, Jackie, and Earl hadn't gotten back yet.

The next day after breakfast we went down to the creek, and there was still a little snow on the ground and quite cold. We started discussing what we had done on our vacations, and we were all glad to see our families but had been anxious to get back. I asked, "Has anyone seen Jackie?"

Eddie said, "We haven't seen him yet, but he may still be over at the big boy's house.

The days went by and still there was no sign of Jackie and when I saw Buddy I said to him, "You know, it's been two weeks since we've all gotten back, and I'm worried that Jackie might not be returning to the school."

Buddy said, "Yeah, I think we all miss him. Things are a lot more fun when we're all together, but I still think he'll show up."

With the cold weather a lot of the lower trees had no leaves, and from where we stood you could see for miles. Buddy said, "There are farms we can see now we couldn't when the trees are full of leaves."

I said, "Yeah, maybe we can find them this summer, and maybe even spend the night." "And who knows, even find another swimming hole," said Buddy.

"Damn, Buddy, don't you ever think of anything else?"

"Well there are creeks over there too, and we might as well take advantage of them," he said.

We were over in the pasture just fooling around and we started throwing dried cow piles, as there was nothing else to do. I thought I heard someone yell and Eddie said, "Look over there at the top of that hill."

It was quite a ways off and we couldn't make out who it was, then we heard another yell, louder this time, and we heard; "Hey, you assholes!"

I looked at Earl and Buddy and said, "Who the hill is calling us assholes?"

Eddie said, "I think it's Jackie!"

And as he got closer...sure enough, it was him. I couldn't wait to ask him where he'd been these two weeks, and when he got here I said to Buddy, "Do you believe it...here's an asshole calling us assholes. Jackie laughed and asked, "What's going on?"

I said, "We're just out here throwing cow piles because with you gone we can't find any trouble to get into, but now you're back, and by-the-way, where in the hell have you been?"

"I went to see my uncle in Washington."

I looked at him and said, "Don't tell me that you ran away again?"

"he laughed and said, "No, I learned my lesson on that...he came and picked me up and we had a good time."

"Weren't you still mad at him for what he did to us?" I asked.

"Yeah, at first, but he explained that he was trying to teach us a lesson...and he was so good to me that all that stuff was forgotten."

After supper that night we all sat around and talked more about vacations, and some of the things we were going to do when the weather got a little better.

The next morning, at breakfast we had fun pointing out which kids came back, and the new kids were joining the school. Jackie pointed out some of the girls that came back, and I looked for the one that had bugged me so much about my art. I didn't see her, but that didn't mean that she wasn't there.

I thought about the stupid nasty pictures that she drew and decided that I would draw some pictures that would make her leave me alone or show her that I could be just as bad as she was.

After breakfast we had the whole day to roam around the mountain, and of course we went down by the creek and everywhere we went the creek went there too. It was too cold to go swimming but there were a lot of other things we could do, such as; looking for arrowheads, exploring old cabins, or just hiking around and looking at the scenery. As we got near the swimming hole I could see Buddy's eyes light up, but it was definitely too cold, even for him or Harold.

Eddie wanted to build a bridge across the creek. "What in the hell do you want to do that for?" I asked, and added, "Jesus Christ, we can almost jump across it!"

"Well, I thought it would give us something to do."

"It would give us something to do, all right, but I don't want to work…I want to have fun," I said.

"Why don't we go up in the mountain and find a big boulder and roll it down the hill?" Jackie asked.

That got our attention so we started up and after awhile we found a boulder that was just the right size and we started digging the dirt out from the front edge. There was a cluster of small trees about halfway down the hill, and we wanted to see if the boulder would go through them.

We started to dig.

"This reminds me of the time last year when we dug around that boulder went the wrong way, when Daniel got that brilliant idea to damn up the creek," Buddy said.

"Was it worth it?" I asked.

"Hell no, all we did was dig for a month and got nothing for it!"

The boulder started to move.

"Lookout!!" Jackie shouted. We all jumped back as the boulder started out real slow, and then it started to pick up speed. By the time it got to that small clump of trees, it flattened everything in its path and in the process it started other rocks to slide down the hill. We watched because it tore down the hill and cut a path all the way to the bottom.

"I have an idea," I said when it stopped. "If it snows again we can use this for our sled ride."

I guess it took most of the day doing all that digging for less than a minute of fun, but we all agreed it was worth it.

At supper that night all the girls were in their catty mode. We couldn't tell what they were saying because they all talked at once. After supper I saw Buddy talking to one of them and later I asked him what the clamor was all about.

"They wanted to know when we were going on our next hike," he said.

"I hope you didn't tell them anything!" I said.

"No I wouldn't tell them what we do and besides, we haven't planned any hikes."

"Yes, you're right, Buddy, I guess I get a little jumpy when I think about them girls following us."

On the way back to the dormitory it started to rain, and I thought, boy, here we go again, it's either too cold or it's snowing and now the rain. Between the rain and the mud we're going to be stuck in the house for another week. And boy, did it rain. I could hear it pounding on the roof when I went to sleep and when I awoke. As we were putting on our rain slicks to go to breakfast the rain turned to sleet, and just to walk to Mayo Hall was a major chore, as we were slipping and sliding all over the place.

We watched as the girls were trying to get there, and they had one hell of a time, sometimes falling down as soon as they got up.

Naturally we were laughing at them, and we saw enough bloomers and underpants to last a lifetime. There were a few of the girls that thought it was funny but for the most part they thought we were nasty little bastards for watching them, particularly without helping, but that didn't stop us from looking. At breakfast they stuck their tongues out at us but that just made us laugh more.

The following day was a school-day and the girls were still pissed at us. I tried to concentrate on a drawing for Mrs. Pierce, and Jackie who was killing time as usual, kept tapping me on the shoulder. I finally turned around.

"Take a look at the two girls in the back, by the window," Jackie whispered.

I looked back and the two of them sat with their legs wide open, showing us their bloomers, and you could tell that they didn't care if we got an eye full for they were smiling as we looked.

"Now that's a couple of little bitches!" I said.

"Do you know who they are?" Jackie asked.

"No, but they sure like to show us their bloomers."

"I wonder what else they'd like to show us," he said.

"I don't know about the other one but one of the girls knows Sally and she was one of the girls that came down to the creek the time you and Jackie played that trick on us," Buddy said later at recess.

"Buddy, we didn't play a trick on you guys! You just happened to be naked when the girls came by," I said. "And besides we think that you liked it."

"How can you say that? You know I didn't!"

"Buddy, that water was so cold that your dally-whacker was hiding up in your belly," I said.

Jackie busted out laughing and I did too.

Buddy tried to be philosophical about it.

"Well, if they've never seen one, then they didn't know what they were looking at, and if they've seen one before then they shouldn't be embarrassed."

"I don't think they saw one," Jackie said, and I busted out laughing.

The bell rang and we had to get back to class. I was tired and couldn't wait for class to be over. The sleet was still there but started to melt, and that made it even worse. Now we would get mud on our shoes every time we went outside, and the housemother would always make us clean up our muddy tracks, so rather than go outside, I just stayed in the house and got some drawing done.

When we were at Crawford House there was the front room where we could play games, color, or just sit around and shoot the bull, but here we only had the dormitory. Sometimes the housemother would unlock one of the classrooms downstairs and let us go in there but she would stay with us, which wasn't so good becuase for we couldn't cuss, which normally we all did.

After the terrible weather had us cooped up for three or four days, at noontime, the housemother came into the dorm.

"The cook is bringing sandwiches for you boys and I'll do the entertaining. I'm going to read a story to help pass the time."

"Ma'am?" Buddy asked, "You tell such good stories. Would you tell us one?"

"Okay, who wants me to tell a story?" she asked. We all raised our hands.

She started out by saying that her grandfather fought in the civil war and he would tell her about how fierce the battles were. Then Jackie raised his hand.

"Sorry to interrupt you ma'am, but you told us that before."

"I don't think so," she said.

"Tell us a spooky story," I said. Everyone started saying, "Please."

"A spooky one it will be, then," she said, relenting.

"I don't know if this is spooky enough for you guys," she said, "but here goes...there was a time when I was a girl when a friend of my mother's had passed away, and about a week later she took me to church. It was a warm summer night and the parents allowed us kids to play outside, in the churchyard. Behind the church was an old graveyard, and as we were playing hide-and-go-seek, the only place to hide was among the tombstones. The light from the stained windows of the church was just bright enough to spread an eerie glow over the graveyard."

"Now, I had gone to hide behind this old above ground vault, and one of the other girls had come along with me, and as we were squatting down to hide, the girl said, "There's an older woman hiding behind one of the tombstones behind us."

"When I turned to look I didn't see anybody, then I heard somebody talking and the girl was over at the other tombstone, and heard the old woman say that she was cold. Now, I didn't see anybody, but I did hear them talking so I was thinking, It's probably just too dark to see her."

"After we were through with our game and we went inside the girl said, "It's so warm that I don't see how that old lady could have been cold."

"As we were leaving we saw a picture of an old lady in the back of the church, and I asked my mother who it was and she told me it is my friend that had passed away last week. It was a few days later that the girl told me, "That was the picture of the old lady that I saw in the graveyard."

"Now, I tried to tell her it couldn't be, as that woman was dead, but she insisted that she saw her."

"I don't know about you boys, but that was pretty spooky for me," she said.

I looked at Jackie and he was kinda shaking his head.

"I don't believe all that crap! Do you?"

"I don't know but it sure makes me wonder," I said.

Buddy was not to be outdone.

"Now, there were times when I've seen things like that."

"Come on Buddy," I said, "you see all sorts of things! I remember one time when we were out catching frogs and you swore that you saw something that was ten feet tall watching us, that nearly scared the shit out of us. Bullshit! You've got an imagination that runs wild, and do you remember the night that you went to the outhouse and you told us that something was rocking it? And the next day, when we went to look, you swore it had moved. Well, moved, my ass! That was nothing but bullshit!"

The next day the rain had stopped and the sun was shining bright, and I for one was hoping that winter was finally over. And I said to Buddy and Harold, "I don't think it will be too long until you two can go swimming again," and that made their eyes light up.

A week or so later we saw Sally at school and we asked her how Mike and Betty were doing.

"They made it through the winter storms just fine, for the most part, but one night the heavy snow and high wind caused his outdoor shower contraption to come tumbling down, out of the tree and the tub broke."

"What are they going to do for a shower now?" I asked.

"Aw he's building a new one."

"I think the weather is warm enough to visit the farm," I said to Jackie. "I want to see how Mike is building the new shower."

Saturday morning we left for the farm and didn't get there until noon. When we got there Mike was down at the barn, making all kinds of racket, and as we walked in the barn, we saw that Mike had this old galvanized metal bathtub turned upside down and he was using a hammer and a large nail to punch holes in one end of the tub.

Mike turned the tub over and put a piece of leather in the tub to cover the holes that he had just punched out. I asked him, "What can we do to help?"

Mike said, "I had to build a new platform as the old one broke, and I will probably need some help hoisting this new tub upon the platform."

Then Mike got what he called a block and tackle, and tied one end to a tree branch, several feet above his platform and the other end to criss-cross ropes that he had tied around his tub. Mike went up on the ladder and we pulled on the rope that was threaded through the block and tackle. When it got up to the right height Mike pushed it in place and as pretty as you please, his shower tub was in place.

As we stood on the ground and marveled at what we had done, Jackie asked, "How are you going to get water up to the tub?"

Then Jackie said to me, "That seems like a lot of work just to take a shower."

As Mike was untying his ropes and throwing them down, Betty walked out, looking at Mike's new handiwork.

"It looks nice honey, but will it work?"

"I don't know yet," he said, "but we'll find out as soon as we can get some water up in it."

"So if you boys want to give me a hand...I'll stand on the ladder and if you'll hand me a few buckets I'll dump them in the tub."

We carried him about five or six buckets, then Mike said, "Stand back!" and pulled on a rope that he had tied to the leather piece, and the water came down just like a shower. When he released it the water stopped. He tried it a couple more times.

"That's a job well done! I can't wait for the weather to get warmer to try this baby out."

"I might try it out too," Betty said.

We had spent the whole day helping Mike and then we had to get back. On the way back, Jackie remarked that Mike sure was smart, and I said, "I agree with you but if you mean book learning, I don't think he had much of that because he didn't spend much time in school, but if he sets his mind to do something, he always figures it out. Even Betty never had much schooling, and can't read or write."

"You're joking," Jackie said.

"No, I'm not, but they know how to run their farm pretty darn well, even if they had to learn the hard way.

It was several weeks later and the trees all had put on their leaves, the weather had started to warm up nicely, and we had started to do the fun things we had been looking forward to. The first weekend we had a chance, we made arrangements to go and see Betty and Mike. Mike had bought a bull and the first thing that he wanted to do, when we got there, was to show it off. It was black and just looking at it scared the hell out of us. Mike said, "Don't be afraid, he's tame, and wouldn't hurt a fly."

I said, "I ain't no damn fly!"

Mike just laughed.

"Come on you guys and pet him." I did but you can be sure I was careful.

"Are you boys going to spend the night?" Mike asked.

"We were planning to but I don't know about that bull being in the barn with us."

"You boys worry too much. You will definitely be alright,"

I told Mike and Betty we were going for a hike and would be back later, so we spent the day wandering around the woods then Buddy and Harold went to the swimming hole and Jackie and I looked for arrowheads. This time we found a couple of real beauties.

"Mrs. Pierce would be proud to have these," I said to Jackie.

Before we headed back to the farm we stopped by and got Buddy and Harold, they had been in the water for quite a while and were about to freeze by the time we got there. This was one time that they were glad to see us.

Jackie showed them the arrowheads we had found. Buddy wanted to go and find some, but it was getting late and we had to get back to the farm. On the way back we stopped to have a cigarette break

"The water in the creek was cold but we were still able to get all the trash out from the bottom, and it was deeper now," Buddy said.

"I'd like to try out Mike's new shower when we get back but I wonder how warm the water is," Jackie said.

"Bullshit!" I said. "I'm not going to haul buckets up to that damn tub just for you to try out a shower. Mike said if we use it we have to leave the tub full of water for the next one."

After we got back to the farm Mike said the he was going to try out his new shower, so we sat around in the barn until he was finished.

"There's still some water left in the tub if someone wants to use it," he said.

And in no time flat, Jackie was getting undressed and was in the shower. Mike started putting on his clothes and after four years of knowing him, this was the first time that I had seen him naked. He arms, neck, and face were tanned, but the rest of his body was as white as could be.

After Jackie had finished his shower he announced that the tub was empty, and that he was about to freeze to death.

"Come on you guys," Mike said, "let's fill her up again." We spent the next half hour or so carrying buckets of water and handing them up to Mike to pour in the tub. Meanwhile Betty came down to milk the cow and asked if we liked the shower.

"Mike and Jackie were the only ones to use it," I said.

"Tomorrow I'm going to try it out," she said. "I'm going to wait until the sun heats up the water. I can do without getting frozen." She finished milking the cow. "Come on up to the house, in about an hour, and get something to eat."

Then I noticed that Buddy had walked over to Mike's new bull and started to pet it on the head, and I was surprised that the bull didn't even move. I was glad about that because I had still been worried about sleeping in the same barn with that animal.

"I guess it's been about an hour. Let's go on up to the house," Jackie said.

Betty had made up some biscuits, sausage, and gravy…now I have to say; to this day I have not tasted biscuits and gravy to match hers.

"How do you do it?" I asked.

"Do what?"

"Make things taste so good."

"Just love, Pat. Just love."

Afterwards we had a smoke with Mike while she put the kids to bed.

That night, in the barn, we had a lot to talk about; the new shower, Mike's new bull, what we were doing tomorrow, and then again back to the bull. It was hard to go to sleep; hearing it snort and move around. When I finally dozed off it wasn't long before I felt the warm breath of something standing over me and since it was over my head I was about to go into a full blown panic.

Jackie wasn't too far from me and I tried to awaken him, but to no avail, then Buddy crawled over and said that the bull was out of its stall, and that he would take him back. Then Jackie woke up.

"What the hell is going on?"

At that point I was still scared shitless.

"That damn bull thought I was his breakfast," I said. "I'm going up to the loft and maybe I can get some sleep!" Everyone laughed and thought it was funny but me.

The next morning I heard Betty milking the cow and when I looked down through the cracks in the loft, I saw she had on her nightdress and I thought I might as well get up and help feed the animals. It was still dark but I could make out how to climb down the ladder.

"Why are you up in the loft?" Betty asked me.

"Mike's bull got out of his stall last night, and after that I didn't trust him."

She laughed.

"he wouldn't hurt you."

"Just the same, I felt better up in the loft."

After Betty was done milking she went to put the cow back in its stall, and when she came back, the lantern was behind her and I could see all of her through that thin nightdress, and I thought, I bet Jackie would like to see that!

The day was warm day but not quite warm nough to go swimming, except for Buddy and Harold, who headed over to the creek. Jackie and I decided just to wander around the woods, but before we left the farm Betty said that she was going to take a shower, and wanted to know if the tub was full. I told her it was and we left. As we walked along I told Jackie about Betty and the show that she put on with the lantern.

"Why didn't you wake me up?" he asked.

"It would have been too late," I said. "It was there one minute and the next minute it was gone. Besides Betty said that later on today she was going to take a shower."

Jackie was a tad confused.

"What does that mean?"

"I was thinking, if we go up in the woods behind the house we will be able to watch her."

"But, there's that tarp around the shower," Jackie said.

"That only goes around half of it," I said. "The half that's open faces the woods. If we stay just inside of the tree line we will be able to see her."

"How do you know that?" he asked.

I had never talked about it, but since me and Jackie was in this little adventure together I felt that he wouldn't blab it around.

"Two years ago," I said, "Mike had put a tub in the tree for a shower, very similar to the one now. The one that last winter's storm tore down. Anyway, I was out hiking in this same area and accidently came upon what I thought was Betty taking a shower, but I was so far away that I couldn't be sure, and later I found out it was Doris."

"Why, you little devil, why didn't you ever tell me?"

"Actually, I didn't think of it until this thing came up about the shower, and it really wasn't a big deal, I was so far away that I couldn't even see any hair down below."

Jackie and I wandered around for awhile and ended up behind the barn, and I guess we were about fifty yards from the shower area. We were at least twice as close as before and could see the barn, house, and shower plainly.

"I hope we're not too close so that she will see us," I said to him.

"I wouldn't worry about that. Just don't move around and give her a reason to look this way."

So we lay real still in the grass and waited, and before long Betty came out and went to the barn. A few minutes later she came out of the barn with just a towel wrapped around her and before she got under the shower she looked all around, unwrapped the towel and hung it on a tree limb. We watched with wide-eyed anticipation as she stepped under the tub, pulled the rope to release the water, and I don't believe either one of us said a word until she had dried off, re-wrapped the towel, and was safely back in the barn.

"Well, did you see some hair that time?" he asked right off the bat.

"Oh my God, *did I!*"

We were still not too talkative as we went to find Buddy and Harold.

"I feel a little funny about what we did," I said finally.

"Me too," Jackie said. "You know, it's not like we walked in on her. We were far enough away that anybody could have walked by and seen her. It was better we *saw her* than some stranger."

I wasn't completely convinced with Jackie's reasoning but it did take some of the guilt feelings away. Finally we got to the creek.

"Let's not tell Buddy and Harold about what we did," I said, and he agreed.

They both said that they were about to freeze and were ready to head back to the farm and I said we had been at the farm all day, so I quietly told Jackie that I wasn't crazy about seeing Betty right now and he said me neither.

"Why don't you guys go back to the farm and me," Jackie told them. "Pat will be waiting right here at the creek until you get back. We might even go swimming."

"Do you think that Betty saw us?" he asked me.

"I don't think so but, at least I hope she didn't," I said. "The next time we go to the farm it will be hard to look her in the face, no matter if she saw us or not."

"Yeah, you can say that again!" he said.

Jackie and I fooled around, looking for arrowheads along the creek banks, and even got in the water for awhile, and before long we saw Buddy and Harold coming on the trail from the farm, and the four of us headed back to the school.

"Betty asked me where you two were," Buddy said.

I looked at Jackie, who was slowly shaking his head. I knew that he was thinking the same thing that I was. When we got back and had supper Jackie and I went off by ourselves to have a smoke.

"We need to talk to Buddy or Harold," Jackie said on the way to the creek. "Let's see what Betty meant when she asked where we were."

"You know, I don't see how that will do any good," I said. "Besides, we don't want them to know what this is all about, and one of them is as bad as the other…they will make a big deal out of it, and before you know it, it will be all over the school."

"I guess you're right, we'll just have to wait until we can get back to the farm."

It was a couple of weeks before we had a chance go back to visit Betty and I didn't want Buddy and Harold to go with us so, we had to figure out how to get away without them, then Jackie suggested we just try and discourage them.

"Since we can't spend the night," I told Buddy, "we've decided to just go and look for arrowheads, and it wouldn't make any sense going all the way to the farm, since it would take up most of our time."

Buddy responded exactly as planned.

"You know, I think me and Harold will just spend the day at the swimming hole. You never know whose going to walk by."

"I'm a little reluctant to visit Betty right now, how about you?" I said to Jackie after they left.

"Me too."

After we roamed around the mountain side, looking for arrowheads, most of the day we headed over to the swimming hole to check on Buddy and Harold, and to our surprise, they weren't there. So, we headed back to the school, and the two of them didn't make it back until just before suppertime.

It was after supper when we all went down to the creek.

"We went to see Mike and Betty today," Buddy said. "Betty asked about you two and wanted to know why you didn't come with us."

"Why didn't you tell her we were looking for arrowheads?"

"I did, but Betty said that she wanted to see you guys."

"Betty must have seen us," Jackie said later that night. "If she did there's nothing we can do about it. Let's just get some sleep and worry about it tomorrow."

"I guess you're right," I said. "Let's just wait and see...you know, she squats and pees right in front of us, so what's the big deal?"

A few days later all of us were down at the creek looking for frog eggs so we might determine the best place to look for frogs, and our search paid off as we found some side pools were full of eggs and tadpoles. We all agreed that Friday night would be the time to go frogging, since we hadn't gone this summer. Saturday was a couple days away, the weather was nice and warm, and we could hardly wait for the weekend. We sat on the bank and we all lit up a smoke.

"You know, we haven't seen Sally in quite awhile," Buddy said.

"That's probably a good thing," I said. "We really don't need her around, we get into enough trouble all by ourselves."

The next day was Friday. We didn't have too much to do in class: it was hot outside and not much better inside. The girls were even quieter except for a few whispers and a giggle now and then. One of the girls had fallen asleep and had slumped down in her chair. Buddy tapped my shoulder.

"Look at that girl back by the window!"

When I did I saw that her dress was hiked up to her waist and her panties were showing. I turned around to Buddy.

"Who cares?"

After school when we all went down to the creek, we planned our frogging trip that night. We were a little disappointed that Earl and Harold both had bad colds and wouldn't be able to go with us. That meant there would only be the four of us, and no one to carry the frogs.

After we got back to the dormitory we got everything we need-ed to go and headed over to the creek. It was still daylight when we got there, so we had to wait awhile until it got dark.

Meanwhile, Buddy was limping around and looked like he was about to die. I asked him what happened, hating to lose another frogger.

"I cut my foot on a sharp rock!" That let Buddy out.

It was up to me to take Buddy's place, so I stepped into the water.

"Shit, this is colder than a witch's tit," I said. Then Jackie got in.

"God damn, how the hell can Buddy stand this cold water?" he asked.

Buddy started laughing.

"That's not cold!"

That kinda riled Jackie.

"Shut up you little bastard or I'll throw you in, hurt foot and all!"

After awhile we got used to the cold water, and we started to catch a few frogs then we decided it was time for a break, and we got out and sat on the bank. We only had six or eight frogs, and that wasn't enough. I looked at Jackie.

"It looks like we're going to have to get back in if we're going to get enough to give to Mike."

"Well, let's do it then," he said.

I got back in the water and it was even colder than before. After fifteen minutes or so, Eddie said that he would get in, and let one of us get out, and Jackie jumped out before even I had a chance to think about it. Eddie had only been in the water about twenty minutes when he stumped his toe and when he reached down to grab his foot he fell into a big boulder and hit his elbow. I turned to Jackie.

"Come on and get back in!"

"Why in the hell did I even get out?" he said.

Before long we had accumulated quite a few frogs and decided to take a break, and as we were lying on the bank having a smoke.

"What was that?" Buddy asked. A few seconds passed. "What was that? I heard a noise!"

"Okay, Buddy, don't start that shit again!" I said.

"But I did hear a noise…there it is again!"

"I didn't hear anything," I said. "What did it sound like?"

Buddy was getting shook up at this point. He stood up.

"I don't know what it sounded like, but I think we should get out of here and start back! We have enough frogs and my foot hurts."

"You know, Buddy, the next thing that you're going to say is there's a bear close by."

That remark got Jackie's attention.

"Be real quiet and listen," he said. "I think I might have heard something, but I'm not sure."

Buddy looked like he was ready to run at any moment.

"That bear that Mike shot at that night just might have come back," he said.

At this point, Buddy's scaredy-cat ways got under my skin.

"If you start to run you'd better not drop those damn frogs," I said to him. "Remember you have a sore foot so shut up about that God-damned bear or we will run off and leave you!"

"I was just saying."

"Well, don't say it!"

All of this bear talk had frightened Eddie, for he looked in every direction as we started on the trail back. It was pretty dark by now and our flashlights had gotten dim, and it was hard to make any time walking. Before long we all heard something like someone was following us, and all of a sudden it didn't make any difference whether it was dark or not…we ran.

After we got close to the school we stopped and listened, and none of us heard anything. We were all tired and out of breath so we took a break. We had just sat down and were going to light up, when we heard the bushes, about twenty feet from us start to move. At first we were frozen with fear, since it just about scared the shit out of all of us. All we could see was this large animal, and with our dim flashlights it made it appear even larger.

"Hey guys, it's Mike's bull," Buddy said. He went over to it. The bull just stood there while he petted it on the head. I didn't like that damn bull and somehow I had a feeling it didn't like me, and I sure the hell didn't trust him, but it liked Buddy.

"You know that you have to take the bull back to Mike," Jackie said to him.

"Well, let's get started," Buddy said.

"What the hell, Buddy, are you nuts, we're not going back there in the dark!" I said to him.

"Yeah, Buddy, Pat's right," Jackie said. "Let's tie him up at the school and take him back in the morning."

The next day being Sunday, we had to wait until after church to return the bull to Mike, and we still had a bunch of frogs to clean.

"Since you get along with the bull so well," I told Buddy, "there's no question that you have to take it back."

Buddy was a little reluctant.

"I don't mind taking him back, but I'm still not so sure that a bear isn't out there."

"Jesus Christ, Buddy," Jackie said. "If Pat will walk along and hold your hand then me and Eddie will take care of cleaning the frog legs!"

I agreed and we were off. When we got to the farm, Mike was overjoyed to see us.

"How did you guys find him?"

"We didn't find him, he found us!" I said.

Mike got a big laugh when we told him how we thought it was a bear, and it nearly scared the shit out of us. He secured him back in its stall.

"Why don't you boys come into the house and have a glass of buttermilk?" he said.

Now I didn't care too much for buttermilk but I took a few swallows anyway, and noticed Betty out in the back yard, hanging out clothes. SoI walked out to say hi, and she asked me where Jackie was. I told her about us frogging last night, and that he and Eddie were cleaning them, but would be here later to give her and Mike some of them.

We hung around the farm for an hour or so, helping Mike reinforce the bull's stall, when we saw Jackie and Eddie walk up. Jackie handed Mike a bag full of frog legs.

"We might have gotten more but that bull of yours kinda put a stop to things."

"Sorry about the bull," he said, "but I know I'll enjoy the frog legs even more since you guys went to all the trouble."

"No trouble," I said, "but we have to get back to the school, because we need to be there by suppertime."

On the way back Jackie had something funny to say.

"You know, I think Betty didn't see us watching her, at least she didn't say anything."

"Well, I hope you're right, but I don't think she would say anything anyway, and damn, Jackie, I hate waiting around for something bad to happen."

The next day at school Buddy was blowing spitballs at the girls. Since he was doing it on the sly so they didn't know who was doing it, and Jackie and I caught the blame. Buddy just sat there and smiled when Mrs. Pierce started reprimanding us. We didn't rat on Buddy but when we went down to the creek at recess, I told him that he would be sorry and we weren't going to forget what he just did.

Buddy just smiled.

"I was just getting even with you guys for all the dirty tricks that you played on me and Harold."

"It looks like we are going to have to think of something real good to get back at Buddy," I told Jackie. "You can bet your last marble it will be something good."

The rest of the day, in class, Jackie and I would just look at Buddy and whisper like we were planning something. We would smile at him and turn away. That got to him. Buddy was a little bit paranoid anyway and it didn't take too much to get his imagination worked up.

After school Jackie and I went off and left all the other guys.

"Buddy is probably worrying about what we might be up to," Jackie said. "It won't be long before he comes to find us."

"You're right," I said. "He's a worry wart, anyway and he won't trust anything we do now, and that's probably the best way to get even with him; just let him wonder."

I looked behind us. There was Buddy, walking slowly, acting like he looked for arrowheads.

From that day on, no matter what we did, Buddy thought we were conniving some sort of a trick to get even with him. When we went by the swimming hole he wouldn't go in with us there, but would wait for us to leave. Before long we got to thinking that he had gone through enough as swimming was his favorite past time.

Girls Like to Swim Too

With the weather getting hot, we ran out of things to do. Betty and
Mike's farm was about a mile from the school. I don't think we had
gone farther than that, which meant there was a lot of the countryside we hadn't seen. One day I asked the guys if they wanted
to go on a hike past that area. They all wanted to give it a try. We
planned to go to the farm, spend the night there, and get an early
start to go far up in the mountains. We would leave just enough
time to get back to the school before suppertime.

On Friday we had gotten permission to spend the night at Mike
and Betty's farm. The group of us - Jackie, Buddy, Harold, Eddie,
Earl, and I - set out right after supper. We got to the farm just as it
got dark. We helped feed the animals that evening and turned in
as early as we could. The next morning I was awakened early when
Betty came into the barn to do the milking. It was still dark.

"What are you doing up so early?" she asked me.

"We're all taking a long hike up in the mountains, to areas we
haven't been before."

"Good luck on that," she said. "Be careful that you don't get
lost. If you guys go far enough you might run into Doris."

I walked outside to have a smoke and Betty came out carrying
her pail of milk, and I offered to carry it into the house. She asked
me to check and see if the tub was full of water because I was
standing on the small apple crate with my hand reaching down to
the water.

"Since you guys are heading up in the mountains, I thought it
would be a good time to take a shower," she said.

I just about fell off the apple crate. What in the hell did she
mean by that? *She's going to take a shower because we're going up in the
mountains?* Maybe she didn't mean it the way it sounded but then
I thought; she did say it in a strange way. I looked at her and she
was smiling.

When the other boys got up it was almost daylight, so they wanted to get started. After we had walked for about an hour or so the sun came out. As it started to warm up we reached the tree line, so we were all ready for a break. I pulled Jackie over to the side and told him what Betty had said to me earlier.

"Well if she did see us, I don't think we should say anything in front of the other guys," he said.

It was getting hot now so we took off our shirts before we started off again. We were getting a little hungry so we stopped and ate some apples, then we found a big cherry tree and ate our fill. We were seeing things we had not seen before. When we came upon a small waterfall that fell into a large pool, we couldn't wait to jump in and cool off.

Between the orchard, taking smoke breaks, and enjoying the pool we took a lot more time than we had planned.

"Hey guys," Jackie said, "I think it's about time we get back. Let's take a different way back. I think it's shorter and we may see some new stuff."

I didn't pay a whole lot of attention to the way we were going until I looked down the mountain. We were behind Betty's farm. I saw the tree we stood behind while we had watched Betty take a shower. That's when I figured out that Jackie knew where he was going all along. I turned to him.

"Do you really want to do this? You know that the other guys will tell everybody about it, and before long it will be all over school!"

"I don't think that they will spill the beans because they would all be in trouble too," he said.

"But you know Buddy," I said, "There's no way that he's going to keep his mouth shut!"

So, we just sat there, had a smoke, and kept an eye on what was happening below.

"I see Mike and Betty's farm," Eddie said. "Let's go and visit them before we go back."

"Wait, let's have another smoke," Jackie said.

Before long we saw Betty come out of the house and head to the barn. She was in there longer that I expected, but then we saw her come out of the back and start feeding the chickens.

"I think we should go on down," I said, so we walked down.

"Did you guys run across Doris?" she asked us.

"No, we didn't run across her, but we didn't go near as far as we had planned," I said. "We found a waterfall and a great swimming hole, and we spent most of our time there."

"I can understand that," she said. "It was a great day for a shower, but I used up all the water. I wonder if you and your friends would fill the tub again?"

"Sure!" I said. We all pitched in and had it filled in no time.

She gave us each a glass of milk and some freshly baked cookies, and we started the trek back to school.

We barely made it back in time for inspection before supper. The way the housemother looked at us I knew we had cut it close. Most of us made it through, but Earl had to go back and rewash. After supper Jackie and I walked down to the creek.

"I wonder why Betty didn't take a shower when we were up in the hills, like we thought she was going to," I said.

"I've been thinking about that...and if we could see her, don't you think that she could see us?"

"I suppose so."

"Do you think that she would strip down naked in front of all six of us?"

"You've got a good point. I guess if we ever want to see her naked again, we'll just have to sneak off by ourselves."

"I don't even know if that will work anymore...now that she's caught on to us," Jackie said.

We were all pretty bored with school because we had gotten a taste of some of the things we could find if we hiked farther away from the school like we did last Saturday. We wondered what we might have seen if we hadn't stopped at the waterfall.

Buddy wanted to go the other way next week. We planned to go to the store, get our cigarettes and candy, and continue past that area to see what lie ahead. When we left early it was just Buddy, Eddie, Jackie, and me.

We followed the dirt road past the store for about a mile and then cut off, up in the woods. The woods were thick and it was tough going. Just when we were about to turn back Eddie saw a cave, so we couldn't pass up the chance to explore it. There were quite a few small caves in the area around the school, but it figured to be a big one, because we could hear a pretty good echo through the opening.

We could walk in for the first ten feet but then it narrowed down. We had to duck, but it went way back. Buddy saw some bones.

"Maybe a bear has been living here," he said.

"Buddy, don't start that shit again!" I said.

"Well, there could be a bear back there. Why don't you crawl back there and see?"

"That'll be the God-damned day when I do some shit like that!" Jackie said.

And as it turned out; our little group produced no volunteers to check out the back of the cave.

"You see what your damn bear talk caused," I said to Buddy. "Now everyone is scared shitless to go in the cave."

Then Buddy actually said something that made sense.

"Why don't we come back later when we have flashlights."

Of course we never did go back while I was at the school, but it gave us a good reason to walk away without feeling guilty about it.

"I'm getting a little tired of just sitting around here doing nothing," I said. "Why don't we head down to that small creek we crossed coming up here."

Everyone agreed so we walked down to the small creek and started looking for frog eggs. When I started to put my foot in the stream a large snake slid off the bank and into the water. It must have been at least five feet long. A snake that large deserved our full attention; there was no way we could just walk away without at least trying to catch it. Buddy and Eddie went on one side of the creek and Jackie and I went on the other. As we closed in on it, it backed off and started to hiss at us. We knew we had made it mad so we had to be extra careful. Jackie got its attention while I got behind it. When I put a stick near its head it struck at it and then recoiled back into a defensive position, that's when I very carefully came up from behind and grabbed the back of its head. It quickly coiled itself around my arm and stayed that way then we took it out onto dry land to figure out what we had caught. It was a water moccasin, poisonous but not to the extent that you would die from the bite. At one time or other we had all been bitten by one, but not be one this big.

We were only about a half a mile from the country store.

"I'll run over to the store and get a sack to put him in," Buddy said.

When Buddy returned we put the snake in the bag to make it easier and safer to carry. As we unwrapped it from my arm, I marveled at its beauty: it was a shiny solid black with yellow eyes. I thought it was too pretty to hurt anyone. When we caught something like this it was a big thing to us. We couldn't wait to get back to the dormitory to measure its length and do a little bragging to the other boys.

We messed around the creek for the rest of the day. When we got back to the school Eddie got a yardstick and we went about measuring it, which wasn't a very easy task. There was no way we would stick our hand in to get the snake, so we had to let it out and catch it again, but we knew how to do that. When we got it where we could handle it we stretched it out, to six feet and three inches long.

"What are we going to do with this monster?" Eddie asked.

"I dunno, I guess we'll just turn him loose," I said, "but before we do, maybe we could find a way to scare the hell out of the girls."

Jackie's face lit up.

"Pat, you're always thinking. Let's get them when they pass the tool shed on their way to eat and show them how long it is."

"I bet when they see this baby, I bet they will yell and scream their little asses off," Buddy said.

"You all know we will catch hell for this," I said, "but it'll definitely be worth it!"

"Maybe we should put something on its mouth to keep it shut," Eddie said.

"I know just the thing!" Buddy said. He rushed off and came back with a roll of black friction tape.

"God-damn, Buddy, I knew you were good for something," Jackie said. We wrapped the tape good and tight around the snake's mouth.

"You guys know we got it done just in time," Eddie said. "I see a group of girls coming down the walk now."

We stayed behind the shed until the girls were right in front of us. Jackie jumped out with with the snake in his hands, and the rest of us right behind. It was like a bomb went off. The girls ran in all directions screaming, and some were even crying.

We laughed our asses off.

"Damn! This worked even better than I thought!" Buddy said.

"Yeah it sure worked alright," Jackie said. "I see Mrs. Todd and Miss Flintmyer heading this way and they don't think it's funny at all."

"Oh my God," I said, "When did teachers start walking with the girls?"

We all took off running but it didn't do any good. As soon as we walked into the dining hall the housemother was waiting for us.

"Is this the four?" she asked Miss Flintmyer.

"That's the four, alright!" the young gym teacher said.

"Well, what do you have to say for yourselves?"

"Nothing, Ma'am," I said. "We were wrong."

"You darn right! You all were wrong! And guess what? You won't leave this area for a week, and the ones of you that sneak out to have a smoke – forget it! Do without!" The housemother was pretty upset. "That is a water moccasin…and it is poisonous. I want it disposed of, now!"

"Pat, you and Buddy are the oldest and should be setting a good example. I want you two to take that moccasin out in the woods and kill it before it strikes one of the kids."

Buddy and I took it out in the woods and walked to the creek.

"Look at this beautiful snake," I said to him. "How could we possibly kill it?"

"I can't, you'll have to do it."

"Let's compromise and turn it loose in the creek," I said. That's what we did, and told the housemother we killed it.

It was a couple of weeks later that Jackie, Eddie, Buddy and I were just out wandering around when Jackie wanted to go on the other side of the school where the cow pasture was. There wasn't much to do over there, but since Jackie had never been over there, we went with him. The school had about thirty milk cows and two big bulls. The bulls were kept in a separate pasture so we didn't have to worry about them. In the area beyond there was just open fields, a small creek, and a large patch of woods that stood at the bottom of the mountain.

Just to get to the woods was almost a mile and Buddy was getting tired already, but Jackie wanted to go so we tagged along. We had passed the cows and were in a field where the grass came up to our armpits. The walking was bad enough but there were all kinds of bugs in the grass…then we hit a marshy area and we had slimy mud to contend with.

"Hey guys, it's dry over here!" Buddy said.

By the time we got to him we had this black mud up past our ankles. When we got to the small creek we had a chance to clean our feet, and boy, did it stink. I looked at Jackie.

"Do you want to continue?"

"Well we're almost to the woods," he said, "so I think if we stop and have a smoke then we can give it another try."

We agreed. No longer had we lit up when we heard it. It was almost like thunder in the distance, but then we saw a smoke cloud build up and Eddie stood up and said, "Look at that!"

We all stood up and we could see that the smoke cloud was moving towards us...then I saw three or four horses galloping in our direction. We all started to panic because we thought they were coming after us, so we ran toward the woods. As we were nearing the woods, I looked back and saw that they were running on past us.

"Look what's behind the horses!" Buddy said.

"What in the hell are you talking about? I can't see anything for the tall grass," Jackie said.

I looked and all I could see was the top of something's head.

"It's a God-damned mountain lion!" someone said.

And that did it for me.

"I'm getting the hell out of here! If anyone wants to come with me, I'm leaving now! I'm not going across that damn muddy field... if I have to walk twenty miles, I'm going around it."

I looked at the other guys and they felt the same way. It took us over an hour to get back. We were late for supper. When we walked in the housemother was waiting.

"Oh, it's you four again!"

"Yes Ma'am, just us four," answered Buddy.

You could see that his remark bothered her. One thing that most of us had learned about her was: while she was reprimanding you, you kept your mouth shut.

She gave a mean look at Buddy.

"That was rhetorical!"

"Ma'am, I don't know what rhetorical means."

We kept nudging Buddy and trying to tell him to shut up as he was just getting in deeper, but he was a little bit stubborn.

"Okay, by tomorrow at this time, I want you to find out what rhetorical means, and write the definition twenty times for me."

But Buddy just wouldn't shut up.

"Ma'am, how do you spell rhetorical?"

"I'm done, Buddy. You figure it out!"

I guess we should've thanked Buddy for taking her attention completely away from the rest of us – or at least so we thought. No sooner did we sit down than she stood up like she had just remembered something important.

"The four of you are grounded for another week!"

Jackie and I talked about it after supper.

"If you hadn't wanted to go all the way over to those woods, we wouldn't have gotten into trouble again," I told him.

"It's not nearly as bad as it sounds," he said. "Sure we were grounded for a week but when you look at it, we go to school for five days and it only hurts us on the weekend, and that's only two days, so what's the big deal?"

"Since you put it like that, okay," I said. "We can't do anything about it anyway. We'll go visit Mike and Betty next week."

Saturday and Sunday we had to stay around the school. No matter what the situation, we were always looking for some kind of mischief to get into. Even when we weren't looking for it, somehow it found us. The girls' building was about fifty yards from the schoolhouse where we lived. They had a small playground with swings in it. Normally we never used this playground but it was the only thing left to do, and besides it would give us a chance to tease the girls.

None of the girls had come down yet so, Jackie, Buddy, Eddie, and I went down and sat in the swings, talking about some of the things we planned to do this summer. Eddie had on a pair of pants that he had trouble keeping up because he had no belt.

Before long the girls came out to play and were surprised to see us as hardly any of the older boys played there. When we got to talking to some of the girls, one of them wanted to know why we were here on the weekend. Jackie told one of his big lies about how we were chased by a mountain lion.

"We could have gotten killed but the housemother didn't believe us, and that's why we got grounded," he said. The girls were scared because they thought there was a mountain lion close to the school, but by now I was getting bored. I looked at Buddy, who had one of the girls on the teeter totter. Every time he had her up, he would stop and keep her up until she complained.

Eddie came over and wanted to go back to the dorm and try and find a belt, but Jackie heard him. Hhe turned, grabbed Eddie's pants and pulled them down to his knees. Two or three of the startled girls jumped back and screamed with laughter. Eddie pulled them up and got real pissed at Jackie, but by now everyone was laughing but Eddie.

Buddy got off the teeter and came over.

"What happened to your little irl friend," I said, "did she get tired of you, already?"

"Well, first off, she's not my girl friend! And secondly, she caught on to what I was doing."

"What were you doing?"

"Okay… she wasn't wearing any underwear, so when I got her up in the air I would keep her there and just enjoy the view."

"You little devil, I wondered why you kept her up there so long," I said. I told Jackie what Buddy was doing.

"Why that little bastard, he's sneakier than we are!" he said.;

While we talked one of the girls came over and took Buddy over to the side. I couldn't hear what they were saying, but I could see Buddy's face light up. He came over to us.

"Do you guys know what that girl wanted me to do?"

"No, what?" I asked.

"She wanted me to pull Eddie's pants down again."

"Go ahead and give them an eye full!" Jackie said.

"No way," Buddy said. "I don't want him pissed at me."

Jackie grabbed Eddie's pants in an attempt to pull them down, but there was no way that Eddie would let that happen again. Even one of the girls tried, but Eddie wasn't going to put on another show, and he kept away from everyone after that.

After we thought we had caused enough trouble in the girls playground we decided to sneak over to the area where we used to run the track and have a smoke as we hadn't had one all morning, and on the way, we almost died with laughter at what had transpired with the girls... all but Eddie who was still miffed at his so called friends.

"Those girls are as bad as we are!" Jackie said.

"If you ask me, they're worse," I said. "If they came down to the swimming hole with us they would be the first to jump in naked!"

"Do you really think they would do that?"

"I would bet my last marble on it," I answered.

Later Jackie said we should get them to go to the swimming hole with us.

"And just how do you think we can do that?" I asked.

"Well, I have an idea. You know the girl that asked Buddy to pull down Eddie's pants? I think she would be the one to ask. Ssince she was the one that Buddy has talked to, let's see if he will ask her to go swimming with him. What do you think?"

"I think it's a great idea."

And when we asked Buddy, he was all for it.

We still had a few days until we were off our restriction, but after we would be able to try our plan. Friday night came and we were wondering how we would spend the weekend when Buddy walked into the dorm, looking like the cat that swallowed the canary

"What's up?" I asked him.

"I got the job done!"

"What job?"

"I've just been talking to the girls we met at the playground," he said. "They're going to the swimming hole tomorrow."

"So, what kind of a lie did you have to tell them?"

"No lie, I just didn't tell them we were going in naked."

"You did well, Buddy."

Saturday morning after breakfast we started out to the swimming hole. When we got there Buddy got in the water with his pants on. Jackie and I just lay on the bank and had a smoke. I guess it was around noon when the girls showed up and walked over to where we were lying.

"Does your housemother know that you smoke?" one of them asked.

"Jesus Christ, is that why you girls came out here?" I asked back.

They both started laughing.

"I was only teasing," she said.

"Aren't you girls going to come in the water and cool off?" Buddy asked.

"We can't get our dresses wet," the other girl said.

"Well, take them off," Jackie said.

They just giggled.

"We have underwear on and it would be just like a bathing suit, so why not?" one of the girls said to the others. She slowly and rather tentatively pulled off her dress, and stuck her toe in the water.

"This is so cold!" She stood there. "What are your guy's names?" she asked. We all gave our names. "I'm Bobby Jo, that is Emily, and over there in the red dress is Stella," Bobbi Jo said. She was probably eleven or twelve and was a little skinny with not too much on top. I noticed the other two start to pull their dresses over their heads. One was a little overweight and had larger breasts. The other was slim and pretty, and also had small breasts. I watched the last one get in the water.

"There ain't no way that Buddy is going to have all the fun, I'm going in," I told Jackie.

Before you knew it, we were all having a good time and we didn't pay too much attention to the fact we were naked, and the girls were almost naked. Then after awhile we got out of the water to have a smoke. The girls got out and lay on the bank and we all talked while Buddy stayed in the water. One of the girls stood up. When I looked at her from where I was laying you could see right through her underwear. When I was about to say something one of the girls laughed.

"You guys can see right through our underwear," she said.

Buddy laughed too.

"Well it looks to like you might as well take them off and let them dry on the rocks."

"That's not fair!" Bobbi Jo said. "You guys have your pants on."

Buddy got out of the water and stripped off his pants.

"Now, we're all even."

And sure enough, the three girls slipped out of their underwear, and I looked at Jackie.

"Oh, what the hell, let's join the fun." We too stripped down and got back in the water.

We played around the rest of the day, almost like it was an everyday thing. We didn't touch the girls and surprisingly, we didn't tease them. We just had a good time.

The next day we had a smoke down at the creek.

"Did you guys see the one with those nice big breasts?" Buddy said.

"You must mean Emily," Jackie said. "They were big alright, she must have been a little older than the other girls. I saw what the cold water did to their nipples."

"Yeah, but did you see what the cold water did to our peckers?" I said, and we all laughed.

"I wonder if they are sitting around talking about us the way we are about them," Eddie said.

"I'll bet anything they're sitting there laughing the asses off at our shrunken up peckers," Buddy said with a moan, but then Jackie had to add his two cents.

"You know, I was surprised to see that they had hair down between their legs, like we do."

"But did you notice that they had a lot more than we do?" I said.

Before long other girls started coming to the swimming hole. In fact it started getting crowded.

"Maybe you will have to make it bigger," I told Buddy.

"The swimming hole farther on up the creek, where the mountain girls go swimming is a lot bigger...we could all start going up there," he said.

, "We don't want to get those people involved," Jackie said. "That might get us in trouble."

Going to the farm was the last thing on our minds now that we had naked girls going to the swimming hole. Swimming took all of our time. One day Jackie pulled me aside.

"You know, we haven't seen Mike and Betty in a long time."

"Yeah, I know and I bet they wonder what has happened to us. Maybe we should go visit them next weekend," I said. Jackie agreed.

"That's a great idea!"

The next Saturday we told Buddy and Eddie we were going to the farm.

"We've made plans to go to the creek with the girls," Buddy said.

"Well, you do that but Jackie and I are going to visit Mike and Betty...maybe we will see you on the way back."

We left early and got to the farm at about eleven. Mike was busy working in the barn, so we went in to help him. He was glad to see us and asked us where the other boys were. We told him that they were swimming with girls, so we came alone.

Mike asked us if we would fill the tub for Betty so the water would have enough time to warm up before she takes her shower. While we were in the process of carrying buckets of water Doris came into the barn. We hadn't seen her in almost a year, and we were glad to see each other.

"Sally and I had gone to the store when they heard all the noise from the swimming hole," she said. "We went to check it out and we saw you guys swimming with girls, and all of you were naked."

"Why didn't you stop and say hi?" I said.

"Sally wanted to walk up and say something, but I said, don't bother them, so we just stood behind the bushes and watched awhile. It looked like you had such a good time we didn't want to embarrass you." She laughed. "It was kinda funny."

I wanted her to shut up. The more she talked, the redder our faces got.

"What are you guys going to do the rest of the day?" she asked.

"We have to get back to the school today, but we'll come back when we can stay overnight," I said.

Doris went back in the house and Jackie and I went out in the woods. After about twenty minutes Jackie spoke up.

"I wonder when Betty will take her shower." I laughed.

"I wondered when you were going to say something about that. We might as well walk on up to our favorite watching spot, since we really don't have anything else to do."

As we sat there in the woods I thought about Buddy and the rest of the guys, wondering what they were doing.

"Hey, look, here comes Betty," Jackie said. I caught a glimpse of someone going into the barn. In a couple of minutes I saw Doris come out and walk to the makeshift shower. She took off her dress and hung it over a limb. She looked around and stepped under the shower, and as we were watching Doris washing herself, and we saw Betty walk over by Doris, disrobe and join her in the shower. In a few minutes Doris got out and dried off.

"God-damn, we got two birds with one stone!" Jackie said. I laughed.

"This has got to be better than the swimming hole!" After they were done I told Jackie, "We should go down and see them before we leave."

We wandered around and came back behind the barn, and Betty and Doris were standing out in the sunlight drying their hair when we got there, smiling.

"Where have you guys been?" Doris asked. To my surprise Betty answered her.

"They were up in the woods watching us take a shower."

I was simply taken aback, not so much that she knew, but the way she blurted it out in front of Doris.

"Why you little devils!" Doris said to us, then turned to her. "How in the world do you know that? I didn't see them."

"One day while I was showering I saw them...they didn't know it, but I saw them moving around up there."

"What did you do?" Doris asked.

"Nothing, I just went on taking my shower. They were way up in the woods so it didn't bother me."

We wanted to get back, and away from this embarrassing situation as soon as possible, and we did want to stop at the swimming hole, so I said, "We are going to leave now, but will come back when we can spend the night."

Betty asked, "When will that be?"

"I hope, in a week or two." I said while I walked. I think Jackie was already at the corner of the barn.

Doris said, "Good, I'll be looking out for you."

When we were on the trail back Jackie said, "I *thought* she had seen us watching her when we were here before but I wasn't sure."

"Are you sure now?

"Well yeah, how could I not be? But what I'm worrying about now is: what did Doris mean by; *I'll be looking out for you?*"

"Jackie, I think that she was just trying to get under our skin because we both know what she meant."

When we got to the swimming hole the girls were still in the water so we sat on the bank and had a smoke, and they got out and began dressing. Buddy stood there watching Emily, the girl with the large breasts.

"Why does your thing get so small when you get in the water?" she asked him. Buddy's face turned red.

"That water's damn cold and that's why your titties shrink and your nipples look like little rocks." I couldn't believe that he had the nerve to say that, but we all laughed, even the girls.

When I look back on those days with the girls, I don't remember us ever doing anything bad with them but there are shenanigans were done out of curiosity more than anything else, and the girls felt the same way we did. Before long we didn't pay too much attention to the nakedness.

The week after our embarrassment with Betty and Doris, Jackie and I were down at the creek and I said, "You know, Betty might have told Mike about us spying on her in the shower."

And Jackie said, "I never thought about that, and if she did, I don't think he would like it."

"Well, what's done is done, but I have an idea; let's have Buddy, Harold, Eddie, and Earl go and visit them the next time, and see if Mike says anything about us.

"Well, that may work but none of those guys know about what we did," he said.

I said, "I guess we'll just have to take that chance."

So, Jackie and I made up excuses as to why we didn't want to go with them to visit Mike and Betty, so they left without us. We hung around the school most of Saturday, except for a couple jaunts down to the creek to have a smoke now and then. We were bored because normally we would hiking to the farm, but I guess it was worth it if we got the information about Mike we wanted. The trouble was, we couldn't tell the boys what we were trying to find out, so it was at best a hit or miss proposition.

Near suppertime the boys got back. We had no chance to talk to them before we washed up for supper. Later that evening we all headed down to the creek. I couldn't wait to see how things went and what they might have found out. I pulled Buddy over and asked him if Mike had mentioned Jackie and I.

"Mike was glad we came by and thanked us after we fed the animals," Buddy said.

"Did Mike or Betty take a shower?" Jackie asked Eddie.

"No, because the tub was empty and Mike had a sore back, so we filled it for him."

After we went back to the house I got with Jackie.

"Well, we sure didn't find out if Mike knew anything, so it looks like we wasted a perfectly good weekend for nothing."

"The way I see it, there's nothing we can do...if we're asked about what we did, let's just say it was an accident, and we'll both stick with that story."

No Going Back

Jackie and I hadn't visited Mike and Betty at the farm in a couple of weeks. To be honest, we weren't crazy about going back after that last confrontation with Betty and Doris. Finally we had to go for fear they would think we were avoiding them.

Friday was upon us and we got permission to stay overnight, and Buddy, Jackie, Eddie and I left right after school, and got there a couple hours before dark. Mike and Betty were not at the farm, but Doris came out and met us. I asked Doris, "Where's Mike and Betty?"

Doris said, "They've gone to visit some friends and aren't coming back until tomorrow, but you guys are always welcome and can sleep in the barn."

Jackie said, "There's still daylight left, could we help you with some chores?"

"Well, now that you mentioned it, the wood boxes are empty, and if you big strong boys wouldn't mind," she said, and added, maybe I can rustle up some cold milk.

"That would be great!" I said.

We carried firewood; enough to fill the boxes and sat around, drank milk and joked with Doris until it got dark. Eddie said, "I guess we should go out and start spreading out straw for our beds."

Doris said, "Take the lantern to see what you're doing."

I said, "Thanks! See you in the morning."

Morning came sooner than I wanted it to. I could see Doris milking that damn cow there in the dark. For the life of me I could never figure out why that cow had to be milked so early. I didn't want to get up but there was no way that I was going to get back to sleep, so I got up and went outside to have a smoke. She had finished milking when she came outside and asked me what we were going to do today. I said, "I'm not really sure...probably hike around the mountains and look for arrowheads, and maybe go down to the creek and fool around."

"Why?.. Will your girlfriends be there?

"I doubt it," I said.

And as she was putting the cow back in its stall, she said over her shoulder, "Would you see if there's water in the tub…I might take a shower while you guys are gone."

Then she laughed, "You'd like that…wouldn't you?"

I thinking, what in the hell did she mean by that? Is she going to take a shower and show herself off, or was it just a little dig?

Later on she made us some pancakes with molasses…not quite as good as Betty's but still it kept us from going hungry. Later on we went down to the creek while Buddy and Eddie walked up to take a look at our old fort. I told Jackie what Doris had said about taking a shower.

"She's either teasing us or tempting us," he said, "and either way I guess we'll have to find out, but we'll have to sneak away from the other boys if we're going to spy on her, because it would do no good for Buddy to find out what's going on. The whole school would probably find out as soon as we got back."

"Of course getting rid of Buddy would be difficult to do," I said.

Jackie said, "I don't know, since we're being sneaky, why stop with Doris?" and said, "You know, all we have to do is mention swimming, and he's the first one in the water."

That gave me an idea so I said, "I'll handle Buddy."

Then we started walking up the hill toward the fort and met Buddy and Eddie halfway. I said to them, "Jackie and I are going to replace a lot of the sagebrush in the fort and will meet you guys later at the swimming hole."

"And just as I figured, Buddy jumped at that plan."

But we couldn't just start walking towards the woods, so in order to fool Buddy and Eddie we had to go almost to the fort then circled around to the tree line and come down to the spot where we could see the shower which took us at least a half an hour.

When we got to the *spot* I stood behind a clump of bushes and started looking for Doris and sure enough there she was with one towel wrapped around her and another wrapped on her head... walking toward the barn. I said to Jackie, "You know, old buddy, "I think we're just a tad late."

He said, "Yep, just a tad...I guess we can forget all this and head back to the school."

Jackie and I had found a few arrowheads down by the creek so when we went to school Monday we gave them to Mrs. Pierce. We had been at the school for three and a half years, and between us and the girls, had given her a lot of arrowheads, which she had attached to a large plywood board. They were all laid out in rows and labeled as to what they were and how they were used.

On occasion she would take the whole class down to the creek to look for arrowheads. She said, "The best time to look for them is right after a good hard rain because the rain would wash away the dust and sand that had hidden them," and she was right. Every time we went out with her we found a few.

A week after we had seen Doris Jackie, Buddy, and I were down at the creek having a smoke when we saw Sally. Now we hadn't seen her for almost a year, and she said, "What have you boys been doing?"

I said, "Just the same old thing...hiking around the woods and trying to stay out of trouble. What have you been up to," I asked.

Then she said, "Doris and I went by the creek a week or so ago and saw you and your girlfriends swimming and you seemed to be having a good time."

Then she laughed and said, "We watched you guys for awhile and left."

Jackie said, "Why didn't you two come on and get in the water?"

"I wanted to." She said, and added, "But Doris would let me."

"Well, we might be back there swimming, this Saturday," I said.

"She said it may be different this Saturday because of what she had heard."

"What did you hear?" asked Jackie.

She just smiled and said, "*Wait until Saturday.*" Then she left and we went back to the dormitory. I asked Jackie, "What do you think Sally heard?"

He said, "I've no idea, but didn't we just go through all of this shit so I guess we'll have to wait until Saturday...I wouldn't be a bit surprised if those girls are trying to scare us into *thinking the worst.*"

"I believe their scheme is working," I said, and added, "I know that her and Doris have been spying on us at the swimming hole, and even Betty has been with them...so what's the big deal about what we have done? And what's the big secret about what she heard? But, I'll tell you one thing...she'll make it nasty, you can bet on that!"

Friday rolled around and I caught up with Jackie and asked him what he wanted to do tomorrow. He said, "Well, Sally said that she was going to the swimming hole but all the guys will be there, and who knows about the girls, and I don't want to find out about her little secret with all the others around."

"Well," I said, Why don't we try and find something else to do, and if she shows up at the swimming hole and starts making a big deal out of what we might have done...we'll just say that she made it all up."

Jackie said, "That sounds alright but you know Buddy and Eddie...whatever they hear about us they will make a big deal out of it."

"You're probably right but I don't see any other choice," I said.

Saturday, Jackie and I, instead of going to the creek with the others wandered on up the mountain trail and ended up at the fort. There wasn't much to do, after we had cleaned the debris that had blown in on the floor, so we mostly just lay around, and occasionally looked down to see what was going on at the swimming hole. At one point Jackie shuck his head and said, "I don't see Sally down there."

I said, "That's a good thing... I wonder if she was just playing with our minds."

Jackie said, "Probably, she's good at that sort of thing! I see Buddy, Harold, Eddie, and Earl but none of the girls are there."

With nothing else to do, I said to Jackie, "Why don't we go over to the small creek by the school and see if we can find the snake we put there?"

He said, "I don't think it will be there, but let's give it a try... it's better than lying around here."

We had to cross over the pasture, and on the way we saw Sally coming down the path. I said, "Let's hide before she sees us," so we went behind some rocks and waited until she went by.

We watched as she headed for the swimming hole...I told Jackie, "I bet she will hide and watch the guys."

Jackie said, "I don't care, let's just go and find that snake."

It didn't take us long to get to the small creek but we couldn't find the snake, so we sat down and had a smoke. I was a little bit upset about wasting the whole day, worrying about what Sally might say about us, and I said, "Dammit, Jackie, do you know where we made our mistake?" Then I answered it myself, "We had no business hiding from Sally when we met her. Wwe could have easily found out her little secret, butnow she thinks we're afraid to see her."

"You may be right, but what's done is done."

I dreaded Sunday morning. It seemed to mess up every weekend, because we could have been spending two nights at the farm instead of only one, having to always hurry back before supper on Saturday. I don't think any of us boys were getting anything out of church. I felt it was a waste of time! Be that as it may, we had to go tomorrow and the housemother was laying out clothes for the boys to wear the next day. After she was done she went back down stairs to her room. It was early evening and only Jackie and I were in the dormitory. He came up with this brilliant idea we change the clothes around so that all the boys would have clothes that didn't fit.

After supper nobody noticed what we had done. We hoped they wouldn't notice until everyone was on their way to church. After breakfast Sunday morning Jackie and I finished eating first and hurried back to the dorm. We got dressed up and ready for church, standing outside waiting for the others, when the house-mother walked by.

"My, you boys are getting better about church...that's very good!" she said, and went on inside. Jackie and I had a hard time holding back our laughter.

We had to march to church in a group, with the housemother in front, and the girls had to do the same. The group that was ready first got to go first. On this particular day the boys were in front. At first everything was going alright, until some of the boys had trouble keeping their pants up. Then some whose pants were too tight started wiggling around, trying to get comfortable. After awhile the girls noticed this and started to giggle. By this time we could hardly contain ourselves. Bby the time we got to the church the housemother was thinking she had made a mistake and put the wrong clothes on the beds. In any event it was too late now and they would just have to suffer until we got back home. Every time I looked at Jackie he was smiling. I could barely keep from busting out laughing in church.

When we were back in the dormitory, Jackie told Buddy and Eddie what we had done, and Eddie got a little pissed but he got over it. Buddy thought it was funny. After church we only had about four hours before we had to wash up for supper, so we couldn't go too far but we still had time to go down to the creek and fool around.

Jackie and I were standing there smoking when Sally walked up.

"Oh, there you are!" she said.

"What do you mean, *there you are?*" I said. "We come here all the time!"

"Oh, I don't know, I kinda thought you two were hiding from me."

"No, you just missed us," Jackie said. "Tell us what you heard that you've been so secretive about."

"Doris told me about you guys watching her and Betty take a shower!"

"It was an accident," Jackie said quickly. "We were up in the woods when they were in the shower and we couldn't help but see!

"Betty told Doris that you guys had done it before and it was no accident," Sally said.

"What about you?" Jackie challenged, which surprised me. "There were times that you did the same thing, watching boys at the swimming hole."

"That was different."

"What was so different? You sneaked up on us and hid in the bushes," Jackie shot back.

Her whole demeanor changed.

"Well don't tell Buddy or the other guys because they will tell everybody and it will be all over the school," she said, suddenly nicer. "I would surely get in trouble."

I wanted to get away from Sally.

"It's about time to go back to the school and get ready for supper," I said, so we said good bye to Sally and left.

That night at the supper table one of the girls said that she didn't like some of the girls were going to the swimming hole.

"We better not go to the swimming hole for awhile!" I told the other guys.

"Why?" Buddy asked.

"Well, it looks like somebody has ratted on the girls and all of us could get into trouble." I said.

"I don't care," Buddy said, asshole that he was. "I've done nothing wrong. I'm going swimming anyway!"

"Well, don't say that I didn't warn you," I said. "And don't rat on the rest of us if you get in trouble."

The next day Buddy said that he found out it was Sally that told on us. I just looked at Jackie.

"I damn well knew that she would be trouble!"

"It doesn't surprise me either," Jackie said. "She's about as nasty as they come, and here she is ratting on us! Why don't we talk to Doris. Maybe she can do something with her, since she's her sister."

"That would probably be a good idea," I said, "except I think Doris is still mad at us for watching her and Betty in the shower."

"Well we have to do something! We can't just sit around and let her get away with this!"

The next Friday we got permission to stay overnight at Mike and Betty's. Eddie, Buddy, Harold, and Earl left earlier than we did and were already at the farm before we got there. When we walked up I asked if they had seen Doris.

"She isn't here!" Buddy said. I looked at Jackie.

"Damn, there goes our plan!"

Later on, I had a chance to talk to Betty when she came out to milk the cow. I told her that Sally had told some of the girls at the school about us meeting the girls at the swimming hole. And it looked like we wouldn't be able to see them anymore because the school will probably ground us.

"What did you boys do with the girls?" she asked.

"We met several of them at the swimming hole and we all went in together, naked," I said. Betty laughed.

"I don't see why that should cause any trouble for you guys. It's only natural for young boys to do that sort of thing. I will have a talk with Sally but it might not do any good, since she's probably mad at you boys and wants to get even."

After a week went by and we didn't heard anymore about the problem with the girls. Apparently Betty spoke to Sally and got her to take back what she had said. I asked Buddy if he had seen Sally; he said one of the girls at the school told him that Sally had gone back to live with her mother.

"Damn, that's good," I said. "Let's hope that she stays there."

After school the next day we all met at the creek for a smoke.

"We better plan a way to go get some frogs," I told them. "It's getting late in the summer."

"I know of a place that one of the older boys told about," Eddie said, "but we would have to get an early start because it was a long hike just to get there."

"Where is this place?" Jackie asked. "I'll tell you right now, I don't plan to walk all over the countryside and come back empty handed!"

"It's a way past the country store, where we get our cigarettes, and from what he told me, the creek is wider and deeper than the place where we usually go frogging."

I looked at Jackie and could tell he didn't like the idea of walking that far. Neither did I. We didn't like being far away from the school at night. We always felt safer when we were closer. Going to a place that was a lot farther away, I was afraid would put us in a scary situation. The next day someone pointed out that we had been to just about every part of the creek, so we decided this was a challenge we couldn't resist. We couldn't leave after supper since we wouldn't have time to get there and back before it was too late, so we left Saturday at around noon. First we stopped at the country store and bought our cigarettes and candy. The walk was a good long trek. We didn't know how far, but we walked for hours and it got dark.

"Are you sure about where we're going?" I asked Eddie.

"If we just keep on walking we will come to the creek," he said. "We can't miss it!" Then I heard the sound of running water. A couple of minutes later we ran up to the bank.

"They were right," I said. "It *is* a big creek, more like a river!"

"My God!" said Eddie. "I don't know about this!"

"This was your big Idea, Eddie," Jackie said, "so you can get in first."

"We should get in and see how deep it is," Buddy said. He got in with his pants on. The water came up to his armpits, and the current was so swift it almost pushed him over, so I grabbed his hand and helped him out.

"We aren't going to be able to catch any frogs in this kind of swift current," I said. Jackie was pretty upset.

"This was a damn big waste of time," he said. "We should have gone to the creek we knew. This was a lot of walking for nothing!"

We had a cigarette and talked about what we could do to salvage the night. Earl, who had walked a little farther up the creek, came back and told us about a tide pool off to the side. We decided we might be able to get some frogs there, so we walked up the creek, about fifty feet, to the side pool. Right away, Buddy spotted a frog; Earl caught it but it wasn't too big so he let it go.

Jackie was unhappy with coming all the way here. He said he wanted to go back to our old frogging creek, but it was too late. By the time we got there we wouldn't have time to do anything, so we headed back to the school. By the time we got to the country store it was closed, but we could hear somebody cussing. We walked closer and could see that two people were fighting in front of the store, which had a beer sign in the window. We could see two dunk women. After we stood there a couple minutes, they started ripping off each other's clothes, pulling hair, and cussing up a storm.

I had never seen women fighting before. As we stood there watching, it was kinda funny and a little scary, too. We didn't stay there too long, because we felt like intruders and they might come after us. After we had walked away, Jackie was laughing.

"They were a hell of a mess with their clothes half torn off and their hair hanging down."

"I wonder where their husbands are," Eddie said.

"They're probably sitting in the car, having a beer, and wondering which one will win," said Earl, and we all laughed at that. We didn't have too much farther to go but we were getting tired when we passed the girl's building. I was anxious to get in bed, so I couldn't believe Jackie's idea.

"Let's get up close to a window, make some animal noises, and scare the girls," he said.

"It's late and they're probably asleep by now," I said, but we didn't want to miss the opportunity. We sneaked up and got right under the window. Earl could make noises that sounded just like a large animal, so we let him alone to do his thing. After that we started scratching on the window with our fingernails. That got the girls up and we could hear them moving around, and then the screams started. We took off running to the dormitory.

"I guess the night wasn't a complete failure, after all," Jackie said at the door. I looked at him.

"Don't get anymore bright ideas like that one!"

In a week or so the leaves were turning all sorts of colors, which told us that soon they would be falling off, and the weather would start turning cold. I didn't like this time of year and the other boys felt the same way. One day after school Jackie, Buddy, Eddie, and I sat down and talked about what we wanted to do before the rains and cold weather was upon us. We still had a few short weeks of warm weather left, so of course we had to go visit Mike and Betty, but there were a few other things we wanted to do. Buddy wanted to go swimming before it got too cold and the rest of us wanted to repair the old fort. That would make sure we had a place to get in out of the rain if we got caught on one of our hikes. Sometimes we would be off up in the hills on what started out as a nice day, and all of a sudden we would get caught in a summer storm. It would happen so fast we would have no place to go. The fort solved that problem. It worked out so well we decided to build another one about halfway to the farm for a rest stop and a shelter from the rain.

We found a spot next to the tree line that was just right, so we started to dig out a place in the small hill. We worked on it for about a week. We had all kinds of dead tree limbs to make the top, and we put broom sage on the limbs, and then another layer of limbs to keep the broom sage from blowing away.

"We should dig a trench all around the fort to keep the rain water from coming in," Eddie said. After we got the trench done we waited for a chance to use it.

Before long we got permission to spend the night with Mike and Betty. We found Mike plowing up the vegetable garden in the back of the house. Betty was finishing up with the canning.

Buddy wanted to see if he could plow. He got behind the plow and said, "Giddy up," and we watched as the mule started to go. I guess Buddy wasn't quite ready and because he tripped, but continued to hold on to the reins. The mule kept on going as Buddy was pulled along the furrows. We all laughed until Mike finally stopped the mule. Buddy got up with a mouthful of dirt and dusted himself off.

"That was pretty good Buddy," Mike said. "Would you like to try it again?"

"Maybe at a later time, Mike," Buddy muttered.

Mike finished plowing and put the mule away.

"Tomorrow I'm going to get a load of firewood," he said. "I could use some help."

That night we slept in the barn. Mike's bull was moving around, kicking the boards in his stall and snorting just about all night long, so I got very little sleep. I had just closed my eyes when Betty came in to milk the cow. Betty wasn't too quiet when she did the milking and at some point she would even cuss the cow. I just lay there and watched. After awhile I got up and started feeding the animals. She said that Mike would be here in a few minutes to get the mule hitched up to the wagon to go get firewood.

"Before you go come up to the house and eat breakfast because it's going to be hard work," she said. The other boys were getting up by now. It was still dark when Mike came out and we went in to have breakfast. After we ate Betty gave us a big pail of cold milk to have while we were out with Mike. We all got in the wagon and started off, but we didn't have to go far before we found some good limbs and loaded them. We continued farther into the forest until we found enough limbs to completely fill the wagon. When we got back we had a huge pile of wood to unload.

"I'll start cutting this up tomorrow, but we've done enough for today," Mike said. While the others were getting water, I remembered that I had left my small knife in the barn. When I walked in I saw Betty stepping out of the shower. She was drying off, but she covered up when she saw me.

"I thought you guys were gone!"

"I'm glad we weren't!" I said. I don't know why I said it; it just came out. "We would have left but I had to get knife," I said after an embarrassing silence.

"Well, I have to get dressed," she said.

"We'll be going, now," I said, hurrying out. Jackie and the others were waiting for me at the house, so we left. I don't think we had been gone over twenty minutes when it started to rain, so we took off for the fort. We got a little wet but the rain quickly into a drizzle by the time we got there. Then it started to come down hard. We must have stayed and watched the downpour for an hour or so, counting our lucky stars that we had built the fort. It held up pretty good except for a couple drips here and there. The rain didn't look like it was going to let up anytime soon, so we started debating when we were going to start back to the school. In about an hour it would start getting dark, so we were worried about getting back before supper.

"It looks to me like the rain has let up," Jackie said at one point. "If we want to stay out of trouble I think we should get on the road." None of us wanted to go through the silly penalties of being late for supper, so we all got up and started out in the light rain. We started in a slow trot. As the rain stopped we got close to the dormitory, so we all ran, soaked to the skin but in time for supper.

For a week it rained and we were stuck in the dormitory, getting out only to go to Mayo Hall to eat. What I hated was having to clean the mud off our shoes. After the rain stopped we were finally able to go out and play. With the leaves fallen off the trees, the hills looked a lot different. We were sad to see that summer was gone and everything looked so dead and quiet. Since it hadn't snowed yet there wasn't much to do, but we did get out of the house with our slingshots to look for rabbits. We ever hit one but it was fun trying. We also got to the fort a couple times but there wasn't much to do there either except lie around and smoke. We were anxious for it to snow so we could take the sleds up the mountain.

We spent a lot of time inside listening to the housemother telling her stories but after awhile that got boring too, since we had heard just about every one of them. Jackie, I and the rest of our little roup would huddle in a corner and talk about all of our escapades of the last summer. I told nary a one of them about my last encounter with Betty, although I was dying to.

For about three weeks we laid around doing nothing but argue and get on each other's nerves. Finally one of us got up and looked out the windows, and we all saw it at once – it had snowed! After breakfast we got our sleds and went to a small hill not too far from the school, just to get a feel of the first snow. Buddy had found an old piece of corrugated roofing that he had bent up the front of.

"This ought to do just fine if I can get it started in a straight line," he said. He managed to go in a straight line until he came upon a large rock. Being unable to steer, he went ass end over teacups. I tried it too.

"If I start my slide about ten feet to the left," I said, "I will show you how it's done," but alas, somehow I got the same results. Jackie found a large cardboard box in one of the school sheds, during his ride one of the sides caved in and he rolled the rest of the way down. We tried just about everything we could get our hands on, just to make it more exciting. For the most part we were just sliding down on our backsides or not going at all, but we had so much fun we forgot how cold it was.

After awhile Buddy wanted to go and get warm. We all were about to freeze so we went into the dormitory…the housemother made us some hot cocoa and wanted to know if we were alright. Of course we wouldn't say how cold we were or she wouldn't have let us go back out.

We hung around inside for a short time then headed back to the hill and continued to play, and by the time suppertime rolled around we were so tired it was a chore just to eat.

The next day at school, we could look out and see that the snow was still coming down…I whispered to Jackie, "That hill we were on yesterday was nothing compared to the old route twenty-nine hill we used to slide down that was up closer to the old Crawford House."

Jackie said, "I know but it's such a long walk pulling the sled back just to give someone else a turn."

"I said, "Not only that, but it's a long hike in the snow just to get up there, in the first place. So, if you don't mind a lot of walking, just to get a couple of rides, let's give it a try."

The next Saturday Jackie, Buddy, Eddie, and I got the sled and went up the mountain, on the other side of Crawford House, and with the snow as deep as it was, and the drifts even worse, it took us a half of the day just to get there.

Now we hadn't used this old slope in a year or two and we weren't sure where the best sledding path was, but we had a pretty good idea, so when we got to the summit, Jackie said, "Damn, that's a long way down!"

Buddy wanted to take the first ride. We were all glad to hear someone volunteer as the slope was even more intimidating than I remembered.

So, he got ready and we gave him a shove and down he went... he went out of sight for awhile and then we saw him a way down the hill. I had to hand it to Buddy he made it look easy, especially for the first ride with no sled tracks to follow. While we waited for Buddy to bring the sled back we stood around and had a smoke, and Jackie said, "Damn, that looked like a hell of a lot of fun... I think I'll go next, if there's no objections."

By the time we got the sled back, Jackie was chomping at the bit, and he took a belly-flop on the sled and was off like a racecar at the starting line, and was doing great until he slipped off of Buddy's track, and a few seconds later he hit a big rock that pop up after about three feet, and luckily he stayed on the sled and came down on the trail...and was okay until we saw him heading towards the split rail fence and as we watched he dumped the sled just before he got to the fence.

When he brought the sled back, he said, "That was one hell of a ride!"

I took my turn after Jackie and did almost the same thing that he did but I managed to get back on the trail before I came to the fence. We could only make a couple more runs before we had to start back. All the effort was worth it, and although it took the whole day, we all had a great time.

At school, on Monday, Mrs. Pierce found some pictures that I had drawn the year before so I didn't have too much drawing to do for Halloween this year, so for the most part I just sat around and daydreamed about going home for vacation. I wasn't that crazy about going but it all my friends would be going, even Harold, so I knew it would probably be boring here.

Halloween was just another day as far as I was concerned… I would be thirteen years old and it seemed like I had spent most of my life here at the school, and when I left here it felt like I was lost…I wasn't used to the world outside of here, and I didn't have any friends except the guys here at school.

Jackie had only been here a couple years but the other boys had been here with me the whole time. You know they could be real assholes at times, but they were like my own brothers and whatever I did, they were right there beside me.

The bell rang and took me out of my revelry and it was time for recess and although it was cold, we went down to the creek for a smoke anyway. The creek was frozen over so we sat with our feet dangling on the ice.

After school we had a short time before supper to have a snowball fight and since we were close to the girl's building we threw snowballs at them and mostly they returned the fire but some just ran into the house.

Later on that evening my brother Jack came over to the dormitory and told me that pretty soon we would be going home for Christmas. I said, "Yeah, I know but that doesn't make much difference to me."

Jack didn't say so, but I had the feeling that he felt the same as me…*this was his home*. During the four years we had been at the school Jack and I only saw each other occasionally as we lived in different houses and had a complete different set of friends, but every month or so I would find Jack waiting at my bed area in the dormitory…he would always ask me how I was getting along, and if I needed anything. Although those meetings were always short, I did have the feeling that he looked out for me.

The time for the Halloween carnival had finally arrived, and it was old hat for me as we did the same old things we had done for years, but as usual we had some good pumpkin pie and I was turning thirteen and in my mind I was quite the veteran here at the school. The dancing I didn't much care for but it was fun watching the other guys mess it up. Jackie, Buddy, Eddie, and I would laugh when they fell down.

We had a break in the weather, warming up to almost fifty, so we were able to make one more hike that year to visit Mike and Betty. We left early Saturday morning and had to be back before supper, but not before the housemother gave us a stern warning.

"You boys would be wise to get back early," she said, "because you know the weather this time of year, and I know that you don't want to try and walk back in a blizzard. Do you all understand?"

"Yes Ma'am," we all said in unison.

When we got to the farm we found that they were getting ready for the holidays…Betty had baked a pumpkin pie, had made a big fruitcake, and we could smell the aroma of cookies in the oven as we neared the back door. I told Betty, "Now we can stay only a short while for we have to get back this evening and the housemother is worried about us getting caught out if it would storm."

She said, "We're really glad that you all came, and what a surprise…we thought we wouldn't see you again until spring."

Mike built a fire in the fireplace, got out his banjo, and opened a jug of cider… Betty cut us a piece of fruitcake, and we all had our own little party. I can't begin to tell you how much we enjoyed being with them albeit for such a short time. After a couple hours we all said good bye to Mike, Betty, and Doris…telling them how much we enjoyed the afternoon and we'd see them next year.

Betty gave each of us a warm hug and said, "We're going to miss you guys."

Thanksgiving turned out to be a great time at the school...all of the kids came to Mayo Hall and together we had turkey with all the trimmings and after we went to the dance hall in the main building where they gave out awards to students for accomplishments throughout the year. Of course that didn't mean anything to the kids in our little group, since we never came close to getting one. Then they had a dance and a group singing thing, which were both useless as far as I was concerned.

The following day the housemother told me it was time to leave on my holiday vacation. I knew it was getting close for that time to come, but I certainly wasn't ready for it.

Jack came over and helped me get my things packed.

"We're going to leave in two days...the train leaves at noon this Monday," he said.

After Jack left I went down to the creek and had a smoke with the other boys, and they asked me when I was leaving. I told them, and Buddy said we would all be back after Christmas.

"It will probably be boring but it will be good to get back!" I said.

Monday, after breakfast, we all said our goodbyes, Jack came and got me, and we went to the main hall where the car was waiting to take us to the train station in Charlottesville.

My mother picked us up as usual in Miami and wanted to know how things had been going at the school. Jack filled her in on most of what was going on while I sat and listened. And also as in vacations in the past, she saw to it we were dressed properly for Florida weather.

Christmas was a little more of a "big deal" this year, since just about all of our relations were there, and Christmas eve mom made what she described as big announcement, "As you may have heard; my divorce from Jerry was final a couple of months ago, and Roger has decided to make an honest woman out of me…We're getting married after the first of the year!"

Everyone liked the idea as they cheered and lifted their wine glasses, and offered a toast. I didn't think it would make much difference to me, since I would be going back to school in a few days and my life would stay the same.

The following morning mother sat down with Jack and me at breakfast and said, "Boys, your father wants to see you and also wants you to spend some time with him."

That upset me a little, because I didn't know my dad and I couldn't even remember what he looked like. What worried me even more was how it would affect us going back to school.

"Mom, how long will we be there?" I asked.

"I don't know. That will be up to your dad." I was upset and got the feeling that this wasn't going to work out well at all.

A couple of days later Jack and I took a bus to Greenville, South Carolina where my dad lived. He picked us up at the bus depot and the three of us went to a restaurant and ate dinner. He was nice enough.

"I've always loved you boys," he said. "Things haven't ever worked out between your mother and me, and being in the Air Force and all, I couldn't ever spend any time with you."

We spent three pretty good days with him, we always ate out, he gave us money, and bought us all kinds of gifts. After the third day he sat us down.

"I'm leaving on a short trip and I want you two to stay with a good friend of mine," he said.

"Who is that?" Jack asked.

"A Doctor Richardson, he lives in Simpsonville."

The next day we got up early so Dad could drive us to Simpsonville, South Carolina to meet the Doctor. We hadn't been on the road long when Jack spoke up.

"Dad, did you know that Pat and I thought we were to go back to the boarding school right after New Year's Day?" he asked.

"I've been giving that some thought and I believe it's probably a waste of money. You boys are old enough so as that you don't have to be watched twenty-four hours a day. School will start back, in Simpsonville in a few days, and the doctor will get you both registered. And that's the last we will talk about that!"

My heart sank, right then and there...just to think that I would never see my close friends again made me sick and I almost vomited right there in the car. What would Mrs. Pierce think when I didn't come back...she told me, at one time, "Pat, you're my favorite pupil." And what about Jackie, Buddy, Eddie, Earl, and Harold? Would they think something had happened to me? The more I thought about this the less I was liking my dad.

I wondered about Mike and Betty...would I ever see them again? Then I thought about how we got that one warm day in November to go see them for the last time, and how their good-byes seemed so special at the time. I'd like to say that Mike and Betty were two of the nicest people that I have known...*to this day.*

At first I was a little frightened of the doctor because I thought that I was going to be examined but I soon found out that I was just going to live with him until my dad found a house big enough for all of us to live in.

Now the Doctor and his wife lived in a very large house and since their kids were all grown, they rented out some of the rooms, mostly to school teachers. But Jack and I had a nice room on the bottom floor of this three story house. I did like these people and everyone was very nice to us, but I was still holding on to a glimmer of hope that somehow I would be going back to school. So, I asked Jack, "Do you think that if you asked dad about going back to boarding school, he might let us?"

"No, you're just going to have to forget about that school...
I talked to him about that, and he flat-out, said no!" Jack said.

That did it...I hated everybody concerned.

I pouted for a few days and then one morning when I decided
to eat breakfast with some of the people that rented the rooms, I
was surprised to find that a girl that lived there was my age, which
I soon found out was the Doctor's granddaughter and was nice to
me...Her name was Martha, and after we got registered for school,
we walked together, and she showed me where all my classes were.
Before long we were going a lot of places together; movies, roll-
er-skating, or just sitting around the malt shop and talking about
our past. I truly liked her because she was very pretty, with blonde
curly hair, and talked a lot about things that I liked.

The old Doc told me that I could go on some of his calls if
I wanted to.

"Sure, that would be a lot of fun," I said.

"Probably not as much as you think," he said.

The first time that I went with him was when he came and
knocked on my door, late at night.

"Pat, are you ready to go?" he asked.

"I guess so," I said.

That night we must have driven twenty miles on a dusty dirt
road, through the middle of a cotton field until we came to an old
wooden shack...Doc didn't even knock and as we walked in I saw
a black man; maybe in his late fifties lying on a mattress who said,
"Hi Mister Richson, I knew it you...you jus walk in...onie one dat
do it."

"Well, Mister Jackson, with them feet of yours, you don't need
to walk if you don't have to."

"Thank ya, thank ya fer dat...da feet are better...thanks to you.
Do ya have sa more ah dem antybotics?" he asked.

"That's why I came here tonight," Doc said . "Take these pills
just like the ones that I gave you before. And listen to me; try to

stay off your feet for another week...I have put you some fresh insulin, a new syringe and some needles in your icebox."

"Thank you for dat too, Misser Richson."

"We're leaving now but tell your old lady to take care of you better."

"What's wrong with his feet?" I asked Doc after we left.

"They're infected and he thinks that they will heal, but they won't...he's diabetic and nothing short of amputation will save him!"

I was on the verge of tears and said. "That's one of the saddest things that I've heard...Where's his wife?"

"Don't know but she'll probably show up sometime this morning to cook something and give him his insulin...you see Pat, she has given up on him and likes to sleep around."

"That's sad, Doc."

"Just a part of life that you may be a little too young to understand."

I wound up going on a lot of such calls with the old Doc...his medical treatments were always interesting, but his stories about how he grew up and the things that he had seen continually fascinated me.

For example: "One day my father took me to the train station in Greenville because he had heard that the infamous train robbers, Jesse James and his younger brother Frank were getting off the train. My dad and I waited for a long time until I finally saw them walking our way, and when they past us I got to shake hands with *Frank James.* My dad and the other people crowded around the depot treated them like celebrities, and cheered when they caught a glimpse of them."

I asked the Doc, "Weren't you afraid?"

He said, "No, Frank was very nice."

One day after one of his stories he said, "Pat, I've been talking your ear off...tell me about how things went at your school."

I couldn't believe that someone wanted to hear about me and my life at school, and I couldn't wait to start talking. I told him about my old friends and our hikes in the mountains, our escapades at the swimming hole, our trips to Mike and Betty's farm and especially about Betty and my fascination with her and her nakedness…I told him about Mrs. Pierce and how she encouraged me to draw. I talked his ear off.

He said, "Pat, you have some beautiful memories that you will keep for the rest of your life but you have to close the door on that chapter of your life…now you have to make new memories."

He said the right things to me because it made some sense, that I should start to grow up and enjoy my new life, but I knew that *I would never forget.*

Then he said, "I've been noticing that you spend a lot of your spare time drawing, and don't take me wrong, you do real good… but every young artist needs some advanced training, so, if you don't mind, I have a friend that's a professional artist and I would like for you to meet him and show him some your work."

A few days later when I came home from school, the old Doc was talking to a man in the front room. When they saw me Doc said, "This is James Taylor, he is a very good artist."

The man said, "Hi there, young man, I understand that you like to draw."

I answered, "Yes sir, more than anything!"

He said, "Would you go and get some of you drawings for me?"

Later on I found out that Mr. Taylor taught school and had an art class that met everyday but the problem was: the cost was five dollars a month and my dad didn't have the five dollars.

But as time went on Mr. Taylor would drop by and bring me art paper and pastels and on occasions would sit and show me how to blend colors and put a more professional look to my drawings.

I got use to the people at the house and learning to like every-one when one day my father came and took Jack and me to live with him.

And that squelched any hope that I had of returning back to the school. I never saw those wonderful people or the school in the beautiful Blue Ridge Mountains again.

The End.

ABOUT THE AUTHOR

Patrick L. Napier is a retired pen & ink artist living in Simi Valley, California. His art may be viewed and/or acquired at www. fineinkart.com .

Made in the USA
Middletown, DE
25 January 2023